THE BRITISH ISLES

Die Fernsehsendungen zu *Inside the British Isles* produzierte der Bayerische Rundfunk 1997/98 für das Telekolleg II.

Die Deutsche Bibliothek - CIP-Einheitsaufnahme

Gottschalk, Hannelore:
Inside the British Isles : a documentary series for advanced students of English / Hannelore Gottschalk ; Joe Hambrook ; Helen Wood. - München : TR-Verl.-Union, 1998
ISBN 3-8058-3268-0

Zu *Inside the British Isles* sind zwei Audiocassetten (Best.-Nr. 33202) erschienen: eine Mitlesecassette mit Originalinterviews und eine Übungscassette mit ausgewählten Übungen.
Die wiedergegebenen Texte sind durch das Symbol gekennzeichnet.

2., durchgesehene Auflage 1999

Fotos: Hannelore Gottschalk sowie Videoprints aus *Inside the British Isles*
Landkarten: Erica Heisinger, München
Umschlaggestaltung: Franziska Schob-Bergmeir, München
Gesamtherstellung: Gebr. Bremberger, München
ISBN 3-8058-3268-0

Inside the British Isles

A documentary series for advanced students of English

Hannelore Gottschalk
Joe Hambrook
Helen Wood

TR-Verlagsunion

Introduction

Join us for a look at life and work in different parts of the British Isles. You'll be meeting people with various occupations. They use everyday language and speak in a variety of accents.

The programme

Each programme is presented by Helen Wood. She takes you to a well-known city or part of the United Kingdom or Ireland, where you meet someone who will tell you about themselves, their work and their home or private lives. Their work provides the main theme or subject matter of the programme, and you will find out more about it from their working colleagues, from members of the public and from Helen.

The book

This book helps you to understand the programmes, provides information about the subject matter and offers language practice. It includes vocabulary, explanations, extracts from interviews and conversations, summaries and a variety of exercises. Each chapter corresponds to a single television programme.

Helen Wood, presenter of the series, in front of the Houses of Parliament

How to view the programme and use the book

When you view the programme, try to follow the main points in what people say rather than chase after the meaning of every word or expression that you hear. In this way, you will learn how to recognise what is important and relevant whenever you listen to spoken English.

After viewing each programme, work through the corresponding chapter and do the exercises. You will find an answer key at the end of the book.

Contents

A JOURNALIST IN LONDON

1

1 A

Introduction

The first programme is about Ruth Gledhill, a journalist working in London as Religion Correspondent of The Times, traditionally the newspaper of the British Establishment.
Ruth talks about herself and her job. We see what she does at work and in her spare time. We hear what people think about the newspapers they read, and we learn more about The Times from *the Editor* Peter Stothard.

editor Chefredakteur(in)

Ruth Gledhill, Religion Correspondent, The Times

1 B

Helen interviews Ruth Gledhill

Helen: Why did you become a religious affairs correspondent?
Ruth: Well, as a child my *ambition* was always to be a missionary. I thought I had a religious *vocation*, and that probably came from seeing my father, who was a *clergyman* in the Church of England. But when we came back from Jamaica, where he was serving as a missionary, I *set eyes on* a *copy* of The Sun newspaper, which had just been bought by ***Rupert Murdoch***. And I immediately lost my missionary vocation and decided I wanted to be a journalist. I liked the wild *headlines* and the lively copy of The Sun.
Helen: Did you go to The Sun?
Ruth: No, I never did in fact. My first job as a journalist was on the Birmingham Post & Mail, which is England's leading provincial newspaper. From there I went to the Daily Mail, which also I would consider one of the country's leading *tabloids*. It's a middle-market tabloid. And then from the Daily Mail I came to The Times. And when I was at The Times, I found out that religion was an *up-and-coming* subject. And it was a way of combining my two vocations of missionary and of journalist.
Helen: Do you think the Editor offered you the job of Religious Affairs Correspondent because of your background?
Ruth: I think he offered me the job because I had *established* myself as a news reporter, and at the time religion was thought to be perhaps by some people a bit *detached from* the demands of ordinary news subjects. And the Editor very much wanted religion to be treated like politics, like social affairs, like health.
Helen: You told me about the first religious story you *covered*, the *ordination* of women.
Ruth: That has been, I suppose, one of the main stories of my work as Religion Correspondent. But it hasn't been the only story. There have also been stories about the Royal Marriage, for example, because in this country *the Church* is *established*: the Queen is *Supreme Governor of the Church of England*, and Prince Charles will one day be Supreme Governor when he takes the place of his mother as head of the country, as King. So it's obvious that the *issue* of the Royal Marriage is very important. It's *crucial* to our *coverage of* Church and State, so I've been very *involved in* that as well as women priests.
Helen: Do you have any other jobs or any other tasks at The Times?
Ruth: Besides covering news on the religious front, I also cover news on the charity front sometimes. Recently I went abroad to Rwanda to cover the *refugee disaster* over there, and I wrote a big *story* about the international efforts of the Red Cross.
Then also I do - my favourite job of all - I visit a church each week, or a synagogue or a *mosque*, and I write about the service. And it's almost like a religious version

of a food *review*. I give stars for the *sermon*, for after-service care. I give stars for the architecture, *felicity of the music* and generally write a review of the service and of the welcome I get, and of how I generally feel about it. I also give stars for the *spiritual 'high'*, the sense of spiritual satisfaction I obtain from the service. And this is widely read, this *column*, and it's even been published as a book recently.

Note:
Rupert Murdoch is an Australian-born *media tycoon*, owner of several newspapers, including The Times and The Sun in Britain, and of television companies in many parts of the world, including Sky satellite television.

ambition	Ziel, Ehrgeiz
vocation	Berufung; Begabung
clergyman	Geistlicher, Pfarrer, Seelsorger
to set eyes on	zu Gesicht bekommen
copy	Exemplar; Text
headline	Schlagzeile
tabloid	Boulevardzeitung; Sensationspresse
up-and-coming	vielversprechend, gefragt
to establish oneself	sich etablieren, anerkannt werden
to be detached from	losgelöst, abgetrennt sein von
to cover	(*Presse*) berichten über
ordination	Priesterweihe
the Established Church	Staatskirche
Supreme Governor of the Church of England	Oberhaupt der Anglikanischen Kirche
issue	Frage, Angelegenheit, Problem
crucial	entscheidend, äußerst wichtig
coverage of	Berichterstattung über
to be involved in sth	mit etw. zu tun haben
refugee disaster	Flüchtlingselend
story	*hier*: Artikel
mosque	Moschee
review	Kritik, Besprechung
sermon	Predigt
felicity of the music	Musikauswahl
spiritual 'high'	Hochstimmung
column	Kolumne, Spalte
media tycoon	Medienmagnat, -zar

I. Vocabulary

a) *Find words or phrases in the interview which could replace the following words in* ***bold*** *letters.*

1. For a while Ruth and her family were living in Jamaica where her father was **working** as a missionary.
2. Every week Ruth attends a religious service and writes **an assessment** of it.
3. The **short titles** that appear at the top of the front page are written by editors not journalists.
4. The **subject** of the Royal Marriage is very important.
5. In her job at The Times Ruth can combine **special interests and abilities** of a missionary and of a journalist.
6. **Suitable choice** of music can make a church service more enjoyable.

b) Give the nouns corresponding to the following words.

1. ambitious
2. to decide
3. to consider
4. to combine
5. to establish
6. to satisfy
7. to publish

II. Understanding

1. What sort of news does Ruth Gledhill cover?
2. Where did Ruth start her career?
3. Who influenced Ruth in the choice of her career?
4. Why did Ruth go to Rwanda?

III. Test your English

Finish each of the incomplete sentences in such a way that it has the same meaning as the sentence before it.

Example: It was wrong of you to speak so unkindly to him.
Answer: You shouldn't have spoken so unkindly to him.

1. She intends to go to Africa.
   She is thinking of ....
2. I said I was sorry that I hadn't warned him.
   I apologised for ....
3. She said that her article must be printed at once.
   She asked for ....
4. Are you still writing your article?
   Haven't ....
5. It wouldn't be advisable for you to go to the meeting tomorrow.
   You'd ....

1 C

The British press - Daily and Sunday newspapers

Some newspapers are called *broadsheets* because they have a large, wide format. They are often *referred to* as quality papers because they are supposed to be serious in the way they treat the news.
The Times is perhaps the most famous quality broadsheet. Its rivals are The Guardian, The Independent, The Daily Telegraph and The Financial Times, Europe's business paper.
Other papers are called tabloids because they have smaller pages so that they can

be handled easily. Most of them are popular papers, each with a *circulation* of more than a million readers a day. And they usually have a rather sensational *approach* to the news.
For a time Ruth worked on the Daily Mail. She referred to it as a middle-market tabloid because it's aimed at readers who want a *fairly* serious approach.
All these are national papers, produced in London. There are also excellent provincial papers, produced outside London. Ruth started her career with a provincial paper, the Birmingham Post & Mail.
Apart from the news, people often choose papers to *suit* their own tastes or interests. So, most daily papers and all Sunday papers have special interest sections and separate *supplements* which look in detail at various subjects such as entertainment, sport, fashion, travel, personal finance and so on.
Some of these sections form part of the paper itself, others are separate supplements. And some supplements are in the form of colour magazines with lots of advertisements. And because each subject is dealt with separately and is clearly identified, you can easily find the supplements you want. And you can get rid of the ones that don't interest you.

broadsheets	*seriöse Presse*	fairly	recht
to refer to	*hier*: bezeichnen	to suit	*hier*: befriedigen
circulation	Auflage	supplement	Beilage, Magazin
approach	*hier*: Aufmachung		

Questions

1. What's the difference between a quality paper and a tabloid paper?
2. Name four national newspapers and a provincial paper in Britain.
3. What's a supplement?

1 D

What papers people read

Helen asked several young people what papers they read and why they chose them. One of them liked the Daily Mail because it wasn't a broadsheet but was nevertheless a quality paper. Most of them chose papers which *reflected* their views and which covered their special interests in ways which they approved of.
Readers of broadsheets claimed that they were *unbiased* and gave objective *factual accounts* of everyday events.
Helen also talked to a well-known actor, Sir Ian McKellen. He said that he was currently buying every paper he could get hold of because they were all giving favourable reviews of his latest film, Shakespeare's Richard III. At other times, he didn't take any paper on a daily basis, but he usually bought The Guardian, the

Independent on Sunday and The Observer. He read the news and arts coverage, but he threw away the sections on business, sport, fashion and travel.

to reflect	(wider)spiegeln
unbiased	unvoreingenommen, neutral
factual account	Tatsachenbericht

Vocabulary

Give a synonym or synonymous expression for the following words.

1. unbiased
2. section
3. accounts
4. to get hold of
5. a review

British press: supplements

1 E

Ruth describes her working day

Because newspapers go to press at around seven or eight in the evening, I don't have to be in my office until ten o'clock.

But when I get there, then it's hectic. I start by opening my post. We don't have secretaries. Everyone thinks The Times is *incredibly* high-tech and we all have millions of secretaries and assistants, but we don't. I go through the post and then I check my *diary* to see if I have any stories to go to. I'll maybe write a story first thing, from a *press release* that I've had. I'll answer the telephone and listen to my telephone messages. Then, after that, I will speak to the *news editor* and discuss that day's stories with him. I'll go through my *schedule* for the week, and we will decide whether maybe a *tip-off* I've had, whether it's worth *pursuing*, or whether I should just what we call 'spike' it - *put* it *on the spike*, which means that it's dead for ever and ever - unless another newspaper does it, and then I have to follow it up again. After that, there might be a conference with the Editor, when I might discuss future plans. I'll discuss what I'll be doing for my 'At your service' column, be discussing the major issues we should be following up and whether I should be interviewing any bishops.

The afternoon is always a busy time. I have to work really hard, be at my typewriter or at my computer terminal, putting in everything that I can. I have to write my *copy* for the first *edition*, and the *deadline* for that is really four o'clock in the afternoon. Real panic will set in if I haven't for example received a phone call that I need in order to stand a story up, or if someone is being *dilatory in* sending me a press release, or if our fax system isn't working, as it often isn't. But after I've finished my story I will input it into the system and from there it goes to the *news desk*. From there it goes to what we call the *sub-editors*, who then check it for commas, full stops, for grammatical errors, for any *contradictions* or errors of style. Then it goes to the Back Bench. The Back Bench are the final *arbiters* of the story. They take a particular interest for any story that's going on the front page. They will put the headlines on the story, and they will determine the final placing of everything in the paper. And they will then what we call 'put the paper to bed': they will press the button on the computer that *sets the presses rolling*, and then you have a newspaper the next day.

incredibly	unglaublich, unwahrscheinlich
diary	*hier*: Terminkalender
press release	Pressemitteilung
news editor	Nachrichtenredakteur
schedule	*hier*: Terminplan
tip-off	Tip, Wink
to pursue	verfolgen, recherchieren
to put sth on the spike	etw. nicht weiter verfolgen
copy	*hier*: Artikel
edition	Ausgabe (*einer Zeitung*)
deadline	letzter Termin, *hier*: Redaktionsschluß
to be dilatory in	sich Zeit lassen mit
news desk	Nachrichtenredaktion
sub-editor	Redakteur(in)
contradiction	Widerspruch
arbiter	Herr, Gebieter
to set the presses rolling	die Druckerpresse ins Rollen bringen

I. Vocabulary

Give a synonym or synonymous expression for each of the following words or expressions as used above.

1. incredibly
2. major issues
3. schedule
4. to pursue
5. conference
6. deadline
7. to stand a story up
8. dilatory
9. error
10. particular

II. Test your English

Complete the sentences with by or until.

1. Ruth doesn't have to be in her office .... ten o'clock.
2. Will she be able to finish her article .... four o'clock in the afternoon?
3. If the conference with the Editor goes on .... three o'clock, you won't be at Westminster .... the time the Prime Minister is due to speak.
4. The sub-editors will stay here .... midnight.
5. The copy was already written .... the time I got the new press release.
6. Will your fax system be repaired .... noon?

1 F

Interview with Peter Stothard, Editor of The Times

Peter Stothard and Ruth Gledhill

Since 1986 many British newspapers have moved from their traditional homes in Fleet Street and Grays Inn Road to the Docklands area of East London. The papers owned by Rupert Murdoch are now based in Wapping, and The Times operates from a former *warehouse* there.

Helen: Mr Stothard, can you give us a brief history of The Times?

Editor: The Times is the oldest national daily newspaper in Britain. We've been printing since 1785. So that's more than 200 years old, and we've printed ever since. The Times was founded by a man who was effectively a printer, and he invented a new printing process which enabled newspapers to be printed in a proper, efficient and for the first time, you know, commercial way.

The Times has always been a technologically innovative paper, right up to the present day, where we are one of the leading *players* on the Internet.

Helen: Could you tell me about the different kinds of news and topics covered in The Times?

Editor: Foreign news coverage has always been at the heart of The Times's advantage in this country. We have more than a dozen full-time correspondents around the world, and we've just recently opened a bureau in Peking. So we have a very strong foreign service, and at a time when other newspapers are *cutting back*, we're keeping very much that going and indeed are expanding it. But of course we have *stringers*, as we call them, across the globe ...

Helen: What is a stringer?

Editor: Well, there are sixty people who get part of their income from working for The Times. There are still huge areas that newspapers can cover, and good newspaper journalists can cover truths that they can get at that aren't available to television or to radio.

Helen: Why is that?

Editor: Well, because we're not driven by pictures. We don't have to compress our thoughts into a very short space. We don't have to make them immediately *palatable* to millions of people. We can campaign day after day; we can uncover a little bit here and a little bit there; we don't have to make it all *packaged up* immediately. There are lots of advantages that quality newspapers have over both tabloid newspapers and over television and radio.

Helen: What other news do you cover in the paper?

Editor: The Times had traditional *authority* in *economics*, *domestic politics*, *foreign affairs* and what one might call the key serious issues. We have the best letters - we still have the best letters, we have the best *obituaries*. And it's really that, the extension of the authority of The Times into areas where previously people didn't think The Times was very strong. So now we have the Fashion Journalist of the Year, who has become the *pre-eminent* fashion writer, who is the Fashion Editor of The Times.

We have the best car supplement, which people wouldn't normally have thought that we would naturally do. Restaurant critics, gardening, general leisure sections of one sort or another.

We have cultural areas, religious areas, artistic and musical areas, and there's a huge readership out there who want detailed knowledge. I mean, just to take religion: we have the best Religion Correspondent in Ruth Gledhill, and we give her a lot of space, and she does a lot of work for us. She's the most respected writer about religion in this country, so when news happens, she hears about it first. So we get the best news coverage.

Helen: Have these new sections actually increased the circulation of The Times?

Editor: Oh, the circulation of The Times has more than doubled in the last three years. So now we sell 800,000 copies on a Saturday, so more than twice what there were a few years ago, and more than four times what we would have been when I joined the paper.

Helen: Tell me about your move to Wapping.

Editor: Well, The Times led the whole of the British newspaper industry out of the old trade-union dominated *plant* up in Fleet Street and Grays Inn Road. It was a very dramatic day, you know. There were *pickets* outside, strikers. Suddenly the strike was on. And within hours we were driving a couple of miles down to Wapping, where this brand-new plant was waiting.

The trade unions didn't even - barely knew that it was there. And we missed that one night's production and were back the following Monday in a completely different world, a completely different newspaper world where we could produce our own papers. All the mistakes were ours instead of mistakes introduced or indeed sometimes even *censored in* by printers.

warehouse	Lager(haus)	economics	*hier*: Wirtschaft
player	Anbieter	domestic politics	Innenpolitik
to cut back	sich einschränken	foreign affairs	Außenpolitik
stringer	(freie/r) Lokal-reporter(in), Bericht-erstatter(in) vor Ort	obituary	Nachruf
		pre-eminent	herausragend
		plant	Werk(sgelände), Produktionsanlage
palatable	schmackhaft, genieß-bar; (*fig.*) attraktiv	picket	Streikposten
to package up	zusammenstellen, präsentieren	to censor in (a mistake)	absichtlich (einen Fehler) machen
authority	*hier*: Kompetenz		

I. Questions

1. What are the main sources of information for a big daily newspaper?
2. What commercial advantage did The Times have over its rivals when it was started more than 200 years ago?
3. Many printers have lost their jobs in recent years. Can you explain why?

II. Understanding

Complete the sentences, using the information from the interview.

1. The Times was founded by ....
2. At a time when other newspapers are cutting back, The Times is ....
3. The Times gets the best .... from its correspondents across the globe.
4. The Times has a .... who want detailed knowledge about politics, domestic and foreign affairs, economics and the arts.
5. About 800,000 .... are sold on a Saturday.
6. Most newspapers have .... from Fleet Street, once the famous home of national papers, to the Docklands area.

III. Test your English

Use the correct form of the verbs in brackets.

1. We've just recently ..... (open) a news agency in Hong Kong.
2. The Times ..... (print) for more than 200 years.
3. It's exactly seven years since The Big Issue, a new magazine, ... (launch) to give homeless people an alternative to begging.
4. The Big Issue ..... (have) growing success, it now sells around half a million copies a month and ..... (win) many awards.
5. A spokesman of the company confirmed yesterday that a meeting ..... (take place).
6. One year ago, the European football championship ..... (take place) in England.
7. Next month thousands of people from all over the world ..... (meet) in New York, at the International Conference on Population and Development.

1 G

The Times

In The Times nowadays, a lot of the news reports are written by the paper's own staff journalists. Some of the foreign news is provided by The Times foreign correspondents who work in many parts of the world. Other news comes from *free-lance* reporters, some of them known as stringers, or by means of press releases from news agencies, such as ***Reuters***.
Then there are feature articles written by well-known journalists and sketch writers comment, for example on politics, in their own regular and often humorous columns.
Even more *light-hearted* is The Times Diary, with its accompanying cartoon. The *leading articles*, or *leaders*, are the responsibility of the Editor and his *editorial*

staff. They appear in the middle of the paper, next to the *Letters to the Editor*. Many of these are written by well-known people who find the correspondence columns of The Times the best place to *air* their views.
Traditionally The Times has always published the *Court Circular*, giving news of the Royal Family's activities and engagements. There are obituaries of prominent people who have recently died and extensive reviews of artistic events and personalities. And, of course, full coverage of sports and of business affairs.

Note:
Reuters is an international news agency originally set up in the 19th century.

freelance	freiberuflich, freischaffend	Letter to the Editor	Leserbrief
light-hearted	unbekümmert, vergnüglich	to air	*hier*: (eine Meinung) verbreiten, darlegen
leading article, leader	Leitartikel	court circular	Hofnachrichten
editorial	redaktionell, Redaktions-		

'Waiting for The Times' by Benjamin Haydon

I. Vocabulary

a) Explain the following expressions as they are used in this programme.

1. circulation
2. coverage
3. stringer
4. obituary
5. column
6. copy

b) Complete the sentences with one of these words.

stringer • sub-editor • freelance writer (*or*: journalist) • editor
foreign correspondent

1. The .... is the person who has responsibility for the contents of a newspaper, and who must ensure that the paper makes money.
2. A reporter who is on the staff of a newspaper and provides news from abroad is a ....
3. A .... is a local journalist who provides news reports when a staff reporter is not available in the area.
4. The .... is the person who checks articles for accuracy, grammar, errors of style.
5. A self-employed journalist who writes for various papers is called a ....

II. Translation

Translate paragraph 1 to 3.

Does Diana rank as the story of the century?

When the biggest news stories break, journalists tend instinctively to react first as news editors and only seconds later as human beings. That may be unfair: perhaps unlike other people we do both simultaneously, reacting with shock and *grief* but also immediately planning what should go in the paper. That was certainly the experience of every journalist when the news broke in the early hours of August 31.

Since then, no story this century has commanded so much space in British newspapers or newspapers across the world. *On that count* alone, beyond its emotional and tragic *impact* or its ability within Britain to *rouse* a nation against a monarchy seemingly *out of step* with its *subjects*, the death of Diana, Princess of Wales has undoubtedly been the biggest news story of the country.

But was it the most *significant*? Within newsrooms, it has *sparked a debate* about which news stories have had the same impact on editors and readers.

We all have our own candidates. Within my *adult* lifetime, the stories that stand out in the memory are the Queen's *coronation* in 1953, Suez in 1956 and (after I became a journalist) Churchill's *funeral*, the Cuban *missile* crisis of 1962, the *assassination* of President Kennedy in 1963, Watergate, the wedding of Prince Charles and Princess Diana, the fall of the Berlin wall and Nelson Mandela's *release*.

Those are stories with a global impact. Among the British candidates must be the Aberfan disaster, the Falklands and Gulf wars, Hungerford, Lockerbie, Dunblane and several IRA bombs.

That, however, ignores half the century. The Times, then a much smaller newspaper, *devoted* as big a proportion of its space to Queen Victoria's death in 1901 as it did last week to the death of Princess Diana - as did the Daily Mail to the flight across the

Channel by Blériot.
The main problem in selecting such journalistic lists is that most are stories of death, disaster and war and never about love and happiness. The 'good news' stories - the discoveries of penicillin, the *X-ray* or DNA, the invention of radar, television or the jet aeroplane, *test-tube babies*, women's liberation, black liberation - cannot be measured by their impact on a single day's or week's news. Yet each has had a more momentous impact on human happiness than any of the other stories. That is the way newspapers work and is, in fact, what readers expect.

(*Brian MacArthur in The Times, Wednesday, September 10, 1997*)

grief	Trauer	adult	Erwachsene(r)
on that count	(*fig.*) in diesem Punkt	coronation	Krönung
impact	(Aus-)Wirkung	funeral	Trauerfeier, Begräbnis
to rouse	aufrütteln, wachrufen	missile	Rakete
to be out of step	nicht im Gleichklang sein	assassination	Ermordung
		release	Freilassung
subject	*hier*: Untertan	to devote	widmen
significant	bedeutend, wichtig	X-ray	Röntgenstrahl
to spark a debate	eine Diskussion auslösen	test-tube baby	Retortenbaby

1 H

Ruth Gledhill

What do you know about Ruth Gledhill from watching the TV programme and reading the interviews in the booklet? Complete the following text.

1. Ruth Gledhill is the Religion .... of The Times.
2. She started her career as a journalist on the Birmingham Post & Mail, a leading ....
3. Then she went to the Daily Mail, one of the country's leading ....
4. Finally she came to The Times, where she now .... religious stories as well as .... from the charity front.
5. Recently she wrote a big story about the .... in Rwanda.
6. Her .... job is to write about religious services which she compares with a religious version of a ....
7. Ruth has a rather unusual ...., ballroom dancing.
8. She married recently in Barbados and when the .... came back to England, they had a .... in St Bride's Church, which is known as the journalists' church, because it's in Fleet Street, which was once the home of British ....

9. On Saturdays Ruth likes .... in Harrods or Selfridges and .... friends for coffee and tea in one of the many cafés along the Kings Road which is still a .... place in London.

Ruth's hobby is ballroom dancing

1 I

Television and radio

Broadcasting in Britain was for a long time the monopoly of the BBC, the British Broadcasting Corporation, which is financed through a *licence fee* paid by everyone who has a television *receiver*. Now there are five broadcast television channels in Britain: two transmitted by the BBC, and the other three by independent private companies which are financed through advertising *commercials*.
There are also cable and satellite organisations which provide television programmes to viewers who *subscribe to* their services.
The BBC has five national radio channels and many local radio stations. There are also a large number of independent radio stations, most of them local.

licence fee	*hier*: Fernsehgebühr	commercial	Werbefilm, Werbespot
receiver	Empfänger	to subscribe to	abonnieren

I. Understanding

Complete the sentences using the information from the text.

1. You have to pay a .... fee for television, but not for radio.
2. You cannot watch cable or .... television unless you pay ....
3. The BBC and many independent companies have a lot of .... radio ....

II. Comment

What are the advantages and disadvantages of newspapers in comparison with television for reporting and commenting on the news? (about 100 words)

1 J

Ruth interviews the Bishop at Lambeth

In the course of her work Ruth went to Lambeth Palace, the London home of the Archbishop of Canterbury, to interview the Bishop at Lambeth, one of the Archbishop of Canterbury's chief assistants.

Asked about the future of the Church in the next *millenium* the Bishop said that, despite pessimistic forecasts that the Church was about to die out, its membership was beginning to rise again, especially in parts of the Third World. He also explained that the Archbishop of Canterbury often took the initiative on international issues which *affected* the Anglican Church.

in the course	während, im Laufe	to affect	sich auswirken, beeinflussen
millenium	Jahrtausend		

The Church of England

The Church of England is part of the Anglican Communion, a group of broadly similar churches throughout the world.

It's the Established Church of the United Kingdom, with Her Majesty The Queen as its head or Supreme Governor. She is also called Defender of the *Faith.*

The Archbishop of Canterbury, the Primate of all England, is its spiritual leader.

The Church of England is a Protestant Church - it was formed in protest against the Roman Catholic Church in the 16th century.

There are other Protestant *denominations* or religious groups in Britain: for example, the Presbyterian Church, which is the largest denomination in Scotland.

Some of the Protestant denominations are Non-Conformist: they do not follow the practices of the Established Church.

The Methodist Church is one of the most famous of these Non-Conformist churches.

faith	Glaube
denomination	Konfession, Bekenntnis

I. Vocabulary

*Find words or phrases in the texts above which could replace the following words in **bold** letters.*

1. The Presbyterian Church is the largest Protestant **religious group** in Scotland.
2. The various churches of the Anglican Communion are **more or less the same as** each other.
3. Membership of the Church of England is starting to **increase in numbers**.
4. The Archbishop of Canterbury often takes the **lead** on issues which affect the Church in many parts of the world.

II. Understanding

1. Who is the Head of the Church of England?
2. Where does the Archbishop of Canterbury live when he is in London?
3. Why is the Methodist Church called Non-Conformist?
4. Why does the Bishop call reports that the Church of England is about to die out 'pessimistic'?

Westminster Abbey

TEACHERS IN CAMBRIDGE 2

2 A

Introduction

This programme is about teachers in a comprehensive school and about education in England.
Phil Evans teaches geography at Netherhall School in Cambridge. He talks about the school and about his work as Head of the Sixth Form, where his Assistant Head, Carolyn Dunn, teaches chemistry. We see him teaching and also taking time off with his family. We see sixth form students during a typical school day, and we hear them talk about school and about their plans for the future.
Nick Williams is the *Deputy Head Teacher* at Netherhall School. He explains some of the most important features of the education system.
At the end of the programme, Nick Williams takes us on a tour of several of the colleges of Cambridge University.

deputy head teacher stellvertretende(r) Schulleiter(in)

2 B

Netherhall School

Netherhall is a mixed comprehensive school for students aged eleven to 19: mixed because it's mixed sex - boys and girls - and comprehensive because the school does not select students according to their academic ability.
Phil's students are in the sixth form, where they spend their last two years at school. They are working for A-levels - advanced level examinations - which they take at the end of their final school year. They have been doing fieldwork - going outside the classroom and *investigating* the *environment at first hand.* This fieldwork is an essential part of the A-level geography course.

to investigate	untersuchen
environment	Umwelt; Umfeld, Umgebung
at first hand	aus erster Hand

I. Vocabulary

Explain the following words or expressions.

1. A-levels
2. comprehensive school
3. to investigate
4. fieldwork
5. essential

II. Understanding

1. Who does Phil teach?
2. What subject does Ms Dunn teach?
3. Who is Nick Williams?
4. What are Phil's two jobs at Netherhall School?

2 C

Helen interviews Phil Evans (1st part)

Phil Evans

Helen: What does the job of being Head of the Sixth Form *entail*?
Phil: Well, it's basically to be in charge of the day-to-day running and the planning and the management of the separate sixth form centre, which operates as part of Netherhall School.
Helen: Tell me what the sixth form is.
Phil: It's a community within a community. I mentioned that Netherhall School was a school for children aged eleven to 19, and the 16- to 19-year olds are the

sixth form within there. And we have very much separate accommodation, a different day to the rest of the students. They don't wear uniform, they have certain other privileges, and really the way in which the whole sixth form *set-up* is managed within the school is very different from those students who are aged eleven to 16.

Helen: So how do you actually become a sixth-former?

Phil: Well, at Netherhall School, it's a fairly simple process in that we only really do offer one type of course post-16. So for a student to *progress* at the age of 16, having done their first really public examinations, which are known as *GCSE examinations*, most students will do eight or nine - in eight or nine subjects. And we would require that they have a minimum of five *grade* C *passes* or better in order to move on and study A-level, although the *recommendation* always is that a student actually gains A or B grades, particularly in subjects that they're studying at A.

Helen: How many A-levels does a sixth-former usually choose to take?

Phil: *Virtually* all sixth-form students would do three A-levels, although a small number would do two if three were too difficult and too *demanding*. But it would be a relatively small number who actually only end up doing two. More and more subjects at university require a combination of subjects: *sciences* or *engineering*, for example, or medicine would require maths, physics, chemistry, biology or a combination thereof. Other courses, like *law* or business studies, you can access those with a much broader range of subjects. They can be sciences, including mathematics, or they can be arts and *humanity subjects*.

Helen: If a student *opts* not *to* go on to further education, will A-level results help him or her to find a job?

Phil: There are many careers that require A-levels as a minimum: for example, *trainee accountancy* or *surveying*. But most jobs that would lead to a position of responsibility - some managerial responsibility - would *invariably* require A-levels as a minimum for entry.

Helen: What sort of grades would a pupil need to get into university?

Phil: It depends on the university, *frankly*, and depends on the subjects that are studied. *Inevitably*, there's a hierarchy of universities in Britain, as there would be in all countries. So for Oxford and Cambridge, for example, at the top of that hierarchy, then it really is as simple as *straight A grades* in order to gain access.

And if one looks at the traditional so-called red-brick universities, ***civic universities*** in large cities, that have long traditions and have been around for perhaps a hundred years in most cases, then the offers are more likely to be three Bs or three C grades, typically.

Note:

Civic universities were founded in the 19th century in large cities to encourage and develop higher education in their local areas.

to entail	mit sich bringen, erfordern
set-up	Organisation, Drum und Dran
to progress	weiterkommen, Fortschritte machen, sich entwickeln
GCSE examinations (= General Certificate of Secondary Education)	*entspricht etwa der Mittleren Reife*
pass grade	Abschluß-, Prüfungsnote
recommendation	Empfehlung
virtually	praktisch, fast, nahezu
demanding	anspruchsvoll
sciences	Naturwissenschaften
engineering	Ingenieurwesen, Maschinenbau, Technik
law	Recht
humanity subjects	Geisteswissenschaften
to opt to	sich entscheiden für
trainee	Auszubildende(r), Volontär(in), Praktikant(in)
accountancy	Rechnungswesen, Buchhaltung; Steuerberatung
surveying	Inspektion
invariably	unweigerlich
frankly	offen gestanden, ehrlich gesagt
inevitably	zwangsläufig, unweigerlich
straight A grade	*entspricht etwa einer glatten Eins*

I. Vocabulary

a) Give the verbs corresponding to the following nouns.

1. accommodation
2. requirement
3. recommendation
4. choice
5. combination
6. option
7. entry
8. necessity

b) Find words in the interview that mean the following.

1. to be responsible for
2. to refer to
3. we would require
4. comparatively
5. professions
6. without exception
7. to be admitted

II. Test your English: reported speech

Put Helen's questions into reported speech.

1. Tell me what the sixth form is.
   Helen wanted to know ....
2. Have you heard what Nick did last night?
   Helen asked me ....
3. Will you be seeing Phil this afternoon?
   Helen asked Nick ....
4. Are you aware that smoking causes cancer?
   Helen asked him ....

5. Why have you painted your bike black?
   Helen asked the student ....
6. When are you going to take your A-levels?
   Helen asked Anne ....

2 D

Examinations

For secondary school students there are two main examinations: GCSE, the General Certificate of Secondary Education, and A-level, advanced level examinations.
They take GCSE when they're about 16 years old. They usually take eight or nine subjects in this exam, and the pass grades go from A to G. A is the best grade.
Provided they get at least C grades in five subjects, they can go on to study for A-levels, which they take in their last year at school, when they're 18 or 19. They choose two or three subjects at A-level. And the grades they get will affect their *prospects* for further education and employment.
For entrance to Oxbridge, as the universities of Oxford and Cambridge are often called, a student should have three A grades at advanced level. Other universities, like Manchester or Liverpool, which are often called red-brick because of their 19th century architecture, would require at least three Bs or Cs.
There are also many new universities, some of them former polytechnic colleges, which have been given university status in recent years. They would require three Bs, Cs or Ds.

prospects Aussichten

Understanding

1. What is a sixth-former?
2. At what age do the pupils take GCSEs?
3. How many GCSE subjects do most pupils take?
4. Which students qualify for entry to the sixth form?
5. What grades should sixth form students have if they want to go to Oxford or Cambridge?

2 E

Phil describes a typical day at school

Assembly at Netherhall School

A typical day would start at 8.40 in the morning when the students arrive. There would be either a registration period with a *form tutor* or a group tutor, or there may be an *assembly* for the particular year group on that morning. An assembly is a *gathering* of students within a particular sector of the school. It's an opportunity for us as a community to get together and to share information.

The first lesson starts at 9.05 and the last lesson of the day - the fifth lesson of our day - ends at 3.40. There are two *breaks*, one in the morning and one in the afternoon, mainly to allow us to move pupils and move teachers from one *site* to another because our buildings are not all on the same site. But of course it also gives everybody a chance to have a *breather* between lessons in those two parts of the day. And then halfway through the day, at 12.25, we actually have our lunch break, a longer lunch break for everyone.

For their lunch break most of the pupils take advantage of the canteen food which is on offer within the school.

There's plenty of opportunity for students to *socialise* - to talk with friends and catch up with school *gossip* while having lunch. The lunch break also allows time for other activities. Some may choose to relax with a *game of pool*. Others use the break for private study in the sixth form *common room*. And there's usually time for an informal game of football.

form tutor	Klassenlehrer	to socialise	sich unterhalten, gesellschaftlich verkehren
assembly	Versammlung; Morgenandacht		
gathering	Versammlung, Zusammenkunft	gossip	Klatsch, Tratsch; Schwatz
break	Pause, Unterbrechung	(game of) pool	Billardspiel
site	Platz, Stelle	common room	Gemeinschaftsraum
breather	Verschnaufpause		

I. Understanding

1. Which games are mentioned in the text above?
2. When do the students have time to take part in these games?
3. What do you think a typical meal in the school canteen would consist of?
4. What is a common room for sixth form students?

II. Test your English: phrasal verbs

Give a synonym or synonymous expression for the phrasal verbs in ***bold*** *letters.*

1. I can't **put up with** all this noise!
2. We **look on** this town as our real home.
3. Phil **asked after** you.
4. Don't worry, you can **count on** me.
5. **Drop in** any time you're passing.
6. They **ended up** doing two A-level subjects.
7. We will **sort out** the problem.
8. Let's **try out** the new computer.
9. I **ran into** Nick at the supermarket.
10. Sorry I'm late. I was **held up** in the traffic.
11. The students are **getting on** very well in their work.
12. Let me explain how all this **came about**.

III. What about you?

Describe a typical day in your life. (60 to 80 words)

2 F

Nick Williams gives a description of the state education system

Despite the fact that these days increasing numbers of *infants* go to nursery schools before the age of five, compulsory school years begin at age five when children go to primary school. They remain at *primary school* until age eleven, and then comes a big change. At age eleven they transfer to secondary.

STATE EDUCATION

5 years	PRIMARY	
11 years	SECONDARY	
	Comprehensive	wide ability range
	Grammar	academic
	Secondary Modern	vocational
16 years	Sixth Form	A-level vocational

Probably the majority of ***students*** will actually go on to a school rather like this one at age eleven, to a state secondary comprehensive school which has both boys and girls, which has ***pupils*** from a *range of* different social backgrounds, and a different range of abilities. But some pupils in different parts of the country may be facing different systems. For example, in some parts of the country they still have selection at age eleven and the pupils will sit for a public examination called the *Eleven-Plus*. And depending on their *performance* in that, they may go to a grammar school, where the *emphasis* is very much academic, or may go to a secondary modern school, where perhaps it's rather more *vocational*. But all pupils will go to a secondary school, whichever one that might be, until age 16. So the *compulsory* school years end at age 16. At that stage there is more choice. Some pupils may choose to go into employment, but I have to say in recent years that has become an increasingly unattractive option; increasing numbers of pupils now remain in full-time education. And most at 16, even if they stay on in full-time education, will change their school and go into a sixth form college. Some will go on to take advanced level courses, some will go on to take one of a range of vocational courses.

Then at age 18 or 19 at the end of their *further education*, if they wish to and if they have the ability, they may go on to higher education, *primarily* university.

Note:

Pupils *and* ***students*** are words which are used to describe children at school, but pupils are generally younger children, and anyone in the sixth form would expect to be called a student, a term that would be used right through university or any other form of further education.

infant	(Klein-)Kind	emphasis	Betonung, (Schwer-) Gewicht
primary school	Grundschule		
range of	*hier*: Vielzahl an; Auswahl an	vocational	berufsbildend
		compulsory	verpflichtend
Eleven-Plus (examination)	*Aufnahmeprüfung ins Gymnasium*	further education	*hier*: Weiterbildung, schulische Fortbildung
performance	*hier*: schulische Leistung	primarily	*hier*: höchstwahrscheinlich

Understanding

1. What is meant by ‘a different range of abilities’?
2. How long does compulsory education last?
3. What do you understand by the expression ‘further education’ here and elsewhere in this chapter?
4. What is meant by ‘academic education’?

2 G

Private schools

Alongside the state education system, there are several hundred private schools. Parents pay fees to have their children educated at these schools, which can therefore usually spend more money than state schools on *facilities*, both for teaching and for leisure activities. In this way private schools can offer their students a different environment from state schools. Many of them are *boarding schools*, where pupils live on the school *premises* instead of coming to school from home every day. And compared with state schools, private schools have a certain amount of freedom to control the *curriculum* - the subjects which are taught and how the teaching is organised - and to decide how the schools should be managed.
The most famous and oldest secondary boarding schools in Britain are private schools. However, they are always referred to as ‘public schools’ because at the time when many of them were founded, private education meant education at home for children of very *wealthy* people. Nowadays parents pay as much as £10,000 a year to have a child educated at one of the top public schools. Like grammar schools but unlike comprehensive schools, a child must pass an *entrance exam* to get into a public school.

facilities	Einrichtungen	curriculum	Lehrplan
boarding school	Internat(sschule)	wealthy	wohlhabend
premises *pl*	Gelände	entrance exam	Aufnahmeprüfung

I. Understanding

1. State three ways in which public schools are different from state comprehensive schools.
2. What makes it possible for private schools to offer their students a different environment from state schools?
3. How were the children of very wealthy parents educated in the past?

II. Say it in English

1. Das ist eine zu schwierige Aufgabe.
2. Das war eine zu gute Chance.
3. Ich bleibe zu Hause und lerne den ganzen Abend.
4. Wir sehen uns morgen.
5. Sie mögen sich sehr.
6. Was hältst du von dem neuen Lehrer?
7. Heute vor drei Wochen bestand er sein Abitur.
8. Die Feier sollte eine Überraschung werden.
9. Einige Leute waren um Mitternacht noch da.
10. Unsere Schule befindet sich in der Nähe des Bahnhofs.

III. Comment

Do you think children have greater opportunities in life when they are sent to private boarding schools? Give reasons for your opinion. (50 words)

2 H

Helen interviews Phil Evans (2nd part)

Helen: Do you think that pupils have changed in the past few years?
Phil: I think their experiences are very different compared to those of people of my *era* or yours, in that I think students nowadays frankly have far more pressures upon them. It's certainly more common for students to come from family backgrounds that don't traditionally have the *stable* two-parent type background. And I think also they are rather more *sensitive* as well, I tend to think, and more informed generally than students were years ago.
Helen: What is the most *rewarding* aspect of your job?
Phil: I think it has to be at the end of every year when the students from my upper-sixth classes finish with us and receive their examination results, and hopefully do well enough to progress onto the next stage in their education.
Helen: What would you say to a pupil who was thinking of becoming a teacher?
Phil: I think the first thing I'd probably say to them is 'Consult a psychiatrist'. But to be serious, I think the same advice I would give to any student who was *con-*

templating any career, which is to research it thoroughly and to be as sure as they can that it really will be the right career for them.
Helen: Do you enjoy being a teacher?
Phil: I certainly do. I've been doing it so long now I really couldn't *conceive* of doing anything else, to be frank. Yes, there are difficulties. And, you know, there are times when the job feels impossibly difficult. But those occasions are far *outweighed* by the rewards of the job.
Helen: What do you do in your leisure time?
Phil: The thing I enjoy doing most of all, I think, the thing that's the perfect *antidote* to a difficult day at school, is playing with the children, especially feeding the ducks when there's an opportunity to go outside. So I think the summer is better than the winter from that point of view. We've got some very lovely local parks in this Cambridge area. And going to the park, or *going on the swings* with Rhiannon, whatever it may be, that's probably my ideal way of spending a free hour.

era	*hier*: Generation	to contemplate	nachdenken über
stable	gefestigt, beständig	to conceive	denken, vorstellen
sensitive	empfindlich, reizbar	to outweigh	überwiegen
rewarding	lohnend, dankbar (*Aufgabe*)	antidote	*hier*: Ausgleich, Gegenmittel
to consult	zu Rate ziehen	to go on the swings	schaukeln (gehen)

I. Vocabulary

Find words in the interview that could replace the following words or expressions.

1. not the same
2. chance
3. to suppose
4. to seek information and advice from sb
5. to get
6. occupation
7. sincerely
8. compensation (for)

II. Understanding

What do you know about Phil? Complete the text.

1. Phil lives in ....
2. He enjoys being a ....
3. Although he feels his job is sometimes ...., he can't .... doing anything else.
4. Many students ask him for .... when they are planning their ....
5. In his .... time he prefers playing ...., ... the ducks or going on the swings with his ....

III. Test your English: participle clauses

Rewrite the sentences, replacing the sub-clause (in **bold** *letters) with a participial construction.*

1. **When I heard this news** I ran home at once.
2. **After he had passed his GCSEs**, he went on to a sixth form college.
3. **When I arrived in the pub**, I found my friend had gone.
4. **Since he is very poor**, he can't afford to buy new books.
5. **As there was nothing to do**, we went home.
6. **Since the weather was fine**, we went for a swim.

2 I

School uniform in Britain

Boy in school uniform

School uniform is still quite common in Britain. Asked about its purpose, Nick Williams said that school uniform is often *justified* in terms of giving students a sense of identity and of developing a *sense of belonging* to a particular school. And a school which has a traditional school uniform is *deemed* by many parents *to be* a school with traditional values, good discipline and good order.
One of the sixth-formers at Netherhall agreed that uniform was a good idea, but another said she would prefer to wear her own clothes in school because she would feel more comfortable in them.

to justify	rechtfertigen	to deem sth to be	etw. erachten, halten für
sense of belonging	Zugehörigkeitsgefühl		

I. Translation

1. I think all careers should be open to women nowadays.
2. He was to become one of the most distinguished scientists of his age.
3. He might come tomorrow.
4. She worked so hard that she eventually passed the test.

II. The language of education

Fill in the blank spaces.

1. The morning meeting for students is called an ....
2. Students in their last two years at school are ....
3. Exams taken at the end of the last year at school are called ....
4. .... are exams taken at 16.
5. The subject Phil teaches is ....
6. The free time between lessons is called a ....
7. The subject Carolyn Dunn teaches is ....
8. Netherhall is a mixed .... school.
9. The traditional civic universities in large cities like Manchester or Liverpool are called .... universities.
10. Phil's students went outside and investigated the environment at first hand. This is called ....
11. Most of the students have their lunch in the school ....
12. Before the age of five infants go to .... schools.
13. If parents choose to send their children to one of the top private schools, they have to pay ....
14. Schools which house their students overnight are called .... schools.

III. Comment

What are the pros and cons of wearing a school uniform? Write an argument between two people, one of whom is for, the other against school uniform. (130 to 150 words)

2 J

A tour round some of the colleges in Cambridge

Cambridge is a famous old university town on the river Cam. The university is an important part of everyday life in Cambridge. There are about 30 colleges *scattered around* Cambridge and about 12,000 students.
Nick Williams, who went to Cambridge University himself, described some of the colleges.

King's College Chapel, one of the finest examples of the perpendicular style of Gothic architecture

Christ's College was *founded* in the early 16th century by Lady Margaret Beaufort, the mother of King Henry VII.

St. John's College was founded in 1511. The *benefactor* was the same as for Christ's College, Lady Margaret Beaufort. The College Chapel was built in the 19th century.

The great romantic poet William Wordsworth was an *undergraduate* here in the late 18th century.

At Oxford and Cambridge and other British universities, students who have not yet taken a degree are called undergraduates.

Trinity College, founded by King Henry VIII with the help of *endowments* from the *monasteries* he'd *dissolved*, is the largest, the richest, and certainly the most famous of all the Cambridge colleges. And Great Court itself is the largest of all the college *courtyards*.

Isaac Newton was an undergraduate here in 1661. He went on to become a *fellow*, a member of the College's academic staff, and also a professor of mathematics at the University. It was here that he made his *calculations* which *transformed* our understanding of the universe.

The wooden bridge that leads to **Queens College** is commonly known as Mathematical Bridge. It was believed, quite falsely, to have been built without *screws* or *bolts*.

Queens College was founded in 1448 by Margaret, the wife of King Henry VI. Cloister Court has a superb late 16th century President's Lodge, and beneath that the 15th century *cloisters*.

The college was *attended* by the great *scholar* Erasmus, who was here from 1510 to 1514. He did not like Cambridge very much: he found it expensive, the weather was *atrocious*, and he thought the beer was what he described as 'weak and windy'. However, he did say the women were of the 'kissable kind'. So nothing really has changed in five hundred years.

scattered around	verstreut liegen in	calculation	Berechnung
to found	(be)gründen	to transform	umwandeln
benefactor	Wohltäter(in), Gönner(in)	screw	Schraube
undergraduate	Student(in)	bolt	Bolzen
endowment	Stiftung, Schenkung	cloisters	(Kloster-)Kreuzgang
monastery	Kloster	to attend	besuchen
to dissolve	auflösen	scholar	Gelehrte(r)
courtyard	(Innen-)Hof	atrocious	grauenhaft, widerwärtig
fellow	*hier*: Mitglied der Universität, des akademischen Lehrkörpers	perpendicular	senkrecht, perpendikular

I. Understanding

Choose the correct meaning of the following words.

1. A scholar is ....
   a) a benefactor b) a learned person c) a poet
2. A degree is ....
   a) an academic award b) an examination c) a pass grade
3. An endowment is ....
   a) a fee b) a present c) a donation
4. A fellow is ....
   a) a student b) a member of the academic staff of a university c) an undergraduate

II. Translation

Translate this article.

Are you ready for student life?

Although more young people than ever now gain admission to university, there is growing evidence that many of them are unprepared for life away from home. University counsellors report dealing with students wanting to give up their courses within the first few weeks of their arrival because of homesickness. Others have no idea of how to plan a work schedule and they fall behind almost immediately. Georgina Newson, who runs the student advice centre at the University of Reading, is amazed to find so many students lacking basic life skills.

(The Times, Tuesday, September 2, 1997)

Queens College

A PUBLICAN IN THE NEW FOREST 3

3 A

This programme is about Steve Croll, a *publican* who runs 'The Rising Sun', a pub in Wooton in the New Forest, near Southampton in the south of England.
The New Forest was created by ***William the Conqueror*** as his hunting ground more than 900 years ago.
Steve talks about his pub and explains how pubs in Britain have changed over the years, *in terms of* what they provide in the way of food, drink and entertainment. The customers have changed, too, and some of them give their opinions of 'The Rising Sun' and what it offers.
We follow Steve through a typical day, which includes a visit to the local brewery to select and order beer. We also look at some English pub signs and take a trip through the New Forest and its surrounding area.
Steve Croll has a slight London accent which you can notice in his pronunciation of *vowels* and the letter 'r'.

Note:
William the Conqueror was the first Norman King of England (1066-1087). He became king after invading England and defeating the Anglo-Saxon army at the Battle of Hastings.

publican	Gastwirt (*und Pächter des Pubs*)	in terms of	betreffend
		vowel	Vokal

3 B

Helen interviews Steve Croll (1st part)

Helen: Steve, England has a very rich pub tradition. What do you think makes the English pubs so special?
Steve: I suppose it's the *focal point*, it's the social meeting place of any area, especially here. We are a little bit *remote* and it is a meeting place, a social place, a social gathering where people meet their friends.
Helen: What part does the pub play in the typical Englishman's life?
Steve: Here it's very much a meeting place, a social place. People come, they stop on the way home from work before they go home. It's their social gathering, their social life. And we do entertain to keep them actually in the community. Yes, it's their meeting place, their social life.

Helen: But that's for this pub specifically. I'm talking about your average English pub. Is it the same in that case?
Steve: I think that's generally the same, that you have in each area or in each town, you have pubs that people go to for various reasons. Well, visit it mainly for their social life, to meet people, to mix with them, and they go on from there.
Helen: Would you say that 'The Rising Sun' is a drinking man's pub?
Steve: Not as much now as maybe it used to be. It's far more of a family pub now, where people will actually bring their wives and their children in. I suppose through the relaxing of *licensing laws* it's become that family-type pub rather than just a drinking man's pub.
Helen: What does one drink in a typical English pub?
Steve: I think now we're becoming far more *discerning* with our beers. We went through a stage a few years ago when people went off traditional beers, but now they're very much back *in vogue*. As for one or two of the beers we do, we have the local breweries - I do five traditional ales here, and then each month or week or maybe more often than that we'll do a guest beer as well, so people can taste the different varieties.

Steve Croll behind the bar

Helen: Nowadays most pubs serve food as well as drink. Has the standard of pub food actually improved in recent years?
Steve: Greatly so. The majority of pubs now sell food, and people are very discerning. And they will only go to what they consider to be quality places. And we've made eating out *affordable*, whereas before pubs used to - maybe 20 years

ago - you'd come in for a cheese *roll* and a pint of beer. And it was very much *male-orientated*. It's now that wives and girlfriends are coming out, families are coming out, and they've actually demanded that we *cater for* them.

focal point	Mittelpunkt, Brennpunkt	in vogue	in Mode
remote	entfernt, abgelegen	affordable	erschwinglich
licensing laws	Schankgesetze (*Gesetz über den Ausschank und Verkauf alkoholischer Getränke*)	roll	Brötchen
		male-orientated	für Männer bestimmt
		to cater for	mit Speisen und Getränken versorgen
discerning	anspruchsvoll, kritisch		

I. Vocabulary

a) Give the opposite of the following words.

1. rich
2. remote
3. various
4. male
5. special

b) Find words in the text that could replace the words in **bold** *letters.*

1. I **guess** a pub is the social meeting place.
2. Nowadays traditional beers are **popular** again.
3. People only go to pubs they **regard** to be quality places.
4. **Most** pubs now sell food.
5. Families have **asked** that we cater for them.

II. Understanding

1. How does Steve earn his living?
2. What are licensing laws?
3. What is meant by 'people are discerning'?
4. What is meant by 'eating out is affordable'?
5. Explain the expression 'to cater for'.
6. Why do the British like their pubs so much?
7. In what way is 'The Rising Sun' no longer just a drinking man's pub?

III. Test your English: the passive

Put each verb in brackets into the passive in an appropriate tense.

1. All main courses .... (serve) with vegetables and salad.
2. Your sandwich .... (still, prepare).
3. Luckily by the time we got there the car .... (not sell).
4. The beer .... (not deliver) yet.

5. Steve .... (ask) to organise an evening with country music in his pub.
6. Eating out .... (make) more affordable nowadays.
7. As the new refrigerator .... (deliver) on Wednesday morning, Steve will have to stay there to check that it .... (not damage) in transit.

3 C

Pub signs and pub food

For centuries, pubs have been meeting places for friends, *lodging houses* for travellers, and sometimes even *signposts* for visitors.
The smallest towns and villages usually have more than one pub, each with its own *distinctive* sign outside. In fact, it was the Romans who started the tradition of pub signs in Britain, which has continued ever since.

Pubs have wonderful names. You can drink in 'The Queen's Head', 'The King's Arms', 'The Ship Inn' or you can *pop into* 'The Red Lion'.
'The Snakecatcher' was named after someone providing an essential service here in the New Forest, but there are also many common pub names which can be found almost anywhere in Britain. 'The Tollhouse Inn' shows that the name of the pub was also used to *collect tolls* or taxes from road users.
Many pubs sell beer only from the breweries that own them, but a Free House can sell beer from any brewery. And almost all pubs are *fully licensed*: they can sell every kind of alcoholic drink.
Pubs are not only for drinking. Under the influence of other European countries, there is now a wide range of bar snacks und lunches available. 'The Rising Sun'

serves typical pub food such as fish and chips. The fish is usually fried *plaice* or *cod*, and it often comes with peas and some salad. *Steak and kidney pie*, served with chips, peas and carrots is another typical English dish; a *jacket potato* is a potato baked in its skin with cheese or other fillings on top; and ploughman's lunch is what farmworkers ate when they *ploughed* the fields. Nowadays it's bread and cheese, some *pickle*, and an onion. On the evening menu you can sometimes find *smoked salmon* with *horseradish* sauce, or roast beef with Yorkshire pudding and roast potatoes. And you can finish off with *apple pie* and *custard*.
Since the recent reform of the licensing laws, which regulate opening times, pubs are free to remain open all day.

lodging house	Pension
signpost	Wegweiser
distinctive	unverkennbar, unverwechselbar
to pop in(to)	(auf einen Sprung) vorbeikommen, hineingehen in
to collect	*hier*: einziehen, kassieren
toll	Maut, Straßenzoll
fully licensed	mit voller Schankkonzession, -erlaubnis
plaice	Scholle (*Fisch*)
cod	Kabeljau
steak and kidney pie	Fleischpastete mit Nieren
jacket potato	in der Schale gebackene Kartoffel
to plough	pflügen
pickle	(in Essig) eingelegtes Gemüse
smoked	geräuchert
salmon	Lachs
horseradish	Meerrettich
apple pie	Apfelkuchen
custard	Vanillesoße

I. Understanding

1. What is the difference between an ordinary pub and a Free House?
2. What is a ploughman's lunch?
3. What is a jacket potato?

II. Test your English: prepositions

Give the appropriate preposition where one is needed.

1. .... their way home many people in Britain stop .... a drink .... their local pub.
2. Pubs are welcoming places, with the regulars only too happy to talk .... visitors.
3. Traditionally, the British stand .... the bar to drink.
4. Some pubs sell beer .... the breweries that own them.
5. Nowadays there is a wide range .... bar snacks, and lunches.
6. Steak and kidney pie is often served .... chips.
7. Young children cannot go .... a pub, but .... the age of 14 they can when accompanied .... an adult.

III. What about you?

Write at least two sentences in answer to the following questions.

Do you like going to a pub or the equivalent (eg a bar) in your own country? And what is your favourite drink?

3 D

Helen interviews Steve (2nd part)

Helen: Has there always been a pub on this site?
Steve: We're actually mentioned in the Domesday Book, when this would have been the only building for miles around and the *stagecoaches* would *pull up* here. So it was an old *staging post*. And then it was *done up*, I suppose in Victorian times, and then I did it the way it is now about two-and-a-half years ago, but still *retaining* as many of the old *features* as we possibly could.
Helen: When you say it was mentioned in the Domesday Book, can you explain a little about that?
Steve: That was a register of all buildings at that time, and this was as a stage post, so this would have been one of the main roads from the coast up to London, and I think we had at that time smugglers that we used to get because we're right on the coast. And there were stories about gold coins being found in the *locker* upstairs - true or not, I don't know.

Helen: You haven't found any?
Steve: I haven't found any.
Helen: Do you own this pub, or does it belong to a brewery?
Steve: It belongs to the brewery. I rent it. I have a *lease*, a 20-year lease, and I pay them a rent on it. And *by virtue of that*, I am *tied* to buy a lot of my beers from them as well.
Helen: But can you also go elsewhere to buy other beers?
Steve: I'm allowed to buy my guest beers and the traditional ales, and I'm allowed to buy them outside of that *tie*. So customers do have a choice of beer.
Helen: So does this make you a *landlord* or a publican?
Steve: I'm a publican. Had I been the landlord, then I would own the property.
Helen: What makes your pub so different to other pubs?
Steve: We cater for the majority of people. We changed, because the New Forest tends to be a tourist area - is a tourist area in the summer, and even sometimes out of season as well. We cater for both tourists and the locals alike. We try and get people to mix together; the tourists come in because they want to see a typical English pub; the locals keep coming in because it is their meeting place, so it's catering for everybody, families included.
Helen: So what do you offer to families with children?
Steve: We do entertainment for them. A 'Mister Magic' comes and does a magic show one afternoon a week. We also do a Children's Menu, so parents can come in and bring their children as well. And outside there are rides for them, amusement games for them, and then off the garden we have a big *climbing frame*, a play area. And they've got all the animals as well, and especially for the holidaymakers that come from the cities. These children have never seen ponies or *donkeys* or sheep before, so there's all that *novelty value* as well.

stagecoach	Postkutsche
to pull up	anhalten
staging post, stage post	Postkutschenstation
to do up	herrichten, renovieren
to retain	*hier*: beibehalten, bewahren
feature	Merkmal, Besonderheit
locker	Schließfach, *hier*: Safe
lease	Pacht(vertrag)
by virtue of that	aufgrund dessen, deshalb
to be tied	gebunden, verpflichtet sein
tie	Bindung
landlord	Gastwirt (*gleichzeitig Eigentümer des Pubs*)
climbing frame	Klettergerüst
donkey	Esel
novelty value	Neuheitswert, Reiz des Neuen

I. Vocabulary

Explain the following words.

1. feature
2. stagecoach
3. smuggler
4. choice
5. alike (*eg tourists and locals alike*)
6. locals

II. Understanding

1. What is the difference between a landlord and a publican?
2. What does Steve offer families with children?

III. Comment

Write a conversation between two friends who have come into a British pub at lunchtime. They are deciding what to eat and drink. They make different choices and give their reasons for making them. (100 to 150 words)

3 E

Steve describes a typical day

I get up in the morning and feed the animals. Then I *tend to* go into the office and do the *accounts*, *enter* the *figures up*, enter the *books* up. We all live *in dread of* the VAT man (= VAT inspector) and make sure that our books are up together, and the *wages* of course as well.

I count the *tills*, I then do the money to go to the bank, get change from the bank. I may then go through the menu with the chef and *sort out* the day's menu, and possibly the next couple of days as well. Then I organise some entertainment and I tend to be on the phone quite a bit doing that. I get on to the *suppliers* and organise whatever order with them, and if they have any *promotions* or any *tastings* that they wanted me to do, like the ice-cream people. They phone up and say that they would like me to go over there and taste the new flavour of ice-cream. Or even the brewery could phone up and want me to go and taste beer or *sample* a new ale. When time permits I try and get out on the pony and have a little ride on the pony, that's one of my great loves. And, talking of the pony, then the *farrier* may well *turn up* and have shoes to put on both the ponies. And then of course I suppose there's the most important - I've got to entertain the guests when they come in. I'd be behind the bar serving the drink and food, and generally playing 'Mine Host'.

to tend to	neigen, tendieren zu	supplier	Lieferant(in)
accounts, books	Einnahmen und Ausgaben	promotion	Sonderangebot
to enter up	eintragen	tasting	Kostprobe, Probieren
figures	Zahlen	to sample	probieren, kosten
in dread of	in (ständiger) Angst vor	farrier	Hufschmied
wages *pl*	Lohn, Löhne	to turn up	auftauchen, erscheinen
till	(Laden-)Kasse	'Mine Host'	‚Herr Wirt'
to sort out	besprechen, klären		

I. Vocabulary

Give nouns corresponding to the following verbs, as used in this programme.

1. supply
2. promote
3. taste
4. entertain
5. serve

II. Understanding

1. What is Steve's first job in the morning?
2. What does VAT stand for?
3. What does Steve do if he has any time to spare?
4. What does the farrier do?
5. What is meant by playing 'Mine Host'?

III. Test your English: tenses

Complete the sentences with the words in brackets.

1. Steve .... (go) to the bank when he .... (count) the tills.
2. The pub .... (have) long .... (be) the centre of social life.
3. If you .... (know) Steve's pub, you would like it.
4. What .... (be) you .... (do) last night when I .... (phone) you?
5. Steve said his phone .... (be) out of order.
6. How long .... (he, run) this pub?

3 F

A visit to the local brewery

Traditional English beer is produced from *malt* which is made from *barley*. The colour and flavour of the beer is affected by the colour of the malt. The malt is mixed with water to produce a sugar solution which is boiled with *hops*. The unwanted *grains* from the mixture are taken away. The remaining liquid is cooled and *yeast* is added. It is then *fermented* to give the right degree of alcohol for each type of beer.
The local brewery has several different kinds of beer for Steve and his partner to choose from. Traditional English beer or ale is called *draught* bitter, bitter because of its taste, and draught because it's drawn, or pulled, from a barrel.
The strength of beer is determined by the ABV, the percentage of Alcohol By Volume.
In a pub you can order a pint of bitter or a half, half a pint.
Lager is a type of beer which is brewed with gas like most European beers. And stout is a darker, *smoother* beer traditionally brewed in Ireland, which is also popular in British pubs.

malt	Malz	to ferment	gären, zur Gärung bringen
barley	Gerste	draught beer	Faßbier
hops	Hopfen	smooth	*hier*: weich
grain	Korn, Getreide		
yeast	Hefe		

I. Vocabulary

a) Give the nouns corresponding to the following words.

1. to produce
2. mixed
3. fermented
4. brewed
5. popular
6. remaining

b) Give a synonym for

1. flavour
2. barrel

II. Understanding

1. What is meant by draught beer?
2. Where does stout traditionally come from?
3. When you order a pint of bitter, how much do you get (in litres)?

3 G

Helen interviews Steve (3rd part)

'The Rising Sun'

Helen: Is there a danger that, as people become more influenced by the wines from Southern Europe and so on, that this culture or this beer tradition is going to disappear?
Steve: No, I don't think it ever will. It is a tradition, the way it's brewed. It's *unique* to England, and I suppose we've acquired that taste over generations. Youngsters will try and go on to the wines and people will drink wines with meals, and we do now have a bigger selection by the glass than ever before. But in the main, and interestingly, a lot more women are drinking beer now as well.
Helen: What is it in your opinion that makes English beers so special?
Steve: The way they're brewed more than anything, I suppose, which gives them their unique taste. We haven't got any gas in our traditional ales, which again is unique, that it actually comes in and is pulled through on a hand pump, so there's no gas in the beer. And the other is I suppose that it doesn't travel particularly well, that nobody will export traditional beers because they don't travel at all.
Helen: There's one thing you haven't mentioned. I know that you support *the disabled*. Can you tell me a little about that?
Steve: There are two groups that we support. One is very local - it's just down the road, the Fortune Centre of Riding, and that's therapy for disabled children by riding and it's a residential school for them, tied up with riding horses, but they do struggle very much for their *funds*. We do quite a bit of *fund-raising* for them. The

other, which is in New Milton, two miles away, is adult *mentally handicapped*. Of course they tend to get forgotten by a lot of people. Lots of people will support children but not the adult mentally handicapped. And so we do quite a bit for them, and actually have them here, and we'll do parties for them, and it's to try and make their life a little bit more *worthwhile*.

Helen: What was your job before you came here to 'The Rising Sun'?

Steve: This is all I have ever done since I was eighteen. I've been involved in and run pubs. They are all I've ever done.

Helen: And has it always been in this area?

Steve: No, it hasn't. I moved down here ten years ago, but I was in London before that. I had three pubs in London. But now I've moved down here, I would never move far away from the New Forest. It's a wonderful area.

Helen: What type of guests do you get here? Are they locals or tourists? And are there young people?

Steve: A great mixture between the lot, I suppose. Right through the year we have the locals. The tourists tend to be in the summer months. And they mix well together. The youngsters? Yes, there are quite a lot of young people around here.

Helen: Finally, Steve, what's your drink?

Steve: I used to drink *an awful lot*, and now it's wisest for me to stay on coffee.

Helen: Does that mean you're *teetotal*?

Steve: Absolutely. I am teetotal. I don't touch the drink at all.

unique	einzigartig
the disabled *pl*	die Behinderten
funds *pl*	Mittel, Gelder
fund-raising	Geldbeschaffung
mentally handicapped	geistig behindert
worthwhile	lohnend, *hier*: lebenswert
an awful lot	ziemlich viel
teetotal	abstinent

I. Vocabulary

a) Give the adjectives corresponding to the following nouns.

1. danger
2. influence
3. culture
4. tradition
5. residence
6. selection

b) Explain the following expressions.

1. fund-raising
2. teetotal
3. youngsters

II. Understanding

1. What sort of charity work does Steve do?
2. Has Steve always run a pub in the New Forest?
3. What is Steve's favourite drink?

III. After watching the programme, answer the following questions

1. Who did Helen interview in the evening in the pub?
2. How was this evening different from most others in 'The Rising Sun'?

IV. What do you know about Steve?

Write an account (Bericht) *of Steve's work and activities. (100 to 150 words)*

3 H

The New Forest and its surroundings

The New Forest is the responsibility of the British Forestry Commission. The Commission has to *reconcile* commercial interests *with* the demands of tourism and conservation.

The famous New Forest ponies have the right of way on forest roads, and cars have to give way to *grazing* animals. Millions of visitors, many of them bikers and walkers, come here every year to enjoy a breath of fresh air in this *unspoilt rural* playground.

Although originally set aside as a hunting ground, in the 16th century the New Forest became important as a source of *timber*. Its *oak* trees were in great demand for shipbuilding, and one of the important shipbuilding communities was at Buckler's Hard on the Beaulieu River.

One of the most *picturesque* places in the area of the New Forest is the ancient port of Lymington. It's a lively yachting and sailing town with old *cobbled streets* and many fine Georgian and Victorian buildings.

Nearby, on the edge of the Forest, is Beaulieu, with its Abbey, founded by Cistercian *monks* in the 13th century and one of the most influential English monasteries until its destruction by King Henry VIII.

The grounds of the Abbey now house the world-famous National Motor Museum. Lord Montagu of Beaulieu, who lives in the Palace House, has a collection of about 250 cars, some of them very old, like the Rolls Royce Silver Cloud made in 1908.

to reconcile with	in Einklang bringen mit, miteinander vereinbaren	oak	Eiche
to graze	weiden, grasen	picturesque	malerisch, pittoresk
unspoilt	unberührt; unverdorben	cobbled street	Straße mit Kopfstein-pflaster
rural	ländlich	monk	Mönch
timber	Holz		

Helen in a 'Silver Cloud' Rolls Royce

I. Understanding

1. Who created the New Forest?
2. What were the oak trees formerly used for?
3. When was Beaulieu Abbey founded?
4. Who gave the order to destroy the Abbey?
5. Which museum can you visit in Beaulieu?
6. What is the New Forest area famous for?

II. Letter-writing

You are thinking of spending a week in the New Forest area with your family. Write a letter to the local tourist authority (Address: New Forest, Tourist Information Centre, High Street Car Park, Lyndhurst, Hampshire SO43 7NV) to find out about hotel and bed-and-breakfast facilities.

AN APPRENTICE IN CORNWALL 4

4 A

Introduction

This programme is about Gavin McNerlin, an *apprentice* with Svedala *Ltd*, an engineering company in Cornwall in the south-west of England. Gavin's *apprenticeship* involves both working for Svedala and going to a *further education college* in order to gain a *National Vocational Qualification* and eventually become an engineering technician.
We see Gavin at work and at college. Helen talks to his fellow students, and one of the college *lecturers* explains the different ways of *taking up* a career in engineering. We also see Gavin at home and with his friends, enjoying themselves at a local nightclub and on the beach. Helen asks some of them about their jobs and what they do in their spare time.
The programme ends with a look at Cornwall's industrial past and at some of its major tourist attractions.

Accents:
Gavin and his friends have a soft-sounding Cornish accent.

apprentice	Lehrling, Auszubildende(r)	college	Weiterbildung
Limited liability company (Ltd)	Gesellschaft mit beschränkter Haftung (GmbH)	National Vocational Qualification (NVO)	*etwa*: Staatliches Zeugnis über den Abschluß einer Berufsausbildung
apprenticeship	Lehre, Lehrzeit	lecturer	Dozent(in)
further education	Berufsschule, Schule für	to take up	(*Karriere*) einschlagen

4 B

Gavin's apprenticeship at Svedala

Svedala Ltd is based in St Austell. The company produces and *services* pumps and other equipment for marine engineering and for the mining industry. Gavin sometimes accompanies colleagues on trips to service equipment, for example at the English *China Clay pit* nearby. But the main part of his work as an apprentice is in the service and repair area, where pumps which need servicing are brought in and

stripped down to see what is wrong with them. A *quote* is then given to the owner of the pump so that new parts can be ordered. Then the parts are *fitted* and the pump is sent back to the owner again.
Gavin described how *components* for a pump are made in the factory. The process starts with a wooden *pattern* being made by *carpenters* in the pattern shop. Then a sand *casting* of the pattern is made in the *foundry*. The wood is then removed, leaving a *mould* in the form of the pattern. A plastic *coating* is put into the mould in order to *seal* the casting. Then *molten* metal is *poured in*. Next, the sand is removed. This leaves the finished component. Components are *welded*, or joined together, in the fabrication workshop. Finally in the *assembly area* the pump is *assembled* from all the components.

(to) service	(*Geräte*) warten, Inspektion machen; Kundendienst, Inspektion, Wartung
china clay	Porzellanerde, Kaolin
pit	Grube, Zeche
to strip down	auseinandernehmen, zerlegen
quote	Kostenvoranschlag
to fit	*hier*: montieren, einbauen
component	(Maschinen-)Teil
pattern	Muster, Vorlage, *hier*: Gußmodell
carpenter	Schreiner, Tischler
casting	Abguß
foundry	Gießerei
mould	(Guß-)Form
coating	Überzug, Schicht; Anstrich
to seal	versiegeln
molten	geschmolzen
to pour (in)	*hier*: (*in die Form*) gießen
to weld	(zusammen)schweißen
assembly area	Montagehalle, Montagebereich
to assemble	zusammensetzen, -bauen, montieren

Gavin and his colleague in the assembly area

I. Vocabulary

What do the following words mean?

1. to assemble
2. foundry
3. carpenter
4. workshop

II. Understanding

1. What is an apprentice?
2. What kind of work does Gavin do?

4 C

Gavin talks to Helen about being an apprentice

Gavin: Well, basically an apprentice is someone who is training for a recognised qualification, but rather than going to college full time, is based in a *workplace* as well. The other difference is, you also get paid to work as well, which is an added advantage really.
Helen: How long have you been an apprentice for?
Gavin: I've been an apprentice for ten months now.
Helen: Why did you decide to become an apprentice at Svedala?
Gavin: Well, originally I wanted to be an engineer straight from school. The only option then was to go to college full time. So I did a year there and I found it wasn't very practically based. I prefer to get my hands dirty, get on with the job. When the advert came up in the paper for this apprenticeship, I decided to go for that, thinking obviously that it would be more practical, as well as a little bit of theory, which I don't mind. So I decided to take up the job.
Helen: And how long will you be an apprentice for at Svedala?
Gavin: I'll be an apprentice for five years.
Helen: So being an apprentice means you have to do practical and theoretical work. Where do you do the theoretical work, and what kind of work is it?
Gavin: Well, we're at Cambourne College every Monday. We do maths, which could be anything from *vectors*, algebra, basically things that we do need to know, science, drawing. We also do computer-aided design.
Helen: So what do you like most about the apprenticeship? Do you prefer the practical side or the theoretical side?
Gavin: Definitely the practical, I think. Not only using machines but taking things apart, cleaning them and putting them back together, ordering new parts.
Helen: Do you think you'll remain with Svedala after your five years apprenticeship, or can you imagine going on to do something else?
Gavin: Well, I'm very happy where I am, but at the end of my apprenticeship I would like to work abroad for Svedala if the opportunity arises.

workplace	Arbeitsplatz
vector	Vektor

I. Vocabulary

a) Give the nouns corresponding to the following words.

1. recognised
2. to decide
3. to prefer
4. to imagine
5. to think

b) Give synonyms or synonymous expressions for the following words from the interview.

1. to decide
2. option
3. abroad
4. to remain
5. qualification

c) Give the German equivalent for the following expressions.

1. workplace
2. apprenticeship
3. advert
4. vocational training

II. Understanding

1. Why is apprenticeship so attractive for Gavin?
2. How long will Gavin's apprenticeship last?
3. How did Gavin get the job at Svedala?

4 D

Vocational training at Cornwall College, Cambourne

Every Monday, Gavin and other apprentices go to Cornwall College in Cambourne. Gavin's favourite subject is computer-aided design. It involves the use of computers to draw pictures for designing and making products. Learning how to use a computer is an essential part of an engineer's training. They are also taught *robotics*. But more traditional skills are also needed. In the machine shop, students gain practical experience operating heavy machinery under expert *guidance* and *tuition*. Helen talked to Gavin's fellow students about apprenticeship and the course they were following at the college.
One of them said he had decided on this kind of apprenticeship because he had always been interested in practical work, and he needed the money.

A young woman student said she wanted to be a mechanical apprentice or to have a *craft*. For her there was also a family interest because all the members of her family were engineers.
Another student preferred practical work to the subjects that were taught in the classroom.
And one of the apprentices argued that the course offered a *broad-based* way of learning which was vocational rather than academic, so that you were learning as a *hands-on* experience.

robotics	Robotertechnik	craft	Handwerk, Gewerbe
guidance	Führung, (An-)Leitung	broad-based	breitgefächert
tuition	Unterricht	hands-on	praktisch, aktiv

I. Understanding

1. How often does Gavin attend college?
2. What's his favourite subject?
3. What sort of practical training does Gavin get at college?

II. Test your English: modal verbs

Complete the sentences with must, need to, mustn't, needn't and one of the following verbs: go, pay, take up, leave, attend, check, use.

1. You .... entrance fee for the museum.
2. The pump has just been serviced. You .... it.

3. The apprentices .... the computers without being supervised by a lecturer.
4. If you want to be in Land's End by midday, you .... early in the morning.
5. All apprentices .... college once a week.
6. There are two routes for young people who .... a career: a practical and an academic one.
7. Children .... to school until the age of 16.

4 E

Alan Taylor talks to Helen about qualifications for becoming an engineer

Alan Taylor is a lecturer at Cornwall College.

Alan: Nowadays, the best way to be recognised for your practical skills is to take on a National Vocational Qualification. The standards are dictated by the controlling bodies of the industries concerned.
Helen: And what skills will they have to learn in order to gain their NVQ qualification?
Alan: The NVQ spreads over a number of skills. Apprentices will either be machine operators, or they will be *maintenance* engineers, or they could be in welding and fabrication.
Helen: And what is the NVQ qualification equivalent to? Is there a university degree qualification that is equivalent to it, for instance?
Alan: There are two routes, normally, for young people who need to take up a career in engineering. One is along an academic route, and the other is along a much more practical route.
Helen: What makes the better engineer - the university-trained student or the NVQ-trained apprentice?
Alan: It really depends which level you're looking at. I would believe that for all my customers, when they receive a new graduate straight from university, there is a learning curve that that graduate has to, however, take up. With an NVQ progression, the student has remained in industry for a very long time, already *knows the ropes* and will fit in and provide a much better *output*. But it's *short term*. Obviously, as the years progress, then the graduate would be able to overtake the NVQ man and he would take up the more *senior* posts.

maintenance	Wartung, Instandhaltung	short term	kurzfristig
to know the ropes	sich auskennen	senior	höher, leitend
output	*hier*: Leistung		

I. Understanding

Complete the text.

1. There are two main routes to careers in engineering: academic, based on a university degree, and practical, based on ....
2. The academic route involves passing .... at school and then taking a university degree in engineering.
3. After university, an engineering .... will join a suitable company and will eventually qualify as a Chartered (*staatlich geprüfter*) Engineer.
4. But for many young people the .... route is preferable.
5. It means being a fully-paid apprentice with an .... company for four to five years.
6. The apprenticeship begins with in-house training in the company and a short intensive course, called block release, at a further education ...., in order to get a certificate, known as a foundation award.
7. After that, apprentices are given further training in the company. They also study at college one day every week, which enables them to get a .... usually called an NVQ.
8. The NVQ is related directly to the apprentice's ....
9. NVQs are awarded at various ....
10. For example, Level Three means that an apprentice like Gavin will be .... as an Engineering Technician.

II. Comment

Compare Gavin's apprenticeship and vocational training with the prospects of a student who is aiming for an engineering degree. Why does Gavin think he is better off? Do you think he is right? (100 to 150 words)

4 F

Helen interviews Gavin at home

Gavin lives with his mother and younger brother in the village of Fraddon near the cathedral city of Truro.

Helen: Gavin, where were you born and brought up?
Gavin: I was born in Truro, in Cornwall. I've lived here all my life, in Fraddon.
Helen: And have you ever been *tempted* to leave Cornwall?
Gavin: Not really. I don't think I've been tempted to leave. I like the countryside a lot.
Helen: What's your aim in life?
Gavin: My main aim at the moment is to complete my NVQ Level Three. Hopefully move on to *Technicians* after that, just remain happy and working.

Helen: Did your school-friends opt for further education, or did they become apprentices too?
Gavin: Most of them decided to carry on at school, but I do know of two which are doing apprenticeships.
Helen: Did all of your friends manage to get a job, or have some of them been affected by unemployment?
Gavin: Well, the ones that didn't end up with jobs decided to go back to school or college anyway, which is a better option, rather than being unemployed.
Helen: Gavin, you start work very early in the mornings and you finish fairly early in the afternoons, which must be quite nice in the summer, when the weather's nice. What do you like to do in your spare time?
Gavin: Well, I've got a motorcycle which, when it's nice, I do go riding around the Newquay area. I like going to the beach, playing football. I've just passed my driving test, so I can go for a ride in Mum's car. During the week, of (= *during/on*) an evening, I like to go and play *snooker* at the local club. But most of all I like to go clubbing of a Friday and Saturday night to this brilliant nightclub in Newquay called Talltrees. At the weekend, if the weather is fine, I play football on the beach. Some of my friends go surfing, a popular sport on the Cornish coast.

to tempt	verführen, verleiten
technician	Techniker(in)
snooker	Snooker (*dem Billiard verwandtes Spiel*)

Gavin on his way to college

I. Vocabulary

Give synonyms for

1. brilliant
2. to complete
3. fairly
4. spare time

II. Understanding

1. What is the name of Gavin's birthplace?
2. What has happened to Gavin's friends who haven't been able to get a job?
3. What effect has passing his driving test had on Gavin's use of his spare time?
4. What does Gavin mean by 'clubbing'?
5. What are Gavin's hobbies?

III. What about you?

Cornwall has a large number of unemployed young people. What ways can you think of to tackle (angehen) *the problem of unemployment among young people in your own country?*

4 G

Helen interviews some of Gavin's friends

Helen: What are you going to do once you finish your apprenticeship at Svedala?
Young man 1: I'm hoping they're going to offer me a full-time position doing machining and I hope to carry on there for a very long time.
Helen: What do you do?
Young woman 1: I work for Svedala in Cornwall, and I deal with incoming *invoices* and send them out, get them ready for payment so that we can pay the companies who supply us with parts.
Helen: Chris, tell me, how old are you?
Young man 2: I'm twenty-one.
Helen: You're a little older than the other first-year apprentices at Svedala. Can you tell me what you did before you came to Svedala as an apprentice?
Young man 2: Last year I finished my degree. I was at Cambridge studying geology, but I decided I really wanted to move back to Cornwall. I had also decided I wanted to do something more practical, such as engineering. Moving to Svedala proved the ideal opportunity. I was able to gain a *grounding* by doing an apprenticeship, while I've always kept the degree behind me, so I'll always have that to *fall back on*.
Helen: What do you do?

Young woman 2: I work at Svedala. I'm a secretary to the Manufacturing Manager.
Helen: Did you go to Svedala as soon as you left school?
Young woman 2: No, I went to ECC, which is English China Clays on a YTS, which is the Youth Training Scheme for two years, and then I'd seen a job at Svedala which I applied for and I got. So I've been there for five years now.
Helen: What do you do in your spare time?
Young woman 3: I like to dance, go to clubs. I like music a lot. I like to sing.
Helen: Why do you think so many young people like going to clubs nowadays?
Young woman 3: I'm not sure, actually. It's - there's everyone getting together, and if everyone's really happy it's really nice. A nice atmosphere.

invoice	(Waren-)Rechnung	to fall back on	zurückgreifen auf
grounding	Grundwissen, Grundlagen		

I. Vocabulary

Give the opposites corresponding to the following words.

1. to finish
2. sure
3. happy
4. practical
5. young
6. nice

II. Say it in English

1. Ich hoffe, daß Svedala Ltd mir eine Vollzeitstelle anbietet, wenn ich meine Lehre beendet habe.
2. Gavins Freundin arbeitet in der Rechnungsabteilung der Firma. Sie bearbeitet eingehende Rechnungen.
3. Nachdem Chris sein Studium an der Universität Cambridge abgeschlossen hatte, ist er nach Cornwall zurückgekehrt. Er entschloß sich, sich um eine Lehrstelle bei Svedala zu bewerben.

4 H

What do you know about Gavin?

Complete the sentences.

1. Gavin is 18 years old and an .... at Svedala, an engineering company near St Austell in ....
2. Once a week he goes to Cornwall .... where he has to study both practical and .... subjects.
3. After he has got a National .... Qualification, Gavin hopes to go on to be qualified as an Engineering Technician.

4. Gavin lives with his mother and his younger .... in a small village near the city of Truro.
5. He likes the Cornish .... and often goes riding around the Newquay area on his ....
6. On Friday and Saturday evening he likes going .... in Newquay.
7. When the weather is fine he likes going to the .... with his friends.

4 I

A tour of the Cornish countryside

Tintagel

Cornwall is the westernmost *county* in England. No part of it lies more than 20 miles from the sea. It is famous for its *rugged* coastline and wild inland moors. But because it lies in the path of the Gulf Stream, Cornwall has the mildest climate of any part of Britain.

For over two thousand years the main industry in Cornwall was *tin* mining. South Crofty Mine is the last tin mine in Cornwall that is still working. At one time, Cornish tin and *copper* mines were the most important in the world. Now they're closed, and the landscape is full of the castle-like ruins of their engine houses.

About two hundred years ago, the mining of china clay - used in making pottery - developed, and the area around St Austell looks like a moon landscape with its pyramid-shaped china clay *tips*.

Nowadays the most important industry in Cornwall is tourism.

Cornwall is a land of Celtic legends. The ruined castle at Tintagel is said to have

been the home of King Arthur and the Knights of the Round Table. It was the source of many famous stories, such as the romance of Tristan and Isolde.
Very different is the seaside *resort* of St Ives, which attracts crowds of tourists from all over the world during the summer. The town has managed to keep much of its old character, with cobbled streets and tiny gardens in front of *white-washed* buildings. More than sixty years ago, St Ives became a centre for artists, from the internationally famous, like the *sculptor* Barbara Hepworth, to less well-known painters of local sights.

Polperro

One of the most picturesque villages on the Cornish coast is Polperro. Fishing is still a very important source of income here. But nowadays the customers are often tourists. Indeed, tourism has replaced the old practice of smuggling as an alternative way of making a living.
On an island just off the coast is St Michael's Mount, originally the site of a Benedictine monastery founded in the 11th century. The castle itself dates from the 14th and 15th centuries.
The long thin *peninsula* ends at the *rocky* cliffs of Land's End, the westernmost point of England.

county	Grafschaft	resort	Urlaubsort
rugged	zerklüftet	white-washed	weiß getüncht
tin	Zinn	sculptor	Bildhauer
copper	Kupfer	peninsula	Halbinsel
tip	Spitze	rocky	felsig

Understanding

1. Why is the climate on Cornwall's coast so mild?
2. What was Cornwall's main industry in the past?
3. What is china clay used for?
4. What do you know about St Ives?
5. What is the name of the westernmost point in England?

4 J

Translation

Translate the first two paragraphs.

Secret of good training

For a century or more Britain has had the reputation of being quite good at academic education (at least for the social and intellectual elite) but appallingly bad at vocational training.

That seems to be changing as representatives of 56 countries gather today for a conference in London to explore the merits of NVQs - the National Vocational Qualifications introduced in 1986 to improve work-based education.

The system has had plenty of domestic critics and last week the National Audit Office raised doubts about unacceptably large variations in drop-out rates of students on the college-based components of the programme but increasing numbers of foreign governments are now queuing up to copy the UK's invention of a so-called 'competence-based' approach to training. It may become one of Britain's fastest-growing export earners, providing opportunities for further education colleges and consultants.

In papers prepared for this week's international conference in London, the system is described by David Blunkett, the Education and Employment Secretary, as 'one of Britain's best kept secrets'.

The NVQs and SVQs (Scottish Vocational Qualifications) were developed in the mid-1980s to respond to growing international competition and technological change. They aimed to put greater emphasis on the skills that people needed to do their job properly instead of more general theoretical learning.

(The Guardian, November 4, 1997)

A TOURIST EXECUTIVE IN JERSEY 5

5 A

Introduction

Jersey

This programme is about Sue Daniell, who is a tourist *executive* in Jersey, the largest of the Channel Islands a few miles off the coast of Normandy. Sue talks about her *duties*, her career in the tourist industry, and her life on the island. She also takes Helen on a cycle tour to see some of Jersey's best-known tourist attractions.

Sue and some of the visitors to the island explain why Jersey is so popular with tourists, and Malcolm Lewis, the President of Jersey's Hotel and Guest House Association, discusses the facilities on the island and the way tourism is *promoted* abroad.

We also learn about Jersey's unusual form of government and about its economy as an international banking and financial centre.

Note:

Le Jerriais - English is the language spoken on the Channel Islands, but older residents of some country areas still speak a Norman-French dialect called 'le Jerriais'. The local language is however *preserved* in its place names.

executive	leitende(r) Ange-stellte(r), Manager(in)	to promote	werben für
duty	Pflicht, Aufgabe	to preserve	erhalten, bewahren

5 B

Sue Daniell at work

Sue *is based at* the offices of Jersey Tourism. It's the main centre for visitors coming into Jersey. There are two parts: an information bureau, where people can come and find out about places to visit, and an *accommodation* section, where central *bookings* for hotels, guest houses and camp sites are taken.
Sue's main area of responsibility is the European Marketing Department. Her duties include welcoming journalists from the press and other media. She also meets and greets tourists, and she likes to catch up with them if they are in a group in a hotel, or at a tourist attraction, just to *ensure* that they are having a good stay in Jersey, enjoying themselves, seeing the best sights, and being properly looked after by their *courier*. Sue also attends marketing meetings, for example in order to discuss the advertising brochures for the following year. And she is responsible for arranging how the Channel Islands are to be represented at international travel and tourism *exhibitions*.

to be based at	seinen Sitz (*hier*: Büro) haben in	to ensure	sicherstellen, sichergehen
accommodation	Unterkunft, Quartier	courier	Reiseleiter(in)
booking	Buchung, Bestellung	exhibition	Ausstellung

I. Vocabulary

a) Give a synonym or synonymous expression corresponding to the following words in the text above.

1. section
2. duty
3. stay
4. to attend
5. exhibition

b) Give the noun corresponding to the following verbs.

1. arrive
2. include
3. greet
4. attract
5. attend
6. discuss
7. arrange

II. What about you?

Give one or more reasons why you would (or would not) want Sue's job.

5 C

Helen interviews Sue at Mount Orgueil Castle

Helen: Sue, what kind of tourists come to Jersey?
Sue: Well, really all sorts of tourists. We actually divide our market into two very important sections. First of all, visitors from the United Kingdom and then visitors from *mainland Europe*. And they tend to look for completely different things. For example, the UK tourists tend to be older, tend to be *retired*, or even with families - we have a very big family market from the United Kingdom. From mainland Europe it's completely different. They tend to come in order to *explore* more, to cycle, to walk, to do activities. They really are more *adventurous as a rule*. And the market is a lot younger.
The largest mainland Europe market is the French. We're very close to France and it's very, very easy for them to come across. And after that, the German market is becoming more and more important to us.
Helen: Why would you say do people come to Jersey for their holiday instead of going further south for the sun?
Sue: I think the days of *sun-worshipping* are gone. I don't think that's really what people are looking for on their holiday any more. You know, all the major Spanish resorts and the Mediterranean coast used to be very popular. Now I think holiday time is so *precious* that people are looking for something different. They're looking for somewhere where they can sit on the beach but they can also do something else. And they know that if the weather's not so good there are lots of other, beautiful things to see and do as well. We've really got a little bit of everything.
Helen: What sort of activities do you have here?
Sue: Well, we have for the more adventurous a lot of water sports, as you can imagine. We're surrounded by water, and you can do a *diving* course, for example, or windsurfing, surfing, all sorts of water activities certainly. And also on land, a lot of what I've mentioned before. Cycling is very, very popular. In particular the Dutch tend to leave their cars in France and come over and cycle for two weeks.

mainland Europe	das europäische Festland
retired	im Ruhestand, pensioniert
to explore	erkunden, erforschen, entdecken
adventurous	abenteuerlustig
as a rule	in der Regel
sun-worship(ping)	Sonnenanbetung
precious	kostbar
diving	Tauchen

I. Vocabulary

Find words or expressions in the interview which have the same meaning as the following.

1. to stop work
2. to discover
3. valuable
4. daring
5. especially
6. to be inclined to
7. generally liked
8. usually

II. Understanding

1. What sports can you take part in when you visit Jersey?
2. What is a seaside resort?

III. Letter-writing

Write a letter to Jersey Tourism, Liberation Square, St Helier, Jersey JE1 1BB, Channel Islands, telling them that you will be attending a language course this summer. Ask for accommodation - a single room for three weeks in a small guest house or with a family in St Helier - and inquire about the cost.

5 D

Why do people come to Jersey?

Helen asked several people why they had come to Jersey. This is what she found out.

If you're a tourist, a good reason for visiting Jersey is that the island's large, sandy beaches are never really crowded. So it's an ideal holiday place for families with children. Some tourists *do jet-skiing*, others go and see the ***Occupation Museum*** and the ***Underground Hospital*** if the weather isn't too good. Jersey is a good place for shopping, too. There are lots of duty-free goods to attract visitors. Many *couples* come to Jersey on their *honeymoon*. Other young people come to study English at language schools.

But there's another important reason for being in Jersey. Business people come to the island to work, especially in the finance industry.

Notes:

The ***Occupation Museum*** *commemorates* the enemy occupation of Jersey from June 1940 to May 1945. It contains uniforms, equipment and documents from the Second World War.

The ***Underground Hospital*** was originally built during the early years of the occupation as a *store* for munitions and weapons. Later it was *converted into* a hospital but was never used for this purpose.

to do jet-skiing	Wasserski fahren	to commemorate	gedenken
occupation	Besatzung	store	Lager, Vorrat
couple	Paar	to convert into	umwandeln in
honeymoon	Flitterwochen		

I. Understanding

What kind of people go to Jersey and for what reasons?

II. Comment

What do you think of the so-called adventure holidays offered by some travel agencies? (50 to 100 words)

5 E

Helen interviews Malcolm Lewis, President of the Hotel and Guest House Association

Helen: Is Jersey's *hotel staff* mainly from the island?

Malcolm: No, it's not. No, the majority of our *workforce* in the industry come from Portugal, and that's *been due* entirely *to* a special relationship, a special agreement between Portugal and the island.

Helen: And what are you doing to *rectify* the situation, to get locals to work in the industry?

Malcolm: Well, the Hotel and Guest House Association, together with the Restaurant Owners Association, the *Guild* of *Sommeliers*, and the Jersey *Chef*

Circle, are working very hard in terms of promoting the industry, within the schools in the first instance, demonstrating to the youngsters that it's a great profession. And secondly, in the *catering colleges* themselves, and encouraging the catering colleges to provide *the very* courses that are required by the youngsters of the island, and that would be of *benefit* to them in the future within this industry.

Helen: What do Jersey's guest houses and hotels have to offer?

Malcolm: Well, first of all, Jersey is an island. We have some of the most wonderful beaches that I know of. In fact, they're internationally *acclaimed* as some of the cleanest beaches in Europe. We have a whole variety of different types of hotels and guest houses, from *manor houses* to *farmhouses*, to waterside hotels. A whole variety, there's something for everybody, including conference facilities, which is very important these days. We also have fantastic sporting facilities. Again we have the beaches, all the water sports. We have horse riding, we have terrific golf courses on the island. We have *archery*. Well, you name a sport and we can provide it on the island of Jersey.

Helen: Can you tell me the difference between a hotel and a guest house.

Malcolm: Well, it's primarily a question of size. Guest houses tend to be *proprietor* run. That's to say the proprietor will be there personally welcoming the guests, personally cooking the breakfast, personally providing the dinner, whereas the hotel tends to be that little bit bigger, and perhaps a little less personal. But here in Jersey we do *pride* ourselves *on hospitality* and personality in terms of offering service.

Helen: How do you promote Jersey's hotels and guest houses abroad?

Malcolm: Well, the Jersey Tourism Department has representation in all the major European countries, and this is the first step in *putting* the word *across* that Jersey is here. We have a *backup* of advertising and promotion, we have the brochure itself, the European version of our what we call the 'Where-to-Stay' brochure, which is sent to all *enquirers* who *request* information on the island of Jersey and on accommodation on the island.

hotel staff	Hotelpersonal
workforce	Arbeitskräfte
to be due to	aufgrund, zurückzuführen sein auf
to rectify	verbessern, korrigieren
association	Vereinigung, Verein
guild	Gilde, Verein
sommelier	Weinverkoster
chef	Koch
catering college	Hotelfachschule
the very	genau der/die/das
benefit	Nutzen
to acclaim	anerkennen
manor house	Herrenhaus
farmhouse	Bauernhof, -haus
archery	Bogenschießen
proprietor	Eigentümer, Besitzer
to pride oneself on sth	sich einer Sache rühmen (können)
hospitality	Gastfreundschaft
to put across	verständlich machen, vermitteln
backup	Unterstützung
enquirer	(Nach-)Fragende(r)
to request	erbitten, ersuchen um

I. Vocabulary

Give synonyms or synonymous expressions for these words or phrases in the text above.

1. workforce
2. to rectify
3. to be of benefit
4. acclaimed
5. variety
6. proprietor
7. backup
8. to request

II. Test your English: prepositions

Insert suitable prepositions in the following sentences.

1. We stayed ..... a guest house ..... the coast.
2. The air ..... the seaside is very healthy.
3. We stayed ..... the beach ..... lunch-time.
4. ..... the weekend, the beaches are crowded ..... people sunbathing or swimming.
5. Along the whole coastline ..... St Helier ..... St Brelade's Bay there are hotels, restaurants and cafés, all open ..... the thousands ..... holidaymakers.

III. Comment

Which do you prefer: a crowded beach or a deserted one? Give reasons for your preference. (60 words)

5 F

Sue meets Malcolm Lewis

It is part of Sue Daniell's job to discuss the brochures with Malcolm Lewis.

Malcolm: What do you think about our presentation of the two brochures, in particular perhaps the European brochure which the Hotel and Guest House Association produces? Do you think we perhaps should be looking for improvements?

Sue: I certainly have a few suggestions. I mean, I realise there are always *limitations*. I mean, it's a pity in a way that we can't have the size of the UK brochure, but I realise that the postage and what have you, that's always a problem - every year that comes up. A couple of practical points really. With comparing the two brochures, I know that for us at Tourism this year, the listing in the front has been very useful. It's always a very useful sort of catalogue and guide, I notice it's not in the European version. Is there a way of including that?

Malcolm: Well, that's something we are looking at. As you rightly say, it's the size which is a problem.

Sue: That's right. That's another point I wanted to make. For example, people tend to ask these days for vegetarian menus, and another thing that's quite common is no-smoking rooms.

Malcolm: That's right. I think we'll find something for next year. Having had various discussions with the Jersey Tourism Department, the vegetarian issue is something we've *taken on board*.

limitation	Beschränkung, Einschränkung
to take on board	aufnehmen

I. Understanding

Complete the sentences, using the information in the text.

1. In recent years .... has become increasingly popular and profitable.
2. Many of the visitors are day .... from the UK and France.
3. But there are also a large number of tourists who .... on the island.
4. Every year, more than 600,000 of these tourists stay in Jersey, and they have a wide .... of hotels, ..., camp sites and holiday villages.

II. Comment

Does the tourist trade contribute anything to increasing understanding between nations? (100 words)

5 G

Sue's career in the tourist industry, and her life in Jersey

Helen: Sue, how long have you worked in the tourist industry?
Sue: In total, about seven years. Even going back to my student days, I used to work on the boats that travelled between Jersey and the other Channel Islands and the French coast on day trips. Then when I finished university I actually went to France, and I lived in France, in Antibes, for a period of about four years, where I worked firstly at Nice airport. Then I left tourism and decided to go into teaching, but soon returned. I missed the excitement.
Helen: What do you find most rewarding about your job?
Sue: It has to be seeing tourists come to Jersey. When you spend all winter working, and marketing, and designing brochures, and arranging hotel brochures, it's wonderful when the season starts and you see the figures, the number of tourists mounting again. And it's really rewarding.
Helen: But do you ever have any difficult guests?
Sue: I don't know if you can ever speak to anybody who works in the tourism industry who doesn't have difficult guests. I think that's part of the fun! Of course we have difficult customers. Not actually many. I've spoken to other tourist offices, and I think we're quite lucky that we only get the *odd* ones, for sure.
Helen: And what do they argue about?
Sue: Let me think, let me give you an example. Yes, we had one gentleman, he booked a hotel with us and he wanted to pay a *supplement* for a sea view, which was great. So we arranged a sea view room for him. The next morning, he was back in the office very, very angry, and came up to me and said he had a *complaint* to make. I said, "I'm sorry, sir, what can I do to help?" He said, "The *tide* went out! I paid a sea view supplement and the tide went out."

odd	merkwürdig, sonderbar, komisch	complaint	Beschwerde
		tide	Flut, Gezeiten
supplement	*hier*: Zuschlag		

I. Vocabulary

Give the verbs corresponding to the following nouns.

1. decision
2. argument
3. booking
4. complaint
5. thought

II. Understanding

1. Where did Sue go when she finished university?
2. Sue didn't always work in tourism. What else did she do?

III. Say it in English

1. Sue arbeitet schon seit sieben Jahren in der Tourismusbranche.
2. Wir hoffen, das Wetter ist morgen schön.
3. Sues Kollegin wird im Oktober heiraten.
4. Er kommt (aber auch) immer zu spät.

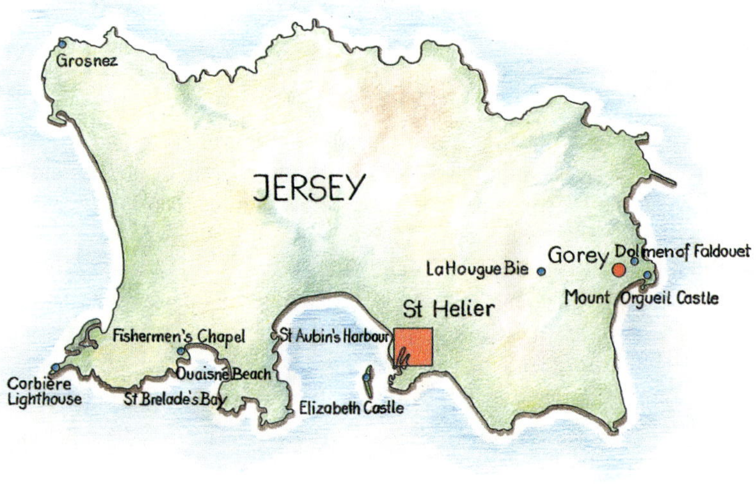

A map of Jersey

5 H

A cycle tour round Jersey

Jersey is famous for its many old buildings and for its beaches.
Elizabeth Castle was built in the 16th century when cannon fire was invented and Mount Orgueil Castle in Gorey was no longer safe. It can be reached on foot at *low tide* and at *high tide* there is a boat.
At the end of St Brelade's Bay is the small Fishermen's Chapel, also called the 'Chapelle des Pêcheurs'.
Next, Sue took Helen to look at some of the island's ancient monuments. La Hougue Bie is a massive *burial ground*, dating from nearly 4000 BC. It's one of the most fascinating ancient sites in Europe. On top of the *mound* there is also a *medieval* chapel.
The Dolmen of Faldouet are a collection of stones to mark an ancient burial site estimated to be about four and a half thousand years old. The main stone, the cap

stone, is estimated to weigh 24 tons. Grosnez is a collection of mysterious ruins thought to have been built in the 14th century to protect the western Jersey people against the French.
Corbière *Lighthouse* was built at the end of the last century and ships have *come to grief* here for hundreds of years. It's the first *concrete* lighthouse to be built in the British Isles. You can reach it at low tide, but there is an alarm that rings when you have to leave.
St Brelade's Bay is one of the most popular bays for visitors to Jersey, and a special favourite with British tourists.
Ouaisné Beach is said to have been used by many smugglers of illegal goods into Jersey in the past. Now the only sign that remains is a little pub called 'The Old Smugglers' Inn'.
St Aubin's harbour was once the island's main port. It used to be a centre for boatbuilding and *knitting*. The ladies who lived in the houses along the port used to knit *stockings* which were famous all over the world.

low tide	Ebbe	lighthouse	Leuchtturm
high tide	Flut	to come to grief	zu Schaden kommen
burial ground	Begräbnisstätte	concrete	Beton
mound	Hügel	to knit	stricken
medieval	mittelalterlich	stocking	Strumpf

Mount Orgueil Castle

I. Test your English: adjective or adverb?

Use the words in brackets correctly in the following sentences.

1. Sue spoke very .... (enthusiastic).
2. He's a very .... (good) surfer.
3. La Hougue Bie is one of the most .... (fascinating) monuments on the island.
4. St Brelade's Bay is .... (probable) the most attractive beach in Jersey.
5. I've read your advertisement .... (careful).

II. What about you?

Do you like travelling abroad? Why (Why not)?

III. What do you know about Sue?

Complete the sentences using the information in the programme.

1. Sue is very busy, but she still has time to do everyday things like .... in the market for vegetables, where she often buys one of the island's most famous products: Jersey Royal ....
2. Sue likes to get away from it all by .... around the island. She invited Helen to go with her.
3. They started by cycling through some of Jersey's Green Lanes. These Green Lanes give priority to .... and walkers, and the .... limit is only 15 miles an hour.
4. Jersey Tourism was the first tourist organisation to join a worldwide scheme called 'Green Globe' which is designed to .... the environment.
5. After the tour round the island, it was time for Sue to join some friends in 'The Old Portelet Inn', one of Jersey's ....
6. That's a perfect place to end a busy day. And anyway, Sue wouldn't be British if she didn't .... to the pub.

5 I

The government of Jersey

Jersey has enjoyed *internal self-government* since 1204. The island is part of the British Isles, but it is independent from the United Kingdom and it is outside the European Union.
Unlike the rest of the British Isles, Jersey is *subject* only *to* the British Crown, not to the United Kingdom parliament. As a result, changes in the island's status have to be confirmed by Royal Charter.

In Jersey the Crown is represented by the Lieutenant Governor, *appointed* by the Queen every five years. The States of Jersey, the island's parliament, *passes the laws* which govern internal affairs.
There are 53 elected members, *presided over* by the *Bailiff*, who is appointed by the Queen.
The present Bailiff is Sir Philip Bailhache. He is not only President of the States Assembly. As President of the Royal Court, he is head of the island's independent legal system. He is also the Chief *Citizen*.
When the United Kingdom passes laws which affect the island, the British Home Office, representing Parliament, *communicates* with the Lieutenant Governor, representing the Queen, who *in turn* communicates with the Bailiff, representing the States of Jersey. The Bailiff is then responsible for communicating with the departments or committees of the States Assembly representing the island's citizens in the *areas of policy* involved.

internal	innere, Innen-	bailiff	Verwalter, Minister
self-government	Selbstverwaltung	citizen	(Staats-)Bürger(in)
subject to	unterworfen	to communicate	in Verbindung stehen,
to appoint	ernennen		sich verständigen
to pass a law	ein Gesetz verabschieden	in turn	wiederum
to preside (over)	leiten	area of policy	Fachgebiet

Understanding

Complete the sentences using the information from the text above.

1. Jersey is part of the ....
   a) European Union b) UK c) British Isles
2. As Jersey is the .... of the Channel Islands it has one of the best sunshine records, because it is warmed by the Gulf Stream.
   a) most southerly b) largest c) smallest
3. Jersey is subject to the ....
   a) States of Jersey b) British Crown c) British Parliament
4. Jersey is free to pass its own ....
   a) local laws b) constitutional changes c) money

5 J

The economy of Jersey

Jersey money

Financial services and banking *account for* 50% of Jersey's *Gross Domestic Product*, or GDP, and of the *revenue* it earns from taxes. There are 31,000 *registered companies* on the island, and 77 banks, which have *deposits* worth £90 billion. A large proportion of these deposits are in foreign *currency*.
This is mostly the result of the favourable taxes *imposed* by the island's government. There is no Value Added Tax on goods or services, and tax on company profits is only about 20%.
Personal *income tax* is also 20% and there is no *inheritance tax* on the money and *possessions* left by people when they die. This makes Jersey an attractive place to keep money or *investments*, and also to live. But *residence* on the island is carefully controlled. To qualify as a new *resident*, a person has to be a wealthy immigrant. Wealthy immigrants must prove that they have an income of at least £750,000 in order to produce at least £150,000 in tax revenue for the island.

to account for	ausmachen, der Grund sein für
Gross Domestic Product (GDP)	Bruttosozialprodukt (BSP)
revenue	Einnahmen, Einkünfte
registered company	eingetragene Firma
deposit	Guthaben
currency	Währung
to impose	(*Steuern*) erheben
income tax	Einkommensteuer
inheritance tax	Erbschaftsteuer
possession	Besitz
investment	Investition
residence	Aufenthalt, Wohnsitz
resident	Einwohner(in)

I. Understanding

Complete the sentences using the information in the text.

1. The main attractions for immigration are the island's low .... and the absence of .... tax and VAT.
2. However, becoming a permanent .... of Jersey today is very difficult, except when you are really ...., or you marry someone who was born on the island.
3. Financial services and banking account for 50% of Jersey's ....

II. Test your English: tenses

Complete the sentences with the correct form of the verb given in brackets.

1. The States of Jersey .... (prove) its commitment to protecting the environment and .... (employ) Conservation Officers for many years.
2. In the last 18 months this commitment .... (strengthen) by the creation of a new post of Environmental Adviser to the States.
3. A strategic policy review and action plan .... (produce) for the island for the next ten years called '2000 and Beyond'.
4. At the World Travel Market in 1995, it .... (announce) that Jersey Tourism .... (become) the first tourism destination in the world to sign and commit to a new world-wide environmental management and awareness programme, 'Green Globe'.
5. A Tourism Investment Fund of £10 million .... (establish) to support new initiatives to improve holidays.

A STUDENT IN BIRMINGHAM

6

6 A

Introduction

Birmingham: The Town Hall

This programme is about David Ginsberg, a student of Law and French at the University of Birmingham. We see David preparing for his final examinations for a ***Bachelor of Laws*** degree and looking for a job. Two months later we return and watch him on *graduation day*, *celebrating* with his family and friends.
David talks to Helen about his life as a student and about his *career prospects*. We follow him during a typical day, and watch him writing his *CV* (*curriculum vitae*), making inquiries at the University Careers Centre and attending an interview with the Rover Group of car manufacturers.
Helen talks to the students who share a flat with David and to other students at the Careers Centre. She interviews the director of the centre, Dr Richard Maynard, and also John Berkeley, who is responsible for training young people at the Rover Group.
Finally, we take a look at Birmingham and especially at the important part it played in the ***Industrial Revolution***.

Notes:

A ***Bachelor of Laws*** degree is a university degree for those who have studied Law, nowadays often combined with another subject (eg French, German, Politics, Business Studies).

The ***Industrial Revolution*** is the period of rapid industrial expansion in Britain at the end of the 18th and beginning of the 19th century.

Bachelor of Laws	*etwa*: Magister der rechtswissenschaftlichen Fakultät	to celebrate	feiern
		career prospects	Berufsaussichten
		curriculum vitae (CV)	Lebenslauf
graduation day	Abschlußfeier (*an der Universität*)		

6 B

Helen interviews David

Helen: David, do you feel that university has prepared you well for life?
David: Well, it's difficult to know at the moment. It's - I mean, I haven't left university yet, but I do feel that I've changed since I've been at university. I mean, you come to a new place, having moved from London to Birmingham, and then you meet new people, and there's new situations, and it's the first time you really have a bit of freedom in your life and make your own choices. And so in that way I imagine it has prepared me for life.
Helen: How long does one have to study French and Law for?
David: It's a four-year course. Three of those years are spent in Birmingham, and we spend our third year in Limoges, in France.
Helen: And apart from French, are there any other languages that you speak?
David: I did a bit of German at school.
Helen: Would you like to become a *lawyer* when you *graduate*?
David: No. I sort of decided after my second year at university that I didn't want to be a lawyer, that I'd like to work in industry or within a business - in commerce.
Helen: Don't you automatically have to enter the law profession if you've studied Law?
David: No. A degree course is - though it deals with law - is left open for people. If you want to be a lawyer, you have to do another year's study following that if you want to be a *barrister* or *solicitor*. But a lot of people who do law don't actually go on to do law, a lot of people actually do accountancy.
Helen: What other *career paths* are open to you if you study a language and Law?
David: Accountancy is one avenue that a lot of people follow. But there are various jobs open to people with a Law degree, especially with the other language - such as working in the *civil service*. A lot of the big firms *recruit* for their Graduate *Schemes* people with languages because of the increasing international dimension of business. So it is really - it's worth having, and it is a help when you're looking for a job.

lawyer	Anwalt, Anwältin
(to) graduate	Hochschulabsolvent(in); graduieren, die Abschluß-prüfung bestehen
barrister	Rechtsanwalt, -anwältin *bei Gericht*
solicitor	Rechtsanwalt, -anwältin, *der/die nicht vor Gericht plädiert*
career path	Laufbahn, Karriereweg
civil service	Staatsdienst
to recruit	einstellen, anstellen
scheme	*hier*: Programm

I. Vocabulary

Give the verbs corresponding to the following nouns.

1. decision
2. choice
3. graduation
4. entrance
5. recruitment

II. Understanding

1. Describe David Ginsberg.
2. What degree is he studying for?
3. How many and what languages does David speak?
4. Does David want to enter the law profession after his graduation or would he prefer to do something different?

III. Test your English: if-clauses

Change the infinitive phrases into clauses with main verbs.

1. If I went to a university, ... (to study Business Administration).
2. If I had intended to study Law, ... (to go to the London School of Economics).
3. If you have done well in your final degree examinations, ... (not need to fear unemployment).
4. If she had been a good student, ... (not to fail her examinations).
5. If you had lived in France, ... (to learn French rapidly).

6 C

The legal profession

There are two separate branches of the legal profession in England and Wales, and two kinds of lawyers: barristers and solicitors.
Barristers work from offices called *chambers*. It's their job to present their client's case effectively *in court*.

To practise as a barrister, you must first join one of the four *Inns of Court* in London and take *Bar* Examinations in order to be called to the Bar. The Bar was originally a *barrier* separating lawyers from the rest of the court.
Barristers are called *Counsel*, and successful barristers may apply to become Queen's Counsel, a title allowing them to put the letters 'QC' after their name. Barristers cannot *have* direct *dealings with* a client. That is the job of solicitors.
You can become a solicitor after two to four years' practical training with a firm of solicitors, followed by Law Society Examinations.
Solicitors usually practise in firms or partnerships with other solicitors. But some are on the legal staff of big organisations, including Central and Local Government departments. They carry out all kinds of legal services on behalf of their clients.
A solicitor may represent a client in court in *minor* cases, but for more important cases the client gives instructions to the solicitor, who *prepares a brief*, a version of those instructions, for a barrister, who then acts as counsel for the client in court.

chambers *pl*	(Anwalts-)Kanzlei	to have dealings with	zu tun haben mit
in court	vor Gericht	minor	unbedeutend, geringer
Inns of Court	*die vier englischen* Juristenverbände	brief	Unterlagen *zu einem Fall*; Auftrag *an einen Anwalt*
Bar	Anwaltschaft		
barrier	Schranke, Sperre	to prepare a brief	einen Fall vorbereiten
counsel	Ratgeber		

I. Understanding

1. What is the difference between a solicitor and a barrister?
2. What are Bar Examinations?
3. What do the letters 'QC' mean?

II. Test your English: the use of <u>may</u>

Translate the following sentences.

1. A solicitor may represent a client in court in minor cases.
2. May I have a look at your pictures?
3. He tries hard and he may succeed.
4. May I come in?
5. The production may prove to be an expensive failure.
6. He may be a nice chap, but he is very ugly.

6 D

A typical day in the life of a student

David lives in Selly Oak, a district of Birmingham where a lot of the students live. He shares a house with three other law students.

David gets up fairly early - about half-seven - and before his *lectures* or classes he likes to go into the *gym* at about eight o'clock.

Then at nine, he goes into the law *faculty* to attend a lecture or study in the law library.

Since he's not far from *campus*, he comes back home at lunchtime and gets together with his *housemates*. They have lunch, watch a bit of TV, *have a chat*.

In the evenings he sometimes goes out with his housemates. One thing they like is going to watch *greyhound racing*.

He often meets up with his girlfriend, Adele, and they go out for a meal, sometimes to a Balti restaurant. There are lots of Balti restaurants in Birmingham.

Note:
A ***Balti restaurant*** specialises in the cooking of Kashmir in the north of the Indian sub-continent.

lecture	Vorlesung	housemate	Mitbewohner(in)
gym(nasium)	Sporthalle, Fitnessraum	to (have a) chat	plaudern
faculty	Fakultät, Fachbereich	greyhound racing	Windhundrennen
campus	Universitätsgelände		

David and Adele in a Balti restaurant

I. Vocabulary

a) Give the meaning of the following words from the text above.

1. campus
2. housemate
3. chat
4. gymnasium

b) Give the opposite of the following words.

1. early
2. sometimes
3. many
4. far

II. Understanding

1. What is Selly Oak?
2. What does David do before he goes to his lectures?
3. Where does he spend his lunchtime?
4. What does he do in his spare time?
5. What is a Balti restaurant?

6 E

Career plans

Helen asked David's housemates what career plans they had.
First, Nick said he was hoping to become a solicitor, which meant that he had to go to Law School for another year after he had finished at university. Then he would have to do two years' training, and then qualify as a solicitor.
Next, Taryn was asked what *hurdles* there were for a woman in the legal profession. She didn't think there were as many as there used to be. She said that big law firms seemed to be recruiting as many - if not more - women than men, and career opportunities were really great. They were much better than they had been for a long time for women. She thought that it was possible now to have both, a good career and also balance it with a family. She hoped that eventually she'd be able to do both.
Finally, Andrew said that originally he wanted to study French, but his father thought it wouldn't be a very good idea to *limit* himself by just studying French. He advised him to do Law. Andrew would like to be a solicitor, so he would start training in two years' time with a firm in Birmingham.

hurdle	Hindernis, Hürde
to limit oneself	sich beschränken

I. Vocabulary

Choose the most suitable alternatives to complete the sentences below.

1. All .... barristers have to join one of the Inns of Court in London.
   a) prospective b) hopeful c) will be d) willing
2. We have .... the post in the press and are awaiting applications.
   a) distributed b) reported c) advertised d) advised
3. We asked David's housemates what kind of .... they were looking for.
   a) business b) career c) vocation d) course
4. The four students get on very well because they have a lot ....
   a) in general b) in particular c) of interest d) in common

II. What about you?

Which subject would you concentrate on if you could study at a university, and why?

6 F

David's CV

David has been busy writing his CV, his curriculum vitae, which he needs when he's *applying for* a job. The CV contains the kind of information which should help David to get a job, even if he's not yet absolutely sure what he wants to do.
David is lucky to have a laptop computer, which he shares with other students. It saves time when he's writing his CV, and the CV looks much better than if it had been typed or written by hand.

Helen asks David about his career plans

Helen: What type of jobs are you applying for at the moment?
David: I've applied for jobs in ***the City*** - *merchant* banking, also with big firms who have a - say a presence in the City.
Helen: Would you consider moving to France, say, to start work?
David: I'm not too sure. It's quite difficult to live there at times. When I was there in Limoges for my *year out*, sometimes there were a few problems - say residency etc, and it's very different to Britain. And I've had a year away and I'd quite like to stay here.
Helen: Do you think that any of your *extra-curricular* activities at university have helped you to apply for certain jobs?
David: I'd like to think so. I mean, I've always - especially in my first and second year - I kept up a lot of extra-curricular activities, particularly in the Students'

Union. I frequently mention them in interviews. Also on *application* forms they tend to look good, and it sort of *sets* you *apart from* everyone else.
Helen: What kind of extra-curricular activities were you involved in?
David: Well, I ran the European Society of the university for a year.
Helen: What's the European Society?
David: The European Society was a group of about 150 members, and we had a political side and a social side, and the political side in particular was organising meetings where we'd get people - politicians, people from *embassies* - to come and talk to us about Europe, and what they thought about Europe.
Helen: So you put something like that onto your CV so that your CV looks better?
David: Yes.
Helen: How do you feel about your CV?
David: I mean it's full. There's a lot on there. You've got to *bear in mind* that how much the extra-curricular activities - er - affect how people see you. Because there are other factors they are looking for, like A-level grades, your *predicted* degree that you're going to get, the subject you studied. So, though they play a part, and it's good to have lots of *stuff* on your - on the CV like that, you've got to bear - you've got to keep a balance, and I think that's what's important.

Note:
The City: the financial and business institutions in the City of London

to apply for	sich bewerben um	to set apart from	sich abheben, unterscheiden von
merchant	Handels-		
year out	einjähriger Auslandsaufenthalt	embassy	Botschaft
		to bear in mind	im Auge behalten, nicht vergessen
extra-curricular	nicht zum Lehrplan gehörend	predicted	vorhersehbar
application	Bewerbung	stuff	Zeug

I. Vocabulary

Use the nouns that are derived (abgeleitet) *from the following words in five separate sentences of your own.*

1. to consider
2. difficult
3. to organise
4. different
5. important

II. Understanding

1. David spent one of his university years in France. Where did he go and what did he do?
2. What are extra-curricular activities?

6 G

How to write a CV

Put suitable prepositions in the blank spaces below.

1. The curriculum vitae or CV is often the most important document written ..... a student about to graduate or by anyone applying ..... a job.
2. It gives details ..... education, qualifications, *work experience* and *suitability* for the job being applied for.
3. A CV should start with personal details such as your name and address, both ..... home and ..... work or university, a telephone number for each address, plus fax and e-mail if you have them. Next, your education and qualifications: your university degree course and the degree you've got or expect to get. You should include study abroad, and particular academic *achievements*.
4. Then, your school A-level subjects and grades, followed ..... your GCSEs with grades. Notice that school comes after university or higher education.
5. Next, your work experience, starting ..... the most recent work. Include: dates, details of *employers*, the title of jobs and positions held, and a description ..... the work you've done.
6. The next part of your CV should cover personal interests, such as: sports, extra-curricular activities ..... school or university, and hobbies or *pastimes*.
7. You should also give details ..... useful *skills*, such as foreign languages, computer skills, and so on.
8. Finally, you need to give references: the names of people the employer can contact to ask ..... your academic and work-related achievements and ..... your personal qualities.

work experience	Berufserfahrung	pastime	Freizeitbeschäftigung, Zeitvertreib
suitability	Eignung		
achievement	Leistung	skill	Fähigkeit, Fertigkeit
employer	Arbeitgeber(in)		

David's CV

DAVID STEPHEN GINSBERG
10/06/1974

Home address: 36 Hyde Park Gardens Mews, London W2 2NX
Tel: 0171-403 7890
Term time address: 24 Exeter Road, Selly Oak, Birmingham, B29 6EU
Tel: 0121-415 4153

EDUCATION

September 1979 - June 1993 Lycée Français Charles De Gaulle

GCSE grades: History (A), Geography (A), French (A), English Lit (A), English Lang (A), Physics (A), Biology (B), Maths (B), German (B), Chemistry (B)

AS Level: Science, Technology and Society (A); Government and Politics (C)

A Level: French (A) with merit in special paper, History (B), Geography (B), English (B)

September 1993 - June 1996 University of Birmingham: LLB Law with French

September 1995 - June 1995 University of Limoges: Diplôme d'Etudes Juridiques Françaises

WORK EXPERIENCE

Summer 1995
7 week placement with Sylvia Jeffrey Ltd, a major supplier of nightwear, childrenswear and leisureware to the major chain stores in Great Britain and Europe. During this time I worked in the accounts department completing projects analysing distribution costs and profiling overseas sales. I also spent a week at a production centre in the north-east learning about the running of an effective production line.

Easter 1994
Admin assistant at Business Systems International, a highly successful computer reseller specialising in the finance community. Whilst there I helped the Managing Director with liaising with clients and suppliers, installing machines with additional hardware/software as well as preparing orders for despatch.

Summer 1993/1994
Work experience for a total period of 10 weeks at Charles Chaplin & Co. This was a busy firm which specialised in commercial property transaction and mortgage repossession. During my two summers there I worked in various positions as part of an effective team.

Easter 1992
Work experience at set of barristers chambers in London shadowing counsel at a criminal trial.

Other work includes recording a French language tape for the BBC and making presentations to up to 250 prospective students at a time during the University Open Days.

HOBBIES, INTERESTS AND ACHIEVEMENTS

School: I maintained an active social and sporting life during my time at school playing second row for the rugby 1rst XV, being part of the 4 x 100m relay team which won the school championships. I was also a founder member of the Debating Society, secretary of the History Society, assistant librarian. In my final year I was particularly proud to be elected editor of the school Yearbook and to be chosen by the student body to represent them on the school's governing body to which end I ensured the creation of a Common Room and better relations with the incoming headmaster.

At the age of 15 I joined 46 F (Kensington) SQN Air Training Corps. I rose to attain my staff cadet classification with a distinction and the rank of Sergeant. During my time there I gained my Bronze Duke of Edinburgh Award, my Basic Gliding Certificate for which I had to fly solo and played rugby for London Wing for 4 consecutive years.
I was also a member of the squadron band, drill team, rifle display team and lead the ATC contingent at the Festival of Remembrance. My duties as a NCO included responsibility for the stores, administrative support for the adjutant and teaching foot drill. I am still an active member of the squadron and teach aeronautics to cadets as a Civilian Instructor.

University: I have maintained a particularly active set of extra-curricular activities. I have been elected twice to the Students Guild Council, managed a successful candidate sabbatical election campaign and been elected to the Guild Finance and Services Committee. This post gave me a valuable insight into the workings of diverse institutions with an annual budget of over £3 million, accounting procedures and the need to sometimes take unpopular but financially necessary decisions.
I have also been an active member of the University European Society being elected president, co-ordinating a trip for over 50 students to Dublin and organising regular speaker meetings which included a debate on the future of Europe which attracted an audience of over 300 people. My involvement in the European Society led to my further involvement in the Young European Movement as Senior National Vicepresident with responsibility for external relations and as a member of the European Movement Management Board.
Since being in France I have rekindled my interest in sport playing rugby for my faculty under the tutelage of Pierre Vilpreuf, one of France's best ever players and by playing fullback for the Ex-pat football team that fellow English students and myself have set up.

I also have a keen interest in popular music maintaining a large CD collection, the cinema, popular French and English Fiction, cooking, Real Ale and Chelsea FC.

Write your own CV.

6 H

The University of Birmingham

David in the Careers Centre

The University of Birmingham is one of Britain's red-brick universities. It was founded at the end of the 19th century and it now has about 17,000 students. Unlike Oxford and Cambridge, it's a campus university. That's to say, almost all its academic and administrative buildings are on one *self-contained* site, which is only five kilometres from the centre of Birmingham.
The University has its own Careers Centre. Most students go there to get information and contacts with potential employers.
David decided to find out about career prospects with the Rover Group of car manufacturers.
Some students use the Centre to get information because they have to prepare for interviews with companies in Birmingham. Other students use the Internet to look for information or for a *work-experience placement* in the summer.

self-contained	separat, unabhängig
work-experience placement	Praktikum, Weiterbildung

Understanding

1. What is a red-brick university?
2. Why do students go to the Careers Centre?
3. What is a work-experience placement?

Graduation Day! Two months have gone by, and David has passed his finals. He's now a Bachelor of Laws.

6 I

Helen interviews Dr Richard Maynard, the Career Centre's director

Helen: What are the job prospects for a graduate today?
Dr Maynard: Right now, the prospects are reasonably *encouraging*, certainly by the standards of the last five to six years, when graduates had a particularly bad time. But at the moment somebody graduating today is faced with a market that is relatively optimistic, and with some *effort* ought to be able to achieve a *reasonable* job in a reasonable time.
Helen: So where do students go after they graduate?
Dr Maynard: From this particular university, about a half of them would go directly into some form of permanent employment. About another 25% or so will go off into some kind of *postgraduate study* - either vocational or academic. A number of people will take the opportunity to visit *far-flung* places - heading off for Thailand or somewhere equally exotic - and obviously there will be some who go into *temporary* work, and a few will remain unemployed for several months after they finish their course.
Helen: So how does a student go about applying for a job?

Dr Maynard: We encourage students to come to the Careers Centre to make the first contact with us in the year before they expect to graduate, so that they can give some really careful thought to what they're going to do and how they will go about applying for what it is they choose to do.

encouraging	ermutigend	postgraduate study	Anschlußstudium
effort	Mühe, Anstrengung	far-flung	abgelegen
reasonable	vernünftig, angemessen	temporary	befristet, vorübergehend
postgraduate	Postgraduierte(r) (*führt seine/ihre Studien nach dem ersten Abschluß-examen weiter*)		

I. Vocabulary

What is meant by the following expressions?

1. postgraduate studies
2. far-flung places
3. permanent employment
4. job prospects

II. Say it in English

1. Er lebt seit mehreren Jahren in Birmingham.
2. Sie hat seit einer Woche ein neues Rad.
3. Ich kenne David seit mehr als einem Jahr, und er ist immer sehr zuverlässig gewesen.
4. Wir haben eine Ewigkeit nichts mehr von ihm gehört.
5. Die Vorlesung dauert nun schon über eine Stunde.

6 J

Applying for a job

When you apply for a job, a CV won't be enough on its own. You also need to write a letter of application saying

- who you are,
- what job you're applying for,
- why you are interested in it,
- why you want to work with the particular employer you're writing to,
- why you are suitable for the job, and
- how soon you can take up the job.

CHARITY GRANTS AWARDS TEAM ASSISTANT

London
c£14,500pa

The Millennium Commission is assisting communities across the UK in marking the end of the second millennium and celebrating the start of the third. The Millennium Awards are grants to enable people of all ages and abilities to achieve personal goals and, in doing so, to make a real contribution to their communities. £200 million will be distributed as Awards by existing grant making organisations working in partnership with the Commission.

We need an Awards Team Assistant who will provide quality clerical support to a small London based team handling requests for grants. This is a key post essential to the smooth operation of the team. The many and varied responsibilities include * dealing with applicants and the general public * responsibility for the team filing and information systems * maintaining up to date information on grants made * setting up meetings and making travel arrangements.

We need someone who has * excellent organisational skills * the ability to work quickly and accurately to meet tight deadlines * the ability to take the initiative and work unsupervised * a flexible attitude and enthusiasm to 'get involved' in all aspects of our work. You will need good written and verbal communication skills and be able to make full use of IT.

The post is offered on a 3 year contract, attracts performance related pay and 22 days annual holiday. Please send your CV with a covering letter describing briefly your reasons for applying and the key skills that you will bring to the post to Margaret Simpson, PO Box 7368, Birmingham B14 3TV, quoting Reference 1564/98. (Details of salary attached)

Closing date for applications is Wednesday 12 November. Interviews will be held in the week commencing 24 November.

An appointment taken from a newspaper

Write a job application.

6 K

Helen interviews John Berkeley who is responsible for training young people at the Rover Group

Motor cars are important to Birmingham. 60 years ago Britain made more cars than any other country in Europe, and for a long time the motor industry was one of the largest employers in this area.
Now it is much smaller and foreign car manufacturers have taken over the original British companies. One of these is the Rover Group, and David Ginsberg has applied for a job there.

Helen: Can you tell me about Rover's *recruitment policy*?
John Berkeley: Yes. Young people are our future. We are developing the next generation for Rover Group. So each year we will recruit between 300 and 400 young

people from the age of 16. And about 80 to 90 of those will be recruited as graduate trainees.
Helen: How do you go about the recruitment process?
John Berkeley: For graduates, as for other young people, there's really no *substitute* for experience. They are choosing us just as we are choosing them. So for graduate trainees we use our student placement scheme. They spend up to twelve weeks with us in the year before they complete their graduate studies. And if they like us and we like them, we make them an offer of employment for the following year.

recruitment policy	Einstellungspolitik
substitute	Ersatz

Summary

Give a summary of how the Rover Group recruits young people, especially graduates. (50 to 100 words)

6 L

David's job interview at the Rover Group

John Berkeley: So, tell me, David, how have you prepared for this interview?
David: Well, I went to the Careers Service on campus at Birmingham University. I got out the *file* on Rover; I read up all the stuff including *newspaper cuttings* dealing with Rover so that I could *trace* how the company has been progressing this year and last year.
John Berkeley: You've made some fairly *sweeping claims* in your application form. That's what application forms are for, such as the fact that you are a highly effective, highly *articulate communicator*. How would you prove that? I mean, is there evidence that you could present - which would convince us of that claim?
David: I consider myself a competent public speaker. I've spoken at the - in the Debating Society at University in front of 300 people. I find that normally I can talk on any subject and express myself to people.
John Berkeley: Okay. Fine. Is there anything about which you hold strong views?
David: Yes. I'm a strong believer in further European integration. I really think that a lot of the way politics is going in this country is very - is very negative, particularly for industry.
John Berkeley: So, like us, you would want to encourage more students from within the European Union to have experience in other member states.
David: Yes, sure. At University I was also president of the European Society, and through that we had a number of members who were from other countries, and we helped to get them fully integrated into student life at Birmingham.

John Berkeley: How would you judge how successful you are in your future life and work? What would be the things that are the most important to you?
David: The fact that I get the job done, and get it done well in that - the *satisfaction* of knowing that you've completed something that's a project - perhaps you've *initiated* - an idea you've come up with is being used and used effectively.
John Berkeley: I think we probably have got enough - enough information - but I'm interested that you should think that that was particularly important.
Thank you very much indeed. I very much enjoyed meeting you. We will let you know the *outcome*, obviously, as soon as possible.
David: Great. Thank you very much.

file	Akte	articulate	*hier*: gut
newspaper cutting	Zeitungsausschnitt	communicator	Redner
to trace	ausfindig machen, auffinden	satisfaction	Befriedigung
sweeping	drastisch, überragend	to initiate	anstoßen, initiieren
claim	Aussage	outcome	Ergebnis

I. Vocabulary

What is meant by the following words and expressions in the text above?

1. file
2. claim
3. outcome
4. newspaper cuttings
5. evidence

II. Understanding

1. What is David's attitude towards Europe?
2. What is David's aim in life?

III. What do you know about David?

1. David is a student of .... preparing for his final degree .... However he doesn't want to enter the .... profession, because he would have to do another year's study.
2. He lives in Selly Oak, a student district in .... and shares a house with three other ....
3. He gets up fairly .... and before he goes to his .... in the morning, he does some physical exercises in the gym.
4. At .... he meets his housemates and has a chat with them.
5. In the evenings he sometimes goes to a .... restaurant with his girlfriend or to .... racing with his fellow students.

6 M

A tour of Birmingham and its surroundings

Birmingham claims to have as many canals as Venice. Certainly an extensive network was needed to transport raw materials and finished goods during the Industrial Revolution. But rail and road transport gradually replaced the use of canals, which became forgotten *backwaters*.

Now everything has changed. Many old canals have been made part of the city's *redevelopment* projects. The canal by Brindley Place, for example, is next to the Birmingham International Convention Centre. One of the buildings in this complex is Symphony Hall, home of the internationally famous City of Birmingham Symphony Orchestra. Nearby is the new Birmingham Repertory Theatre.
The statue to Boulton, Watt and Murdoch commemorates three pioneers of the Industrial Revolution. A model of one of Boulton and Watt's first *rotating engines* is in the Museum of Science and Industry, which has examples of the machinery that made Birmingham famous.
The *iron* for many of the earliest machines came from Coalbrookdale in Shropshire, where the world's first iron bridge was *cast* in 1779. It still *spans* the River Severn today. Ironbridge is the birthplace of the Industrial Revolution.

backwater	Stauwasser
redevelopment	Sanierung
rotating engine	Rotationsmaschine
iron	Eisen
to cast	*hier*: gießen
to span	sich spannen, führen über

Understanding

1. When was the Industrial Revolution?
2. What purpose did the canal network serve in the past?
3. What is the Symphony Hall famous for?
4. What made Birmingham famous in the past?
5. What did Boulton and Watt invent?

Convention Centre

Sculpture 'Forward' by Raymond Mason in Birmingham

A SENIOR CONDUCTOR IN YORK

7

7 A

Introduction

This programme is about the railways in Britain and especially about the work of John Storey, who works as a senior *conductor* for GNER, the Great North Eastern Railway, between Edinburgh and London.
We follow John on his daily *shift*, and hear the views of passengers and staff on his train. Helen talks to him about his work and to Chris Garnett, the Chief Executive Officer of GNER, who explains how the *ownership* and management of the railways have changed in the last few years. She also meets Nigel Stacey, who is *in charge of* three big stations in the North of England.
The programme includes a visit to the magnificent Victorian railway station at York and the National Railway Museum nearby. It ends with a look at the city of York and a trip through the Yorkshire moors in a *restored steam*-driven train.

Accents:
John Storey is Geordie - a person who comes from Newcastle-upon-Tyne. His accent is typical of the North East of England. You may find him quite difficult to understand, but almost everything he says in the programme is included in Helen's interview with him (7 B) so you are advised to read it before watching the programme.

conductor	Zugführer; Schaffner	to be in charge of	verantwortlich sein für
shift	Schicht	restored	restauriert
ownership	Besitz, Eigentum	steam	Dampf

7 B

Helen interviews John Storey

Helen: Was it your childhood dream to work on the railways and become a senior conductor?
John: It wasn't, no. When I first left school I joined the army, and when I came out of the army - it was only through my uncle that I became - worked for the railway. I started off as a *porter*, and then as a *train guard*, in 1980. I became a senior conductor in 1988.
Helen: Do you think that the job of senior conductor has changed much over the years?

John Storey

John: I do, yes. Since ***it was brought out*** in 1988, we're a lot more *focused on* the passengers now on the train, whereas at one time all we used to do was check tickets. As I say we're a lot more involved now.
Helen: What sort of problems do you have to deal with on the train?
John: Well, there's numerous problems we have on the train. You see, you get a lot of people *boarding* the wrong trains. There's - you know, they come into the station, they get confused, and end up going in the wrong direction. And then once they're on the train they *have to* sit in the wrong seat - they have *seat reservations* and they *misread* the seat reservations and end up sitting in somebody else's seat. And we have people that lose their luggage, you know. Quite often.
Helen: And I think you've also told me about a funny *occasion* - something else being left at stations.
John: Oh yes. I had a lady boarded the train. She had two children with her, and it wasn't till about ten minutes into the journey she'd realised she'd left her youngest child on the platform, in the *pram*. I had to deal with that.
Helen: Do you have any passengers with *special requests* or special needs?
John: We have a lot of disabled passengers travel with us. And we have disabled accommodation on board the train. You know, for people in *wheel-chairs*. These people are met at the station and they are *assisted* on to the train.
Helen: How long does your daily shift last?
John: Approximately eight hours.
Helen: What's your favourite route?
John: My favourite route would be the London route.

Helen: Do you get different people getting on the train in London, say, to the people who get on the train at Newcastle?
John: Yes, yes. You get a lot of *commuters* from London that would travel to - like - Peterborough, which is the first station, approximately 45 minutes out of London. But you get a lot of businessmen and that travelling on the trains.
Helen: Finally, are you a ***train-spotter*** in your spare time?
John: I am definitely not a train-spotter in my spare time. Once I leave work I don't want anything to do with trains, although after saying that, since 1980 I've always kept a *log* of the trains I worked with all the numbers and everything. So just in case I need a report on anything. So I've got all the trains I worked on from 1980.
Helen: So you are a train-spotter.
John: Not *intentionally*.

Notes:
it was brought out - John is referring to a change in 1988 when guards on trains were given new duties and were re-named 'conductors'.
A ***train-spotter*** is a person whose hobby is to write down and collect the numbers of trains.

porter	Gepäckträger	occasion	Ereignis
(train) guard	Schaffner(in), Zugbegleiter(in)	pram	Kinderwagen
		special requests	Sonderwünsche
to focus on	sich konzentrieren auf	wheel-chair	Rollstuhl
to board	einsteigen	to assist	helfen
to have to	*hier*: sicherlich, bestimmt	commuter	Pendler(in)
seat reservation	Platzreservierung	log	Aufzeichnungen
to misread	falsch lesen, nicht richtig verstehen	intentional	absichtlich

I. Vocabulary

What do the following expressions from the interview mean?

1. commuter
2. pram
3. request
4. wheel-chair

II. Understanding

1. What did John do when he left school?
2. How long does John's shift last?
3. Which route does he like most?
4. Describe two problems that often arise when people board the train.

III. Say it in English

1. John lebt seit mehreren Jahren in Newcastle.
2. Der Streik der Eisenbahner dauert nun schon drei Wochen.
3. Ich warte schon seit einer Stunde auf den Zug nach Edinburgh.
4. Ich kenne John seit mehr als zwei Jahren, und er ist immer sehr zuverlässig gewesen.
5. Ich habe ihn seit letzter Woche nicht gesehen.

7 C

A typical day

A typical day starts with John *reporting for duty* at Newcastle station, where he's based. The clerk gives John the *schedule* his train will be following, with times and other details.
He then collects his *equipment* for the journey and goes to join his train. In this case, it's the morning train from Aberdeen and John is taking over as senior conductor from Newcastle to London.
Finally, the *catering crew* joins the train, and John's daily shift begins. After each station, the senior conductor has to announce where and when the train will stop. Then he checks tickets and answers questions from passengers. When his shift is over he returns to his base at Newcastle.

to report for duty	sich zum Dienst melden	catering crew	für Speisen und Getränke zuständiges Zugpersonal
schedule	Fahrplan		
equipment	Ausrüstung, Ausstattung		

I. Vocabulary

Choose the most suitable word to complete each sentence.

1. Hurry up! The train leaves in ten minutes. We don't want to .... it.
   a) drop b) lose c) miss d) lack
2. I would be very .... if you could give me the departure times to Newcastle.
   a) grateful b) pleasant c) contented d) satisfied
3. Is John's .... train-spotting? No, it isn't.
   a) sport b) hobby c) job d) occupation
4. It is dangerous to lean .... the windows when the train is moving.
   a) from b) outside c) out by d) out of
5. .... the heavy rain, quite a large crowd of people were waiting at the station.
   a) Even though b) Nevertheless c) While d) Despite

6. You haven't got the right ticket. You'll have to pay the excess .... (*Nachlösegebühr*).
   a) ticket   b) fare   c) journey   d) money

II. Comment

Describe a day in the life of a senior conductor on a train. Use the information given above and in John's interview (7 B). You may include details from your own experience of rail travel. (100 to 150 words)

7 D

Rail tickets and fares

When you travel by train, you can buy a *single ticket* to your *destination*, or a *return ticket* there and back, at First Class or Standard *rates*. But the *fares* you pay can vary a lot.
There are many *discounted* fares and *bargains*, costing less than the regular fare. For example, you can save money if you purchase a ticket in advance. The cost also varies at different times of day. Travel at *off-peak times* is less expensive than during the *rush hour*. And there are often bargains at weekends and on *public holidays*. It also saves money to buy weekly or season tickets for going to work.
There are *railcards* which give discounts to families and young people, and railcards for *senior citizens*, people over sixty.

single ticket	Fahrkarte für einfache Fahrt	bargain	*hier*: Sonderpreis
destination	Ziel	off-peak times	außerhalb der Stoßzeit(en)
return ticket	Rückfahrkarte	rush hour	Stoßzeit(en), Hauptverkehrszeit(en)
rate	*hier*: Tarif	public holiday	Feiertag
fare	Fahrpreis	railcard	Bahnkarte
discounted	ermäßigt	senior citizens	Senioren, ältere Bürger

I. Vocabulary

Give the meaning of the following words and phrases.

1. destination
2. bargain
3. off-peak times
4. senior citizens

II. Test your English: prepositions

Fill in the necessary prepositions.

A letter to a travel agency

Dear Sir/Madam,

I shall be coming ..... England some time in August ..... a month's holiday ..... my wife. I wish to travel ..... London ..... Scotland ..... train early ..... August. Would you please let me know all necessary details, including the difference in fares ..... first class and standard class. Could you please let me know the times ..... the trains and if I have to pay ..... reserving the two seats.
Looking forward ..... hearing ..... you.

Yours faithfully,

7 E

Privatisation

For more than 100 years Britain's railways were privately owned, but 50 years ago they were *nationalised* - taken into public ownership. Now they've been sold back to private *enterprise*. Selling the railways was one of the many big privatisation *measures* carried out by the United Kingdom's last Conservative government.
For many years, some big industries like coal and steel, and also *public services* and so-called *utilities* like water and electricity, were in public ownership. They were owned and *run* by the state, and they were financed or *subsidised* by the *taxpayer*.
In recent years, several of these industries and services have been sold to private enterprise. The companies which own and run them depend on private investment. Newly privatised companies are sold on the London *Stock Exchange* so that *shares* in them can be bought by private investors and institutions.

to nationalise	verstaatlichen
enterprise	Unternehmen
measure	Maßnahme
public services	öffentlicher Dienst
utilities	Versorgungseinrichtungen
to run	betreiben, unterhalten
to subsidise	subventionieren, unterstützen
taxpayer	Steuerzahler(in)
stock exchange	Börse
share	Aktie

Newcastle-upon-Tyne

I. Vocabulary

a) Find expressions in the text that could replace the following words.

1. possession
2. public services
3. firms

b) Give the nouns corresponding to the following verbs.

1. nationalise
2. subsidise
3. invest

II. Understanding

1. Who was responsible for the recent privatisation of the railways?
2. Who paid for the public services and utilities before privatisation?

7 F

Helen interviews Chris Garnett

Chris Garnett is the Chief Executive Officer of GNER, the Great North Eastern Railway. The company operates *the route from London to Edinburgh.*

Helen: When were the railways privatised in Britain?
Chris: The first train *franchises* for operating the trains were *let* at the end of 1995. The *vast bulk* of it, the selling of the *tracks*, the *rolling stock*, and so on, was in 1996, with the last of the train franchises going during 1997.
Helen: You mentioned the sale of the rolling stock. What was actually privatised - the routes, the rails, or the trains?
Chris: There were a number of parts. It was split into an enormous number of different sections, but the *substantial* parts were: Railtrack was a company that was created, and they own all the infrastructure - the track, the tunnels, the *signalling* and the stations. And that got sold - privatised - on the London Stock Exchange during the early part of 1996. The Rolling Stock *Leasing* Companies (ROSCOs) were the people who *took on* - three companies were created to take on the passenger rolling stock, and they own all the rolling stock. Then the main passenger network in the UK was split into 25 different units, and they have been let as management contracts or franchises in periods of between seven and fifteen years. And those *franchisees* - those Operating Companies - pay Railtrack to run the trains on Railtrack's track, and they hire the rolling stock from the ROSCOs.
Helen: So what improvements have you actually seen since privatisation?
Chris: One has been in service to passengers. It's been getting across to everybody, particularly on our route, that nobody has to travel by train. We are in enormous *competition* with the airlines, with cars, with coaches. And so it's been how do we raise passenger standards? How do we give you a good service? There's also been some very *aggressive* marketing. We're like an airline: we have space to sell. So you can sell cheap tickets in advance at discounted prices, and then if you turn up at the last minute, you pay more. So that's filled up our trains. We are taking about 10% more people. So that's been one thing. The other has been about making the system more *efficient* - getting more trains into service, having more *reliable* trains, having clean trains in winter - and so it's been efficiency, it's been service, it's been providing a better railway.
Helen: Can you imagine the railways ever being nationalised again?
Chris: I think not, really. I mean, it's very interesting talking to staff. I was coming down on the train the other day with a driver, and said to him - he's been in the business 44 years - I said, "How do you find it?" He said, "Well, if you'd told me that I would think privatisation was a good thing, I wouldn't have believed you. But now I say, this has come 40 years too late." And he's not alone in saying that. I think the staff have really been quite surprised how much better it all is.

to operate	betreiben	signalling	Signalübermittlung
franchise	Lizenz	leasing	Pacht
to let	vergeben, vermieten	to take on	übernehmen
vast bulk	Großteil	franchisee	Lizenznehmer
tracks	Schienen, Gleise	competition	Wettbewerb, Konkurrenz
rolling stock	rollendes Material, Fahrzeuge	aggressive	hart, aufdringlich
		efficient	leistungsfähig
substantial	wesentlich	reliable	zuverlässig

I. Understanding

Complete the sentences with the information from the interview.

The Passenger Railway System

1. The three parts of the British passenger railway system were .... separately, and now these belong to separate ....
2. The infrastructure belongs to Railtrack, which .... and runs the track, the stations, the signalling systems, and the staff to operate all of these.
3. The ...., consisting of the trains themselves is owned by the Rolling Stock Leasing Companies, sometimes called ROSCOs.
4. The rolling stock is ...., or hired out, to the passenger network through the Train Operating Companies, each of which manages and .... its own part of the network.
5. All these companies hold ...., which are contracts with the government to run their part of the system for a franchise period of between seven and fifteen years.

II. Questions

1. What has GNER done to improve its services?
2. What does Chris mean by 'aggressive marketing'?
3. What are the advantages of privatising the railways?

7 G

York station

York station was designed and built in the 1870s. It's one of the finest examples of Victorian railway architecture, and at the time it was considered to be the largest railway station in the world.
The iron Corinthian *pillars* and the *arched* roof which they *support* are the principal design features. They led to the station being called a splendid monument of extravagance. The station is now owned by Railtrack, and Nigel Stacey, Railtrack's Manager is responsible for the station.

pillar	Pfeiler, Säule	to support	*hier*: stützen
arched	gewölbt		

Helen interviews Nigel Stacey

Nigel Stacey

Helen: Nigel, what are you in charge of? The trains, or the station, or both?
Nigel: Principally, I'm just in charge of the station. I have three stations: York, Darlington and Durham. I don't have any real responsibility for the trains, except when they are here, in the stations, when we are responsible for the safety of the passengers joining and leaving, and the *dispatch* of those trains to time.
Helen: Who are the people that work for you?
Nigel: I have 80 staff. They range from station announcers, one of whom you can hear in the background, to platform staff, customer information staff on the stations and a number of cleaning staff as well.
Helen: Are you also in charge of the senior conductors?
Nigel: No. John has his own manager, who is part of the on-train management organisation. Normally the only contact we would have at the station with the senior conductors is as the train is standing in the station, and of course we need to *relay* information between the train and the station, and we would do that through the senior conductor.
Helen: Can I ask you one last personal question?
Nigel: Of course.
Helen: You haven't always been a station manager, have you?
Nigel: No. I started on the railway in 1985 as a train driver - or a trainee train driver - and I drove trains for about four and a half years, and then moved through a *supervisory* job and eventually into management jobs. And I started here three

years ago, just with York, and then last year I took over Darlington and Durham stations as well.

Helen: What was it like driving trains?

Nigel: It was great. Sometimes I'd love to get back to it, and the *glamour* and the - there's a sort of romance to it, I think, that you can't take away - especially for either the very big *freight* trains or for the *long-distance* passenger *trains*. And so in that sense, yes, I'd love to go back to it. However, I think now I've moved on from it personally in terms of my own development, and I'm much happier really doing what I'm doing now. But it was a wonderful time.

dispatch	*hier*: Abfahrt	glamour	Glanz
to relay	weiterleiten	freight	Fracht
supervisory	beaufsichtigend, überwachend	long-distance train	Fernverkehrszug

I. Vocabulary

Give synonyms or synonymous expressions for

1. to be responsible for
2. safety
3. to relay
4. to move on

II. Understanding

1. Who owns York railway station?
2. For how many people is Nigel responsible?
3. What was Nigel before he became a station manager?

III. Test your English

Fill in the gaps using the following verb forms.

would love • considered • moved • was in charge • started

1. York station was once .... to be the world's largest railway station.
2. Nigel said he .... of the station.
3. In 1985 Nigel .... working on the railway.
4. A few years later he .... into a management job.
5. Sometimes he .... to get back to the romance of driving long-distance passenger trains.

7 H

Passengers and staff on the London to Newcastle line

Helen asked passengers about their travelling *habits* and *preferences*. Most of them definitely preferred travelling by train. Some were travelling *on business*, but one was also travelling *for pleasure* because he was going home from work.
Asked if he had any complaints about the railways, one of the passengers replied that the East Coast line, which was the route they were on, provided a very good service. Another believed that the rail service had improved since privatisation. She thought more trains were on time, but - the prices had gone up.
Helen also talked to a member of the catering staff who spoke about her work on the London to Newcastle line. She started work at King's Cross at 6.30 in the morning. She had to work about 14 hours and would finish at 20.38 when her train arrived at King's Cross.

habit	Gewohnheit	on business	geschäftlich
preference	Vorliebe	for pleasure	zum Vergnügen

Understanding

Fill in the missing words.

An announcement

"Ladies and gentlemen, this is your Inter-City .... We shall soon be .... at Newcastle. Please consult the station departure board for your onward service or request the assistance of station .... Myself and all the train team would like to thank you for .... on Great North Eastern Railway and we look forward to .... you again soon."

7 I

The history of railways in Britain

As a result of the Industrial Revolution in England, canals were used to transport goods around the country as freight. But very soon, *steam engines* began to take freight on fixed rail tracks, and in 1830 passengers were carried by rail for the first time.
By 1850 there were 10,000 kilometres of rail track in Britain, and by 1920 the track had increased to 32,000 kilometres, with 6,500 passenger stations and 2,500 stations for freight. In the last 35 years, however, a lot of track and many stations have been closed down, and now there are only 16,500 kilometres of track and a total of 2,500 stations for passengers and freight.

Rail transport has *declined* as a result of competition from cars and lorries, especially for long journeys. But there have been improvements in rail travel, with faster trains and better service. And the traditional sea ferries across the English Channel now have a rival in the Channel Tunnel, which can take 600 trains every day.

The National Railway Museum in York houses a collection of locomotives from the earliest years to the present day, including a model of the Channel Tunnel next to the Rocket, Robert Stephenson's first steam engine. You can also see the first royal trains, with carriages used by Queen Victoria.

steam engine	Dampflok
to decline	abnehmen

Railway Museum, York

I. Questions

1. When did the age of railways begin?
2. What are the advantages of the Channel Tunnel?

II. Test your English: tenses

Complete the sentences with the correct tenses of the verbs in brackets.

1. How old .... (be, you) next birthday?
2. Yesterday I .... (be) at home all evening. I .... (listen) to a concert on the radio.
3. I haven't seen him for a long time, but I .... (see) him next month.

4. He .... (already ask) her three times and now he's asking her again.
5. She .... (live) in York when she .... (be) a child.
6. Have you had any news from your sister recently? - No, she .... (not write) for about two months.
7. How long .... (talk, we) on the phone?

III. Comment

What advantages does rail transport have over road transport in a country like Britain? (50 to 100 words)

7 J

York

York Minster

York is the county town of Yorkshire in the North of England. 2,000 years of history are reflected in the city's architecture, from the time of the Romans onwards. The city of York was a residence for several Roman Emperors. Later it became a centre of Christianity. The city's most famous building is York Minster, the largest Gothic cathedral in Britain. One of the Minster's greatest *treasures* is the *stained glass* in its windows. One *rose window* commemorates the union of the Royal families of York and Lancaster in the 15th century. Part of the Minster was severely damaged in a fire in 1984. The oldest part of the medieval city is full of narrow streets such as The Shambles, once the street of butchers. York has long been famous for chocolates and *confectionery*.

treasure	Kostbarkeit, Schatz	rose window	Fensterrose
stained glass	Buntglas	confectionery	Konfekt, Süßwaren

The North Yorkshire Moors Railway making its way through the beautiful scenery of the North Yorkshire Moors National Park. The steam locomotives and old carriages have been restored and maintained by railway enthusiasts. The railway itself follows the route of Stephenson's original line opened in 1836.

Question

Which is the most important discovery of our times? Give reasons for your choice.

AN ELECTRONICS ENGINEER IN SILICON GLEN

8

8 A

Introduction

John Houston

This programme is about John Houston, an *electronics engineer* in Scotland. He is responsible for controlling and *supervising* the development of new personal computers at the Mitsubishi PC Division manufacturing *plant* at Glenrothes.

Glenrothes is a new town north of Edinburgh in the heart of an area known as Silicon Glen. Glen is the Scots word for valley, and Silicon Glen is Scotland's answer to Silicon Valley in California.

We see John at work, at home with his wife Charlie, and playing golf with one of his colleagues. Helen talks to another of John's colleagues, Jane Nightingale, about her work as a test engineer, and to Bill Campbell, the General Manager of Mitsubishi PC Division, about the computer industry.

Helen visits the Cyberia Café in Edinburgh, and hears from several customers who pay a small fee to *access* the Internet on the Café's computers.

Finally, we take a short look at Edinburgh, the capital of Scotland, which will become the seat of a Scottish parliament as the result of the 1997 *referendum* vote in favour of Scottish self-government.

Accents:
Apart from Jane Nightingale, who comes from Yorkshire, most of the people Helen talks to in the programme speak with a Scots accent. John Houston's accent is stronger and more difficult to follow than the others, so you are advised to look carefully at what he says in the first interview with Helen (8 B below).

electronics engineer	Elektroingenieur(in)	to access	zugreifen auf
to supervise	beaufsichtigen, überwachen	referendum	Volksentscheid
plant	Fabrik		

Edinburgh, the capital of Scotland

8 B

Helen interviews John and his wife Charlie

John and Charlie live in Clackmannan, a quiet little village in beautiful countryside, about 40 kilometres from Edinburgh.

Helen: John, tell me a bit about yourself.
John: Well, I'm thirty-three years of age, married to Charlotte Anne, also known as Charlie. We've been together for nine years, although we've been married for just four. We moved to Clackmannan about three years ago.
Helen: Why do you live in Clackmannan and not in Glenrothes?
John: Well, actually we used to live in Glenrothes, but Charlotte Anne got a job in Glasgow, which is actually about two hours' drive, so we found that that was just too much. So we tried to look for somewhere which was closer, and would give us

a more equal journey. And Clackmannan is actually half-way, and that gives us both a journey of about 45 minutes each morning. So it's a lot better.
Helen: Charlie, do you work in computers too?
Charlie: No. I'm an *orthoptist*, which is a specialist in eyes and *squints*.
Helen: But I noticed that there's a computer here in the house. Are you *computer-literate*?
Charlie: Yes, I am. I can use a computer if I have to.
Helen: What do you use it for?
Charlie: Usually writing reports, and if I'm doing some research and work, then I may use a *database* or *word processing*, doing *graphs*, that type of thing.
Helen: John, what made you decide to work in electronics?
John: I think basically it was job security. I think, when I was at school unemployment in Britain was quite high at that time. I didn't want to do a degree in something which I would then have to go and search for a job. And electronics was certainly up-and-coming in Scotland then, so it was a good career *move*.

orthoptist	Augenarzt, -ärztin	database	Datenbank
squint	Schielen	word processing	Textverarbeitung
to be computer-literate	einen Computer bedienen können, sich auskennen	graph	Schaubild, Diagramm
		move	Schritt

Charlie Houston

I. Vocabulary

a) Give the noun corresponding to each of the following verbs.

1. marry
2. decide
3. think
4. secure
5. employ

b) Give the meaning of the following words as they are used in the text above.

1. countryside
2. to notice
3. actually
4. job
5. journey
6. to search for
7. specialist
8. up-and-coming

II. Understanding

1. What does John's wife do for a living?
2. Why did John and Charlie move to Clackmannon?
3. How long have they been living there?
4. Why did John opt for a career in electronics?

III. Grammar revision: relatives

Join these pairs of sentences, using a relative clause.

1. I'd like you to meet John. His parents are old friends of mine.
2. Charlie works in a hospital. It is part of the University of Glasgow.
3. They live in Clackmannan. It's a small village in the Scottish Lowlands.
4. John has a colleague called Jim Hain. He is an excellent golfer.

8 C

The company's products

John works at the Mitsubishi PC Division manufacturing plant in Glenrothes. The PC Division makes personal computer systems and products for both home and business use.

The so-called *desktop* PC is small enough for the *keyboard* and monitor, or *screen*, to fit *conveniently* on a desk or work *surface*. Nowadays there is often a separate *tower* to house the components which drive and operate the computer and store information in it. Loudspeakers are for use with computer ***programs*** which include sound. There are several other components which aren't part of the computer itself, like the mouse, which moves on a *pad* to enable users to find their way around the

screen and give instructions to the computer's programs, or the *hand-held remote control* which performs more or less the same function as the mouse.
The server is a larger computer, designed for organisations where several people need to share and use the same computer functions and the same information. It serves a *network* of terminals or workstations, with their own keyboards and monitors.

Note:
A computer ***program*** is always given the North American spelling. It is never called a programme.

desktop	Schreibtisch, Desktop (*liegendes Computergehäuse*)	tower	Turm, Tower (*stehendes Computergehäuse*)
keyboard	Tastatur	to store	speichern
screen	Bildschirm	pad	Unterlage, Pad
convenient	zweckmäßig, praktisch, vorteilhaft	(hand-held) remote control	(handgesteuerte) Fernbedienung
surface	Oberfläche	network	Netz(werk)

I. Vocabulary

Give an equivalent word or expression for the following words as they are used in the text above.

1. plant
2. screen
3. work surface
4. several
5. to perform
6. component

II. Understanding

1. What is the function of a mouse?
2. What is the difference between a mouse and a remote control?
3. In what circumstances does an organisation use a server?

8 D

New products and cross-functional teams

New products for the PC Division are designed at the Mitsubishi Research and Development Centre in Birmingham.
The *design* for a new computer is known as the prototype. The prototype is sent to the manufacturing plant in Glenrothes where the computer will be assembled.
The *large-scale* manufacture of a new computer is planned, controlled and *monitored* by a *cross-functional* team of experts, working under a Section Leader for New Products, such as John.

The team includes a manufacturing engineer, a quality engineer, a test engineer, and a purchasing representative, since many of the components are bought from other companies.
The members of the team bring together the functions of their separate departments in order to ensure the efficiency, quality, reliability, and *cost-effectiveness* of the manufacturing process and of the *final product* itself.

design	Entwurf	cross-functional	multipel
large-scale	großangelegt	cost-effectiveness	Rentabilität, Preis-Leistungsverhältnis
to monitor	überwachen, kontrollieren	final product	Endprodukt

I. Understanding

Are these sentences true or false according to the text?

	True	False
1. John works in a Research and Development Centre in Glenrothes.		
2. The cross-functional team is headed by a Section Leader.		
3. The team consists of three people.		
4. Mitsubishi produces all the components.		
5. The prototype is sent to the factory in Birmingham, where the computer will be assembled.		
6. Efficiency and cost-effectiveness of the final product have to be ensured by the cross-functional team.		

II. Say it in English

1. Wir brauchen einen Fachmann, um das Projekt zu überwachen.
2. Die Computer werden in der Produktionsstätte in Glenrothes zusammengebaut.
3. John gibt das meiste Geld für Computerspiele aus.
4. Ein großer Teil des Computermarktes wird von japanischen Firmen beherrscht (kontrolliert).
5. Das Preis-Leistungsverhältnis muß stimmen.

III. Comment

Many big jobs can nowadays only be done by team-work. What general rules would you consider important for successful team-work in industry and commerce? (80 to 100 words)

8 E

The development of a new computer product

Before a new computer product can be manufactured, the cross-functional team must work on its prototype. The prototype goes through several *stages* or *revisions* before the design meets the *requirements* of mass production.

An important aspect of the team's work focuses on the *motherboard* for the new computer. The motherboard houses the essential electronic components, including the processor which gives the computer its power and *operating speed*. The *circuits* and components on the motherboard may vary according to the requirements of individual customers. They are bought in from all over the world by the purchasing department and assembled and *mounted* on the boards by means of *Surface Mount Technology* (SMT), the actual process of mounting the components on the boards. Diagnostic tests are developed at each revision stage to discover and deal with possible defects in important components. If any new electronic component has a defect, it is most likely to lead to failure early in its product lifetime. So it is essential to test for possible failure before *full-scale* manufacturing begins. This includes testing the finished product for possible defects.

In order to *keep ahead of* new products from rival manufacturers, other development work concentrates on speed and efficiency of assembly, and on providing a product which offers the best value for money and the best quality, for example by introducing improvements in the design of the *chassis* which houses the computer's components.

As a result, an activity known as *Manufacturing Process Proving* (MPP) plays an important part in the introduction of the new product. Several examples of the product are manufactured and tested to ensure that all aspects of the production process will be looked after successfully during final assembly, testing and *dispatch* to the customer.

stage	Phase
revision	Überholen, Revision
requirement	Bedürfnis, Anspruch
motherboard	Hauptplatine
operating speed	Rechengeschwindigkeit
circuit	Schaltung, Schaltsystem
to mount	montieren
Surface Mount Technology	*etwa*: Oberflächenmontagetechnologie
full-scale	großangelegt, umfassend
to keep ahead of	einen Vorsprung sichern vor, einen Schritt voraus sein
chassis	Gehäuse
Manufacturing Process Proving	*etwa*: Herstellungskontrolle
dispatch	Versand

I. Vocabulary

Use the word in brackets to form a word that fits in the space.

1. According to research .... (publication) recently, more people are working from home than ever before.
2. Consequently, there has been an increase in .... (isolated) among those people who no longer have to travel to their place of work.
3. Having their .... (to employ) work at home on computers not only saves big companies money and increases .... (to produce) - it can also help the environment by .... (to reduce) air pollution.
4. The new working arrangement is known as telecommuting, with workers .... (connection) to their firms via computers and telephones.
5. Many employers also believe that people are more .... (to create) when they communicate via electronic mail.
6. Fax and Internet are .... (technology) links that can be used, although they still rely on the written, rather than the spoken word.

II. Understanding

1. What happens to the prototype for a new product after it has been sent to Glenrothes?
2. What is the function of the processor in a computer?
3. Why do circuits and components vary from one motherboard to another?
4. Why do computer manufacturers test for component failure before they begin full-scale manufacture?

III. Comment

Assembly-line (Fließband) *work in factories has been thought of as exhausting and bad for the physical and mental health of workers. Is this view still appropriate nowadays? (80 words)*

8 F

Helen interviews Jane Nightingale

Jane is a test engineer responsible for developing diagnostic tests for new computer products.

Helen: Jane, what did you study at university?
Jane: I did a degree in *Information Technology*. It lasted for four years, and included a one-year industrial *placement*.
Helen: And what made you decide to become a test engineer?
Jane: It sounded like it may be fun, and there would be lots of hardware involved, and also lots of software, and lots of *challenges*. And I thought it must be the thing for me, and so far it's okay.
Helen: Is it fun?
Jane: It is fun, yes. Some people might not think so, but I do.
Helen: Is it still rare to find women in similar jobs?
Jane: I would say so. In the computing industry as a whole it's not very rare, but when you get so close to the hardware as this job is, it does become very rare. Maybe about one in twenty engineers are female. But things are getting better. Maybe in ten years' time, this department will be all women, and there will be just one man here. I don't know.

Information Technology	Informatik
placement	Praktikum
challenge	Herausforderung

Understanding

1. What is Jane's job in the company?
2. What does Jane say about the numbers of women in the computer industry as a whole?
3. What did Jane study at university?
4. What is meant by industrial placement?
5. Is Jane from Scotland?

8 G

Computer language

Jane Nightingale used the words hardware and software.
HARDWARE refers to the parts or components of a computer or any electronic equipment.
SOFTWARE refers to the instructions which tell the computer what to do and how

to do it. Computer software consists of **programs** which either enable the computer to operate, or give the computer a particular job to do, such as **word processing**, or making and using **databases** of information, or using **graphics**, which means images of all kinds. Some programs include **sound** as well.
Good programs should be *user friendly*. They should be *straightforward*, and it should be easy to learn how to use them.

user friendly	benutzerfreundlich
straightforward	einfach, unkompliziert

Vocabulary

Explain the following.

1. user friendly
2. database
3. graphics
4. word processing

8 H

Helen interviews Bill Campbell, the General Manager of Mitsubishi PC Division in Glenrothes

Helen: What part, do you think, will the British computer industry play in hard- and software developments that are taking place in the United States and the Far East?
Bill: One of the things that British engineers have always been very proud of is their *innovation*, and the design of products and the manufacture of products have been made there for many years. Unfortunately, in the computer industry, companies like Intel and Microsoft have become so powerful - they are now *dominating* the *marketplace*, and really *dictating* the way things go forward. And therefore I actually believe that the British computer industry will struggle to try and influence such big players as Intel and Microsoft.
Helen: How many jobs have been created in Scotland in the computer industry since the start of Silicon Glen?
Bill: Since the *inception* of Silicon Glen in Scotland, there's approximately 45,000 jobs, which has really been a large *injection* to the Scottish industry and to employment within Scotland.
Helen: And what are future job prospects in Silicon Glen?
Bill: Very *powerful*. If you look at the *imminent* investment that we have coming into Scotland, it's still continuing at a very high rate. If you look at the infrastructure that we have in Scotland for *distribution*, both in Europe and around the world, it's strong. And if you look at the *calibre* of engineers coming from the universities, again, a very high standard. So I think we're really in a very strong position to move forward.

Helen: And where is the money coming from that is being invested here at the moment?
Bill: A large amount of the money being invested at the moment is coming from the Far East. There's a lot of Far-Eastern companies investing in Scotland to give them a *foothold* in Europe.
Helen: Looking ahead to, say the year 2005, what changes do you expect to see in the use of computer technology?
Bill: I think what you'll see in the communications side is that it will be revolutionised. If you look at the Internet, for example, the changes that it has brought to business today - I think in the future that will make a lot of changes both at home and at work.

innovation	Neuerung	powerful	*hier*: günstig
to dominate	beherrschen	imminent	unmittelbar bevorstehend
marketplace	*hier*: Markt	distribution	Vertrieb, Verbreitung
to dictate	vorgeben, diktieren	calibre	Format
inception	Beginn, Anfang	foothold	Stand, Halt, sichere Ausgangsposition
injection	Spritze, *hier*: Schub		

I. Vocabulary

a) Give the verbs corresponding to the following nouns.

1. distribution
2. innovation
3. creation
4. employment
5. investment
6. communication

b) Give a synonym or synonymous expression for the following as used in the interview above.

1. company
2. to believe
3. to struggle
4. inception
5. prospects
6. powerful
7. foothold
8. to continue
9. it will be revolutionised

II. Understanding

1. Why will the British computer industry be struggling to influence large companies such as Intel and Microsoft?
2. What is Bill Campbell's opinion of the engineering graduates coming into the computer industry in Scotland?
3. Where does the money for new investments in Silicon Glen largely come from?

III. Grammar revision: tenses

Complete the sentences using the correct tense of the verbs in brackets.

1. The mathematician Charles Babbage, who .... (live) in the 19th century, ... (call) the father of the computer.
2. His achievements .... (largely forget).
3. Babbage .... (spend) his boyhood in South Devon near the resort of Torquay.
4. Before .... (graduate) in mathematics at the University of Cambridge, he .... (dream) of a machine capable of calculating number tables.
5. The pilot model of his calculating engine .... (win) a gold medal from the Royal Astronomical Society in 1821.
6. Part of the hand-operated machine .... (finish) by 1832 - and still .... (work) perfectly.
7. The mathematician .... (devote) most of his own fortune to development work.
8. The calculating engines .... (remain) his first love, despite his disappointment at never .... (see) them in operation.
9. He .... (die) in 1871.
10. His achievements .... (live) on, and today in the age of the computer his innovative work .... (recognise) and .... (celebrate) at last.

8 I

How people use computers

Like a lot of professional people, John's wife Charlie finds a computer useful doing some of her work at home.
John uses his PC at home mostly for word processing as part of his work for a Master of *Business Administration* (MBA) degree, *sponsored* by Mitsubishi. The MBA involves part-time study at home and visits to Wolverhampton University near Birmingham.
Jane Nightingale also uses a computer at home. She told Helen she used it for playing games and going on the Internet and for sending *e-mail* to her family and her friends. At work Jane uses the Internet almost every day. One of the main reasons is to record all the changes which she makes to programs on the production line, so that someone else could *take over* in her place, if necessary.

business administration	*etwa*: Betriebswirtschaft	e-mail (short for *electronic mail*)	E-Mail (*elektronische Post*)
to sponsor	unterstützen, fördern	to take over	übernehmen, ablösen

What do you know about John?

1. John is an .... working for a Japanese company in Scotland.
2. He is responsible for controlling and supervising the introduction of new .... at Mitsubishi PC Division's manufacturing plant in Glenrothes.
3. The only woman working in John's cross-functional team is Jane Nightingale, who is a ....
4. John is 33 years old and .... to Charlie for four years.
5. Charlie is an orthoptist, a specialist in .... She works at a hospital in ....
6. John and Charlie live in Clackmannan, a quiet little village in beautiful countryside, about 40 kilometres from ....
7. John is currently preparing for an MBA, a .... degree, sponsored by Mitsubishi. This involves .... study at home and visits to university.
8. In his spare time he likes to play a game of .... with his colleague and friend, Jim Hain at ...., the world headquarters of golf, where the rules of the game are decided.
9. He also enjoys .... in the hills near Clackmannan.

John on his mountain bike

8 J

At the Cyberia Café in Edinburgh

The Cyberia Café gives anyone the chance to use the Internet for £6 per hour. It's especially good for people who don't have access to the Internet through their own computers, or who want to learn about the Internet and how to use it, or who just want to relax and surf the Internet looking for information and entertainment. There are cups of coffee, and help is available.

Helen interviewed some of the customers.

Helen: Do you consider yourself to be computer-literate?
Beginner: Oh no, I'm just a beginner.
Helen: Do you have a computer at home?
Beginner: Yes, I do, but it's still in the box. I haven't unpacked it yet.
Helen: What do you use computers for?
Teacher: I use computers at home basically for word processing. I also teach in primary schools, so I use the computer in a classroom as a teaching tool. I teach eight-year-olds at primary school.
Helen: And are you teaching them to use a computer?
Teacher: I do teach the children to use the computer, but often they teach me to use the computer. There's a two-way process; we actually work together on it. They are becoming more computer-literate, so I really have to try to *keep up with* them.
Helen: In what way do you work with computers?
Programmer: I work with computers as a kind of programmer, working for an insurance company here in Edinburgh.
Helen: Why are you at the café today?
Programmer: I am presently at the café for e-mailing my friends and relatives, who are put up in various parts of the world like India and the U.S. and other European countries.
Helen: Do you consider yourself to be computer-literate?
Banker: Yes, I do. I've done a degree in computing, and now I'm working in the IT department at the Royal Bank of Scotland.
Helen: Do you have a computer at home too?
Banker: Yes, yes. I've got a computer at home. I just use that for word processing and *spreadsheets*, not accessing the Internet.
Helen: What are you doing at the café today?
Banker: I'm introducing my girlfriend to the Internet, who's not used it so much, so we're just going through the *basics*.

keep up with	Schritt halten, mithalten mit
spreadsheet	Tabellenkalkulation(sprogramm)
basics	Grundbegriffe, Grundlagen

Understanding

Explain the following expressions from the text above.

1. to be computer-literate
2. e-mail
3. basics
4. Internet café

8 K

The Internet

The Internet, also called the World Wide *Web*, is a network of computers, *linked* together so that they can communicate with each other anywhere in the world.
If you have the right hardware and software, the Internet makes possible the *exchange* of words, pictures and sounds for a variety of purposes, such as to inform, to entertain, to teach and learn, to buy and sell. This is done in several ways, for example by e-mail - mail that is sent electronically, or by websites - pages with specific locations where information can be stored, accessed and used.
Information from the Internet can be *downloaded* and *filed* for future use in your own computer.

web	Netz	to download	(herunter)laden
to link	verbinden	(to) file	ablegen; Datei
exchange	Austausch		

Comment

How do computers affect your life, and how do you think this effect will change in the next few years? (100 to 150 words)

8 L

A visit to Edinburgh (TV commentary)

Edinburgh is the capital of Scotland, and although it was united with England in 1707, Scotland has always kept its own legal and educational systems. In 1997 the majority of Scots voted for the establishment of an independent Scottish parliament in Edinburgh.
Edinburgh Castle stands on a *hill overlooking* the city. It has played an important part in the history of Scotland, and it's popular with tourists who come here to see the many *reminders* of the country's past, including the Great Hall which is still used for ceremonies.

The magnificent *location* of the Castle helps to give Edinburgh its title 'Athens of the North', though not all the buildings could be called beautiful.
The streets in the newer part of the city contrast with the Lawnmarket, where wool and *linen* were sold in medieval times. Nowadays there are shops selling the *tartan cloth* of the Scottish clans.

Bagpipe player

The Royal Mile is a line of old streets running down from the Castle. Further along the Royal Mile is St Giles Cathedral with its unusual tower in the shape of a crown. John Knox, the great religious reformer and *founder* of the Presbyterian church in Scotland, *preached* here in the 16th century.
At the far end of the Royal Mile is the Palace of Holyroodhouse, the official residence of the Royal family in Edinburgh.
An abbey was founded here in the 12th century, 300 years before Holyrood became the home of the kings and queens of Scotland. In 1745, Prince Charles Edward Stuart, known as Bonnie Prince Charlie, also lived here at the start of his rebellion against King George II, in which he *claimed* to be the true King of both England and Scotland.

hill	Hügel	tartan	Schottenkaro
overlooking	mit Blick, Aussicht auf	cloth	Tuch, Stoff
reminder	Erinnerung, Mahnung	founder	(Be-)Gründer(in)
location	Lage	to preach	predigen
linen	Leinen	to claim	beanspruchen, behaupten

How much do you know about Scotland?

1. The capital of Scotland is .... It's often called the .... of the North.
2. The established church in Scotland is known as the .... church.
3. In 1997 many Scots voted for an independent Scottish ....
4. John Knox was a great .... He lived in the 16th century.
5. Wherever you go in this country, you'll hear the traditional ....
6. A .... is a type of Scottish family group.
7. The official residence of the Royal Family in the Scottish capital is ....

AN ENVIRONMENTAL OFFICIAL IN THE HIGHLANDS

9

9 A

Introduction

Karen Watson

This programme is about controlling *pollution* and protecting the environment in the Scottish Highlands, and about Karen Watson, a Team Leader with the Scottish *Environment Protection Agency* (SEPA).
Karen is based at SEPA's North Region *headquarters* in Dingwall near Inverness. She describes her working day, and we follow her on visits to monitor pollution on a beach, a *waste disposal* site, a factory and a *fish farm*. We also see her at meetings with the regional *licensing* group and with her own team. Karen talks to Helen about her work and about her love of the mountains, and we go with her as she walks up Ben Nevis, the highest mountain in Britain. At the foot of Ben Nevis Helen finds out what several other walkers do about protecting the environment.
In the course of her work, Karen reports to the Director of SEPA's North Region, Professor David Mackay. Professor Mackay talks to Helen about pollution in the rivers which provide water for whisky *distilleries*, and we see how single malt Scotch whisky is produced at the Royal Lochnagar Distillery near Balmoral.

We visit Culloden, the site of the last battle on British soil, and other places of interest in the Highlands, and the programme ends on the beautiful island of Skye in the Inner Hebrides.

pollution	Verschmutzung	fish farm	Fischzucht(anlage)
environment protection	Umweltschutz	to license	eine Lizenz, Konzession vergeben an
agency	Geschäftsstelle, Behörde	distillery	(Branntwein-)Brennerei, Destillerie
headquarters	Hauptsitz		
waste disposal	Müllbeseitigung, Abfallentsorgung		

9 B

Helen interviews Karen Watson (1st part)

Helen: Karen, how and why did you become involved in environmental protection?
Karen: I was really quite *fortunate*. When I was at university, I studied an environmental degree, and I first got a job with the National Rivers Authority. I looked after rivers in part of the North of England. So really my first job on leaving university was in the environmental field. I enjoyed the job, and was fortunate following that - I received further job opportunities in this field. So really all I've ever done is sort of work as an *environmental regulator*.
Helen: Do you see yourself as an *environmentalist*, or as somebody simply doing a job?
Karen: Certainly I see myself as an environmentalist, but it's quite frustrating at times because I have to operate within some *constraints*. We deal with businesses, with budgets; we are dealing with people who have jobs and so quite often we can't get the results we want as quickly as we would like. But yes, definitely I'm an environmentalist.
Helen: What are the main environmental issues here in this part of Scotland?
Karen: Our main *concerns* here in the Highlands are issues such as *forestry*, *agriculture*, fish farming, and waste disposal issues. Waste is a new issue which is causing us quite a few concerns. We've a lot of *fly-tipping* - illegal *dumping* problems. But as well as these we have some major industries, such as Dounreay, which is on the north coast. This is a *nuclear processing plant*.

to be fortunate	Glück haben	forestry	Forstwirtschaft
environmental regulator, environmentalist	Umweltschützer(in)	agriculture	Landwirtschaft
		fly-tipping	illegales Müllabladen
		dumping	(Schutt-, Müll-)Abladen
constraint	Ein-, Beschränkung; Zwang	nuclear processing plant	Atomkraftwerk
concern	Anliegen, Sorge		

I. Vocabulary

a) Find opposites for these words as used in the text above.

1. fortunate
2. quite often
3. quick
4. major
5. to leave

b) Give the adjectives corresponding to the following nouns.

1. protection
2. environment
3. fortune
4. agriculture
5. industry

II. Understanding

1. What are the main environmental concerns in the Highlands?
2. In which part of Britain did Karen work when she left university?
3. Dounreay lies on the northern coast of Scotland. Why have most nuclear processing plants been built near water?

9 C

SEPA

Protecting the environment is especially important in the Highlands. Until 1995 it was the responsibility of several different organisations. Their work has been brought together in a single agency, the Scottish Environment Protection Agency, known as SEPA, which employs 650 professional staff. SEPA's task is to protect and improve the environment in Scotland: on land, in the air, and in the water. It operates through United Kingdom *legislation* and European Union *directives* to *prevent* damage to the environment, by stopping pollution actually happening, and to control sources of possible damage, by making sure that what affects the environment is properly managed and regulated.

On land, SEPA controls the disposal and *treatment of* waste, which is generally dealt with by organisations by re-cycling it, by *landfilling* - *burying* it in the ground - and by *incinerating*, or burning, it. To prevent air pollution, SEPA regulates industrial processes, and controls *discharges* into the air.

In rivers and *lochs*, the Scottish word for lakes, and also along the coastline, SEPA tests and monitors water quality, and *enforces* standards set by the UK and EU. SEPA also enforces regulations relating to radioactivity, and cooperates in *emergency* planning in case of nuclear accidents.

As part of its responsibility for controlling pollution, SEPA deals with applications for permission to dispose of waste on land and to discharge substances into the air or water.

legislation	Gesetzgebung	to incinerate	verbrennen, einäschern
directive	Weisung	discharge	Ausströmen, Ausstoß
to prevent	verhindern	loch (*in Scotland*)	See
treatment of	Behandlung, Umgang mit	to enforce	durchführen, geltend machen, sorgen für
landfill (site)	Mülldeponie, -halde		
to bury	begraben, eingraben	emergency	Notfall, Notlage

I. Vocabulary

Give a synonym for the following expressions from the text above.

1. to control
2. task
3. to incinerate
4. discharge
5. standards

II. Understanding

Choose the correct answer, according to the text above.

1. Before 1995 the work for which SEPA is now responsible was carried out by ....
   a) several organisations b) a single agency c) the European Union
2. SEPA .... to deal with nuclear emergencies and accidents.
   a) regulates processes b) cooperates in planning c) controls applications
3. To prevent air pollution, SEPA controls .... into the air.
   a) dumping b) waste c) discharges
4. SEPA will preserve and improve the .... of water in rivers and lochs.
   a) standard b) quality c) regulation
5. SEPA will provide an integrated approach to the .... of the environment across all Scotland.
   a) protection b) proposal c) pollution

9 D

Karen at work

Karen's job involves correspondence and other office work, but there is also a lot of interesting outdoor activity. She has to inspect waste disposal sites, such as the Longman Landfill Site in Inverness, to check *records* showing the amount of waste brought in to the site and to see that there is no illegal dumping. And she personally monitors the *levels* of pollution *emitted* by a variety of companies which use potentially dangerous manufacturing processes. One of them, RK *Carbon fibres* Ltd, produces carbon fibres used for aeroplanes and *spacecraft*. The process emits *cyanide* gas into the air, and the emissions have to be carefully controlled.
As a team leader Karen plays an important part in meetings of the regional licensing group to discuss *applications* for licences to *dispose of* waste. She also holds planning meetings with the members of her own team in order to organise visits to sites which need to be inspected, such as beaches and fish farms. Fish farming is a rapidly growing industry in Scotland, so she goes with one of her colleagues to check the *cages* where the salmon are *hatched* and kept.
Samples collected during her visits to beaches and fish farms are analysed in SEPA's laboratory.

records	Unterlagen, Aufzeichnungen
level	Grad, Stufe
to emit	ausstoßen
carbon	Kohle(nstoff)
fibre	Faser
spacecraft	Raumfahrt
cyanide	Zyanid, Blausäuresalz
application	*hier*: Antrag, Anmeldung
to dispose of	beseitigen
cage	Käfig
to hatch	(aus)brüten

I. Vocabulary

Find words or phrases to replace the following from the text above, altering the meaning as little as possible.

1. illegal dumping
2. a variety of companies
3. the levels of pollution
4. an important part
5. potentially dangerous
6. analysed

II. Comment

What law (or laws) would you propose for fighting pollution, and what would be your reason for proposing it? (80 to 120 words)

9 E

Karen reports to her boss, Professor David Mackay

David Mackay

Karen: I'm just back from looking at the fish farm in Loch Ness. I tend to go there reasonably frequently to inspect the records, have a look at the site, record things like the rate of fish in cages, how much fish feed they are using.
Prof. Mackay: Did you find any major problems today?
Karen: No. The site was *satisfactory*. It was very tidy, all the records were up to date, and it seemed generally to be very good.
Prof. Mackay: No dead fish lying about?

Karen: Not that I could see. There were no problems at all.
Prof. Mackay: Did you see any problems as you travelled there or back? Any rivers being discoloured or any signs of *sewage* pollution?
Karen: You tend to have a look whenever you're passing, obviously. Certainly there are no farm problems at the moment. We've been quite fortunate this summer, despite the wet weather we've had recently.
Prof. Mackay: Well, certainly, with all the rain we've had, that helped a bit. I went to check on a couple of distilleries myself; I'm going over to Royal Lochnagar tomorrow probably, to see if there are any problems there.
Karen: Are you also going to be discussing the discharge rates or is it more environmental inspections?
Prof. Mackay: I think we have to *tighten up on* a few of the distilleries where they are actually discharging more than the river can comfortably *cope with*. So as we're always *trying for* higher standards as you know, we'll do a bit more in that respect. And I'll *negotiate* with them tomorrow on how much tighter we can make the conditions without putting them out of business.

satisfactory	befriedigend, zufriedenstellend	to cope with	fertigwerden, zurechtkommen mit, vertragen
sewage	Abwasser	to try for	sich bemühen um
to tighten up on	strenger werden, härter durchgreifen bei	to negotiate	ver-, aushandeln

I. Vocabulary

a) Give the nouns corresponding to the following words.

1. satisfactory
2. to discuss
3. comfortable
4. to negotiate
5. to tend
6. to inspect

b) Give synonyms for the following words from the text above.

1. site
2. frequently
3. seemed
4. signs
5. obviously
6. fortunate
7. a couple of

II. Grammar revision: concession clauses

Combine the following pairs of sentences, using these conjunctions:

although • but • even though • while • whereas • yet

1. Our air is polluted. Industry still continues to emit dangerous substances into the air.
2. There is a shortage of paper. We throw away our old newspapers instead of recycling them.
3. Scientists tell us that nuclear power stations are dangerous. The government has decided to build new ones.
4. Environmental agencies enforce strict regulations for the discharge of substances into the air and water. Factories still dispose of waste products in rivers and the sea.
5. Thousands of children in the Third World are suffering from malnutrition (*Unterernährung*). We live in greater prosperity than ever before.
6. Empty bottles could be recycled. Most people throw them away.

9 F

Single malt whisky

Access to *sparkling* clear water is essential for the location of a whisky distillery. On the River Dee near the royal castle of Balmoral is the Royal Lochnagar Distillery. The distillery makes single malt whisky.

Single malt whisky is made from barley which has been *soaked* in highland spring water and dried in a fire which burns *peat*, or *turf*, to give the whisky an important part of its *flavour*.
The malt is mixed with hot water to make a liquid which is fermented with yeast. The liquid is distilled in copper *stills* and then it's put into *casks* made of oak where it will be left to *mature* for more than eight years. During this time it takes on flavour from the oak of the casks.
Each single malt whisky is unique - the product of one distillery. It's more expensive than *blended* whisky which is produced by taking whisky from several different distilleries.
The Scots call a measure of whisky in a glass a *dram*. A small measure is a *wee* dram. And notice that it's always called Scotch, not Scottish, whisky.

sparkling	sprudelnd, perlend	cask	Faß
to soak	einweichen	to mature	reifen, reif werden
peat, turf	Torf	blended	(mit anderen Sorten) vermischt
flavour	Geschmack, Aroma		
still	Destillierapparat	(wee) dram	(winziger) Schluck Whisky

Understanding

1. What happens to the malt for whisky after it has been dried?
2. Where is the Royal Lochnagar Distillery?
3. How long and where does single malt whisky have to be kept to mature?
4. What is the difference between single malt and blended whisky?
5. What is a wee dram?

9 G

Helen interviews Professor Mackay, Director of SEPA's North Region

Helen: Why have whisky distilleries to be monitored, and how do they cause pollution?
Prof. Mackay: Well, the real problem is that these distilleries were built - some of them many centuries ago - on the banks of the purest crystal-clear streams, because they needed extra-quality water. These streams also form the *spawning* and *nursery grounds* for the *noble* fish, the Atlantic salmon, which is of enormous importance for Scotland. So the small quantities of *organic* waste which can be *released* from the process when it's complete, are enough to bring down the *oxygen* levels in these rivers and make quite a dramatic effect on them. There is also some hot water which comes from the distilleries which can - change the rate at which the young fish grow, and *set* them *off* to sea before their *proper* time. So they can have a dramatic effect on rivers, which are extremely sensitive to even small quantities of *pollutants*. *Hence* we have to control them quite *rigorously*.

Helen: How many whisky distilleries are there in your region?
Prof. Mackay: Oh, there are hundreds. I couldn't count them all really.
Helen: And to talk a little about a Scotch whisky now: is all Scotch whisky produced in this region?
Prof. Mackay: No, but this is the *heartland*. This is where originally barley was produced in a coastal region on the *fertile* lands near the sea. And then behind this were the high mountains where the water comes down, as I said already, very pure, very clean. Where these two areas meet, that is where the small malt whisky distilleries were originally built and *set up* - a tradition which has now been *honoured* for many centuries in Scotland.
Helen: And tell me, do all Scots love drinking whisky? Do you enjoy a wee dram?
Prof. Mackay: I doubt if more than half of Scots drink whisky. And certainly very, very few are able to drink the malt whiskies - a pure malt whisky, the 'single malts', as we call them, which are produced in distilleries like this. These distilleries have very small *outputs* of whisky. It's very special; it's kept for many years; it's made only with barley; there is no other grain involved. And so it's a *connoisseur*'s whisky. It's not a whisky for getting drunk on; it's a whisky for people to really enjoy. I certainly do enjoy a dram myself - in moderation like most of the best things in life.

to spawn	laichen	hence	also
nursery ground	Brutstätte	rigorous	streng
noble	edel	heartland	Kernland
organic	biologisch	fertile	fruchtbar
to release	freisetzen	to set up	gründen, errichten
oxygen	Sauerstoff	to honour	ehren, respektieren
to set off	(*zu etw.*) führen, bringen	output	Produktion, Ausstoß
proper	eigentlich, richtig	connoisseur	Kenner
pollutant	Schadstoff		

I. Vocabulary

a) Explain the meaning of the following words as used in the text above.

1. nursery ground
2. distillery
3. heartland
4. oxygen
5. connoisseur
6. output

b) Use the following expressions from the text in a sentence of your own.

1. waste
2. pollutant
3. fertile
4. to be sensitive to

II. Understanding

Why can whisky distilleries cause pollution?

9 H

Karen's views on environmental issues

Karen and her team deal with an area of 6,500 hectares, much of it in very beautiful countryside. She said there was a huge difference between protecting the environment in a town and protecting the environment in the Scottish Highlands. In the Highlands the environmental protection teams were *primarily* concerned with fishing, forestry and fish farming, whereas in a city, they would be looking after industries, factories and *commercial premises*.
Asked if we ourselves were doing enough to protect the environment, Karen argued it was up to all of us to do a little to help. Each of us should think about what we were doing with our water and with our waste. We would have to change our *lifestyles*, think about recycling, change the way we used cars and use more public transport.
Karen was asked about her personal view of *pressure groups* such as Greenpeace or Friends of the Earth, or political parties such as the Green Party. She replied that these pressure groups did a very important job, because they brought environmental issues into the media and *into the forefront* of the public's attention, which the staff of SEPA could not do because they were *confined to* acting within the law. But in the end they were all working together to achieve the same *goals*.

primarily	hauptsächlich, in erster Linie	into the forefront	an die Spitze, *hier*: ins Blickfeld
commercial premise	Gewerbegebiet	to confine to	beschränken auf
lifestyle	Lebensstil, -weise	goal	Ziel
pressure group	Interessengruppe, -verband		

I. Understanding

1. What contribution could each of us make towards a cleaner and more livable world?
2. How would we have to change our lifestyles?

II. Grammar revision: infinitive and gerund

Put the words in brackets into their correct form.

1. Have you ever watched people .... (try, catch) fish?
2. Try .... (persuade) your friends .... (care) more about environmental issues.
3. Can you imagine .... (she, study, be) an environmentalist?
4. They refused .... (allow, we, enter) the building site without .... (put on) helmets.

5. I usually manage .... (escape, be) asked to these meetings, but this time I forgot .... (think up) a good excuse in time.
6. I don't mind the children .... (play) in the garden, but I won't have .... (they, walk) over the flowers.

III. Say it in English

1. Bisher ist sehr wenig für den Umweltschutz getan worden.
2. Die Grünen haben die Öffentlichkeit auf Umweltfragen aufmerksam gemacht.
3. Viele Haushaltsprodukte enthalten Chemikalien, die schädlich für die Umwelt sind.
4. Wir müssen unseren Lebensstil ändern und über Methoden der Wiederverwertung nachdenken.

9 I

Helping to protect the environment

At the foot of Ben Nevis, Helen asked several walkers what they did to protect the environment.
The first walker said that his only *contribution* was to try and *harm* the environment as little as possible while he was enjoying it.
Another thought you needed to respect the environment while enjoying the scenery, to keep to the *footpaths* and make sure that you didn't damage anything or pick flowers or drop any *litter*.
In fact, almost all the walkers talked about litter and how they were careful not to leave waste paper, bottles and other *rubbish* lying around. One woman said that she was encouraging her grandchildren to follow her example, and not to throw down litter, particularly things that were not *bio-degradable*.
Another walker belonged to the Women's Institute (WI), a *nationwide* organisation, which collected *tins* to be recycled and used the money from that to send a *carer* away on holiday. WI members also tried to help by picking up any litter which they found lying about.
One of the walkers taught Environmental Law at Surrey University. *At a professional level* he tried to develop environmental law and policy. At an individual level he was careful about what he purchased, and he tried to live in a way that was less harmful to the environment.

contribution	Beitrag
to harm	schaden, verletzen
footpath	Fußweg
litter	Abfälle
rubbish	Abfall, Müll
bio-degradable	biologisch abbaubar
nationwide	landesweit
tin	Dose
carer	im Sozialbereich Tätige(r)
at a professional level	in beruflicher Hinsicht

I. Vocabulary

Find synonyms for these words from the text above, changing their meaning as little as possible.

1. harm
2. rubbish
3. to encourage
4. to recycle
5. scenery

II. Comment

What do you think are the main threats to the environment facing the world at the end of the 20th century? Are we doing enough to deal with them? (100 to 200 words)

9 J

Karen's leisure time

Helen interviews Karen (2nd part)

Helen: You live in a very remote part of the Scottish Highlands. Can you tell me whether you ever get *lonely*? And what do you do in your spare time?
Karen: I think the main advantage of the Highlands is this wonderful landscape we're *surrounded by*. You're only minutes away from the landscape, so you can go walking, climbing, it's a wonderful landscape for cycling. If the weather's lovely and sunny, there's lots of stuff to do, lots of activities.
Helen: What do you like doing most of all?
Karen: My favourite pastime has got to be hill walking and climbing. There's nothing I enjoy better than on a nice day walking up the *munroe* - that's a hill that's over 900 metres. You walk up one of these hills on a lovely day and get the most fantastic views that you couldn't get if you were travelling by car or by bus. And it's just superb.

lonely	einsam
surrounded by	umgeben von
munroe (*in Scotland*)	Berg

Karen at the foot of Ben Nevis, the highest mountain in the British Isles

What do you know about Karen?

1. Karen Watson is an .... official in the Highlands.
2. She works for SEPA, an environment .... agency.
3. Part of her job is to inspect .... disposal sites, to monitor the level of .... caused by factories.
4. She also has to attend .... of the regional licensing group.
5. She takes samples of .... from the beach or from the rivers and has them .... in the SEPA laboratory.
6. She personally supports .... like the Green Party or Greenpeace because in her view they were all working together to achieve the same goals: protecting the ....
7. In her leisure time she likes .... On a lovely day she often walks up Ben Nevis which is the highest .... in the British Isles.

9 K

The Highlands (TV commentary)

The last battle fought on British soil was at Culloden near Inverness. Here, in 1746, an English army defeated the forces loyal to Bonnie Prince Charlie. This marked the end of his *attempt* to become king.
The Glenfinnan Monument commemorates the start of the rebellion under Bonnie Prince Charlie. At the top is a statue of a highlander, who symbolises the Scottish clans which *gathered* there in August 1745 to support their prince.

Urquhart Castle

On the *shores* of Loch Ness stand the ruins of Urquhart Castle, a medieval *strong-hold* which was finally destroyed by the English to prevent it being used against them. Nowadays visitors come here in the hope of seeing the monster which is said to *inhabit* the deep waters of the loch.
Eilean Donan Castle dates from the 13th century, but like many Scottish castles it has been rebuilt in recent years.
To the West is a new bridge from the mainland to the island of Skye, the largest of the Inner ***Hebrides***. Many of the original inhabitants have left to find work elsewhere, and most of those who have stayed on the island are now involved in sheep and *cattle* farming.

Note:
The ***Hebrides:*** a group of over 500 islands off West Scotland. The Hebrides were settled by Scandinavians in the 6th to 9th centuries, and passed under Norwegian rule from about 890 to 1266 before being *ceded* to the Scottish king Alexander II by Magnus of Norway.

attempt	Versuch	to inhabit	bewohnen
to gather	sich versammeln	cattle	Vieh
shore	Ufer	to cede	abtreten
stronghold	Festung		

Understanding

1. Where did the last battle between England and Scotland take place?
2. Who was Bonnie Prince Charlie?
3. What is the name of the largest island of the Inner Hebrides?
4. What is Loch Ness famous for?

A EUROPEAN POLITICIAN IN WALES 10

10 A

Introduction

This programme is about Glenys Kinnock, a Member of the European Parliament who represents the *constituency* of South Wales East.
We see her at work in her Welsh constituency and in the Brussels headquarters of the European Union. In Wales she opens a European Information Centre, visits a village where there has been a serious gas explosion, and talks to pupils at a local school. In Brussels she *chairs* a meeting with a delegation of Welsh farmers.
Glenys explains how the European Parliament operates, and describes some of the ways in which it differs from the British Parliament at Westminster. She also invites Helen to meet her husband, Neil Kinnock, a former leader of the British Labour Party and now the European Commissioner for Transport.
The people of Wales have voted in a referendum to have their own *National Assembly* in Cardiff, where Helen asks several people for their views on being Welsh and on the Welsh language.
The programme ends with a look at castles in South Wales and at the ruins of Tintern Abbey on the border with England.

constituency	Wahlkreis	National Assembly	Nationalversammlung
to chair	den Vorsitz führen		

The Severn Bridge linking Wales to England

10 B

Helen interviews Glenys Kinnock in her constituency office

Helen: What in your opinion does the job of an MEP, a *Member of the European Parliament*, involve?
Glenys: It involves working in two places; it involves two areas of interest. One is the constituency, where I am now, and the other is my work on *committees* in Brussels. In the European Parliament we are all on two committees; one is a main committee, and on another one we have a sort of substitute status. I'm on - my main committee is the Development Committee, which deals with Europe's relations with the Third World, with the developing world. Europe is the biggest *donor* of aid, and trade relationships are very important. So it's quite a *time-consuming* but very, very interesting aspect of my work.
Helen: What is the most rewarding aspect of your job?
Glenys: I think it has to be the constituency work. My constituency is an area described as an area of industrial *decline*. All the coal mines are now closed; the steel industry has *contracted* very severely. So it's an area with huge needs and big disadvantages, but the people are wonderful. I'm not from South Wales, but I'm sort of an adopted daughter of South Wales, and as such it's been a great privilege to work here with local authorities, with the *voluntary* sector, with communities, women's training issues - all of that is very, very interesting.

Member of the European Parliament (MEP)	Europaabgeordnete(r)	time-consuming	zeitaufwendig, -raubend
		decline	Rückgang, Niedergang
		to contract	schrumpfen
committee	Ausschuß	voluntary	freiwillig
donor	Spender(in), Stifter(in)		

I. Vocabulary

a) Find words in the interview which mean the opposite of those listed below.

1. unimportant
2. time-saving
3. revival
4. open
5. advantage

b) Explain the following words or expressions from the interview.

1. the developing world
2. Europe is the biggest donor of aid.
3. to work in the voluntary section
4. an area with huge needs

II. Understanding

1. What committee work does Glenys Kinnock do when she is in Brussels?
2. Why is South Wales an area of industrial decline?

10 C

Glenys Kinnock in her constituency

Glenys Kinnock's constituency - the part of the country which she represents - covers a large area of South Wales. In fact, the South Wales East constituency in the European Parliament is as large as eight constituencies of the British Parliament in Westminster.

Glenys Kinnock's office in Wales is run by Ceri Evans. Ceri is involved in research, and especially research for *funding*. So she spends a lot of time looking at projects which have applied to the EU for funds.

Ros Harry is Glenys's Personal Assistant. She organises visits for Glenys when she's in Wales. Here are three examples from a typical week.

One of Glenys's visits was to New Tredegar, a village where there had been a gas explosion. It caused a lot of damage and a young mother was killed. Glenys talked to the people directly *affected by* the explosion. Several elderly people discovered they were not *insured*, so they would have to wait for *compensation*.

Glenys is a former school teacher and her next stop was at a primary school, where she explained to the children why a European Parliament was necessary.

Glenys Kinnock

She also went to Ebbw Vale, a former *coal-mining community*, to open a new European Information Centre at the local public library.
It is one of five information centres in public libraries within the South Wales East constituency. The *purpose* of the centre is to keep people in touch with developments in the European Union, and with the language and culture of the member states.

funding	Geldbeschaffung	coal-mining community	Bergarbeiter-Siedlung
affected by	betroffen von		
insured	versichert	purpose	Zweck
compensation	Entschädigung		

I. Vocabulary

Give the nouns which correspond to the following verbs and adjectives.

1. involved
2. applied
3. to discover
4. insured
5. familiar
6. to explain

II. Understanding

1. What is a constituency?
2. What is Ros Harry's job?
3. Why did Glenys Kinnock visit New Tredegar?

4. What was Glenys Kinnock's profession before she went into politics?
5. What did she do at the local library in Ebbw Vale?

10 D

An extract from Glenys Kinnock's speech at the opening of the European Information Centre

"Thank you very much for inviting me to come here. It's for me a unique occasion because as far as Europe is concerned, I think we deal with more *misinformation* than with information. So, I think it's very important that we have here *tangible evidence* upstairs of the kind of useful role which the European Union plays.
We are all parts of our continent of Europe and we do share a common future and therefore we develop *objectives* together.
I think, more than anything, we have to gain that ideal which is that as Europeans we have fought each other, we have destroyed each other's lands in two terrible wars in this century; and the main, main reason for giving a positive view of the European partnerships that we have - the European vision we have - is that never again should we confront each other on any *battlefields* in Europe; and to preserve the peace is the reason why the European Union was started.
Thanks very much, it's a great privilege to be here and many, many congratulations for the hard work you have obviously put in to make this possible. So, it's with great pleasure that I cut the *ribbon* and declare the European Information Centre open."

misinformation	Fehlinformation	objective	Ziel
tangible	greifbar, handfest, real	battlefield	Schlachtfeld
evidence	Beweis	ribbon	Band

I. Vocabulary

Put the appropriate prefixes in the blank spaces.

1. I'm sorry to .....agree with what you say.
2. As far as Europe is concerned, we deal more with .....information than with information.
3. The town was deserted and the countryside almost .....inhabited.
4. It's very difficult to find a good but .....expensive restaurant in Brussels.
5. Glenys Kinnock may be .....elected in 1999.

II. Grammar revision: prepositions

Replace the blank spaces with suitable prepositions.

1. Thank you all ..... coming.
2. He wrote to her ..... a couple ..... problems.
3. When the Queen made her annual speech she said her government would play a leading role ..... the development ..... the European Community.
4. She said her government would work ..... greater trust and confidence ..... East and West, and ..... progress especially ..... human rights.

III. Translation

Translate the speech above into German.

10 E

The British parliamentary system

In Britain legislation is the responsibility of Parliament, which consists of the *House of Commons* and the *House of Lords*. Laws are passed by the House of Commons, and although the House of Lords can influence and help to *revise* these laws, it cannot finally *reject* them.
The 659 members of the House of Commons, known as MPs, represent the *voters* in their constituencies. They are elected every five years, or less if the government chooses to call a *general election*. The House of Lords consists of the most senior members of the Church and the legal profession, and *peers* who hold titles which they have *inherited* or which they have been given to hold during their lifetime in return for *distinguished* political or public service.
The government is usually chosen from the party with the majority of *votes* in the House of Commons, and is headed by a Prime Minister who is the leader of that party.
There are three main political parties in Britain: Labour, a socialist party which has been in government since winning the 1997 general election; Conservative, which was in government from 1979 to 1997 and is now the main opposition party; and Liberal Democrat, which has not been *in power* for more than 70 years. There are also two regional parties: the Scottish Nationalist Party, which campaigns for the complete independence of Scotland; and Plaid Cymru, the Welsh Nationalist party, which aims to preserve the Welsh language and culture as the basis of Welsh identity within the United Kingdom. The MPs from Northern Ireland are split among several parties representing different interests.
Because the candidate with the most votes in a constituency is automatically elected as its MP, there are many *minority* parties, such as the Green Party, which can-

not win enough votes in any single constituency to get any of their representatives elected as MPs. This is one reason why there is considerable *pressure* for a reform of the British voting system to allow for some form of *proportional representation*.

House of Commons	(britisches) Unterhaus
House of Lords	(britisches) Oberhaus
to revise	überarbeiten, revidieren
to reject	ablehnen, zurückweisen
voter	Wähler(in)
general election	allgemeine Wahlen (*Unterhauswahlen*)
peer	*Angehöriger des hohen Adels*
to inherit	erben
distinguished	ausgezeichnet, herausragend
(to) vote	(Wahl-)Stimme; wählen, abstimmen
in power	an der Macht
minority	Minderheit
pressure	Druck
proportional representation	Verhältniswahlsystem

Understanding

The following words concern aspects of politics in Britain. Use them to complete the sentences. Use each word only once.

MPs • Parliament • Opposition • House of Commons • general election constituencies • House of Lords • Plaid Cymru • Labour

1. The .... is one of the two Houses of Parliament.
2. The Welsh Nationalist party is called ....
3. There are 659 .... in Britain.
4. The parties which are not part of the government are called the ....
5. There must be a .... at least every five years.
6. .... is one of the main political parties in Britain.
7. The Government proposes new legislation in ....
8. .... are elected to represent the interests of their constituents.
9. The members of the .... are not elected.

10 F

Helen interviews Glenys Kinnock in Brussels, Headquarters of the European Union and one of the two locations of the European Parliament

Helen: How is your time divided up when you're in Brussels? How much time do you spend in the European Parliament, and how much time do you spend doing other things?
Glenys: I spend almost all my time in the European Parliament. It tends to be my place of work. Obviously we have some social life - see friends, sometimes go to the opera or to the theatre, but generally when I'm here I spend far too much time in this building.
Helen: How does your job differ from that of a Member of Parliament at Westminster?
Glenys: The way of working here is very different from the way that national parliaments work, and I think that's because we have a very different type of committee structure, where all the *reports* are looked at, the legislation is *scrutinised* at that level, and then it goes on to the *Plenary* for voting. And I think more than anything the way of working here is very different because it's not *adversarial.* It's very much a way of working on committees, preparing legislation and so on, *influencing opinion* - in a way that means you're looking for *consensus* and cooperation, and I think many of our national parliaments - and it's certainly true of Britain - the system is much more confronting, *polarised* systems; I think this way of working is much better.
Helen: Is it more effective?
Glenys: I think it is. I think that - um - *picking quarrels*, *strutting at* each other across the *chamber* of the House of Commons and so on is something that really isn't very effective *in the long run*. And I think you achieve far more working together towards a *common* goal.
Helen: How much in contact are you with the local members of parliament in your constituency in Wales?
Glenys: I'm in very regular contact with them, and they share our concerns that may be raised with them by *constituents* about something that involves European issues. And because my constituency is one which receives a lot of European funding, a lot of European support, then they naturally will ask for assistance, should one of their local councils or someone come to them who wants to raise a matter related to Europe. And it can be, for instance, you know, this business of people buying houses in a European country - time-sharing - all of those things we cover, also issues related to pension rights, for instance: people move to live in a different European country what happens to their British pension rights? Those issues are generally raised with me by my members of parliament.

reports	Berichte	to pick a quarrel	einen Streit vom Zaun brechen
to scrutinise	untersuchen, genau prüfen		
Plenary	Plenum, Vollversammlung	to strut at sb	sich aufblasen vor jmdm.
adversarial	gegnerisch	chamber	(Parlaments-)Kammer
influencing opinion	meinungsbildend	in the long run	auf (die) Dauer
consensus	Übereinstimmung	common	gemeinsam
polarised	polarisiert, in (gegnerische) Lager geteilt	constituent	Wähler(in)

I. Vocabulary

Give the nouns corresponding to the following words from the text above.

1. confronting
2. to achieve
3. to scrutinise
4. to prepare
5. national
6. true
7. related

II. Understanding

1. Describe two ways in which the European Parliament differs from the British Parliament.
2. Name two European issues which are treated in the European Parliament.

III. Comment

Explain why you would or wouldn't like to be an MEP.

10 G

The European Union

The main institutions of the European Union based in Brussels are the European Council, the Council of Ministers, the European Commission and the European Parliament.

The European Council consists of the *heads of* member *states*, who hold two meetings each year. The Council gives *overall* direction to the EU's activities.

The Council of Ministers consists of ministers from member states. They represent national interests, and can *commit* their governments to *adopt* EU laws and policies.

The European Commission is headed by a President appointed by the member states every five years. There are 20 Commissioners, also appointed by the member states. They are responsible for particular areas of policy. The Commission makes *proposals* for legislation. It is also the *executive body* of the EU, making sure that its policies are carried out.

The European Parliament has 626 members democratically elected by voters in member states. The elections are held every five years.
There are 87 MEPs from the United Kingdom. MEPs represent the people of the member states, in specialist committees and in the full Parliament. The full Parliament sits for one week each month in Strasbourg. The committees and some full *sessions* of the Parliament are held in Brussels.
Most EU laws go through the following stages: first, the Commission makes a proposal; next, a committee of MEPs examines and often *amends* the proposal; finally the Council of Ministers votes on the proposal in its amended form.

head of state	Staatsoberhaupt	proposal	Antrag, Vorschlag
overall	allgemein, umfassend	executive body	ausführendes Organ
to commit	verpflichten	session	Sitzung(speriode)
to adopt	annehmen	to amend	ändern

Understanding

1. Who appoints the President of the European Commission?
2. How many MEPs are there in the European Parliament?
3. In which cities are the full sessions of the European Parliament held?

10 H

Glenys Kinnock's work in Brussels

Glenys's schedule in Brussels is as hectic as that in Wales. Her work on the Development Cooperation Committee is a top priority and Glenys frequently has to visit Third World countries. She works on several other committees, and on the Human Rights Sub-Committee as well.
In the course of her work Glenys is involved in many other meetings. In the TV programme, we see her chairing a meeting for a delegation of farmers from Wales, alongside another Welsh Member of the European Parliament, Eluned Morgan. Eluned, who represents Mid and West Wales, was the youngest Member of the European Parliament when she was elected in 1994 at the age of 27.
The meeting was called to discuss a report on *BSE*, generally known as *mad cow disease*, which has seriously affected the *prosperity* of farmers in Wales.

BSE (Bovine Spongiform Encephalopathy), mad cow disease	BSE, Rinderwahn(sinn)
prosperity	Wohlstand

I. Understanding

1. Who is Eluned Morgan?
2. What subject did the MEPs discuss with the Welsh farmers?

II. Grammar revision: tenses

Complete the sentences with the correct form of the verb given in brackets.

1. In June 1994 Eluned Morgan .... (become) the youngest MEP.
2. During the election campaign she constantly had to remind people that she .... (can) do the job.
3. Before the election she .... (earn) her money as a television researcher at BBC Wales.
4. She .... (plan) to use her free time to redecorate the house she .... (buy) in February 1994 but her life .... (take) a different turn.
5. She's an MEP now. She .... (feel) that she .... (do) something important that she .... (believe) in.

(*adapted from an article in The European*)

10 I

The future of Europe

Helen interviews Glenys Kinnock in the hemicycle *where larger committee meetings, and some sessions of the European Parliament are held.*

Helen: How optimistic are you about the future of Europe - or how do you see Europe in, say, 20 years' time?
Glenys: I don't feel pessimistic at all. I hope that we can move forward to *enlarge* the community, to bring in countries of Central and Eastern Europe who are waiting to join with the rest of our continent - as they rightly should. A lot of things have to change for that to happen, including changes in agricultural policy and so on.
Helen: How do you think should the countries of Europe work together?
Glenys: I think that the countries of Europe need to work together to develop more of a social Europe, a Europe that actually has much more relevance for our citizens. And that means that on environmental issues, on consumer issues - a whole range of concerns, but particularly employment - we have to work together in order to reduce *appallingly* high levels of unemployment in Europe.
Helen: What does Europe do for Wales?
Glenys: In Wales we are *recipients* of - of large amounts of European Union aid. It's what we call 'solidarity' here. We have looked to Europe - in many ways over the last 18 years more than we've looked to Westminster - for support for creating

jobs, for *re-training* our people, and for improving our environment, for instance as a result of the coal mining and steel and other heavy industry that we've had in the past.

hemicycle	Halbkreis	recipient	Empfänger(in)
to enlarge	erweitern	to re-train	umschulen
appallingly	entsetzlich		

I. Understanding

1. Name two important European concerns.
2. What is Glenys Kinnock's view of the future of Europe?

II. Say it in English

1. Wir müssen die hohe Arbeitslosenquote reduzieren.
2. Viele Menschen werden umgeschult werden müssen.
3. Worüber spricht Glenys auf der nächsten Vollversammlung?
4. Wovon leben die Bergarbeiter, wenn ihre Sozialhilfe nicht ausreicht?
5. Selbst wenn wir verschiedene Sprachen sprechen, müssen wir versuchen zusammenzuleben.

10 J

The Kinnocks

Glenys is married to Neil Kinnock, now the EU Transport Commissioner in Brussels. Neil Kinnock is a former Labour leader. He *resigned* the leadership in 1992 after the Labour Party had failed to win the election. Neil comes from Tredegar in Ebbw Vale, in the mining and steel valleys of South Wales which are one of the party's heartlands.
He is proud of his origins and of his Welshness. Like many Celts, he is a master of rhetoric, and some of his speeches are *memorable*.

to resign	zurücktreten von, aufgeben, verzichten auf
memorable	denkwürdig, unvergeßlich

Helen interviews Neil Kinnock in Brussels

Helen: Do your two jobs *complement* each other or can they get in each other's way?
Neil Kinnock: To a degree, they complement each other, simply because it does mean that I think Glenys has got a *conditional* understanding of the workings of

Neil Kinnock

the Commission, and I certainly have a more intimate *insight* into some of the *moods* and movements in the Parliament. And that can help us in terms of contact, in terms of knowing people and so on. So we don't really get into each other's way, but I hate to imagine what would happen if her major interest - for instance was transport - I'm sure we'd find ourselves *colliding* on occasions then.

Helen: You're from the South of Wales - I've heard you described as a 'Valley Boy'. What is the basic difference between the Northern Welsh and the Southern Welsh?

Neil Kinnock: I suppose the temperament is *markedly* different. The Northern Welsh are mainly still rural people, with a *self-contained attitude*, a fairly *inward-looking* attitude. And they are very substantially, of course, primarily Welsh speakers. In South Wales the characteristic is much more *extravert*, much more external, much more outward-looking. But that too is because of the great internationalisation of South Wales, for all kinds of investments generally got carried out here over two centuries. So, I suppose, as a 'South Walean' I would say all of the poetry and creativity is in South Wales, and all of the *earnestness* and religion is in North Wales. And I wouldn't be all that far wrong.

to complement	ergänzen
conditional	bedingt
insight	Einblick
mood	Stimmung
to collide	zusammenprallen, -stoßen
markedly	merklich, wesentlich
self-contained	distanziert
attitude	Einstellung, Haltung
inward-looking	introvertiert, in sich gekehrt; beschaulich
extravert	extrovertiert, nach außen gekehrt
earnestness	Ernst(haftigkeit)

Glenys Kinnock

Glenys Kinnock comes from Anglesey, an island off the coast of North Wales. She has been a teacher in primary and secondary schools. She has also written books about developing countries and about education, and her collection of interviews with British women, 'By Faith and *Daring*', was published in 1993.
Glenys speaks Welsh. In fact it was her first language. She does some *broadcasting* in Welsh, and two of her colleagues in the European Parliament are Welsh-speaking, so when they get together they are able to exchange a few words. Glenys told Helen that it was quite *handy* in a lift if there were other nationalities, because one could feel fairly certain they couldn't understand what you were saying in Welsh.

daring	Kühnheit
to broadcast	im Hörfunk sprechen
handy	geschickt, praktisch

I. Vocabulary

Complete the sentences with one of the following adjectives.

outward-looking • rural • self-contained • earnest • different

1. The temperament between the North and South Welsh is clearly ....
2. The people from North Wales are mainly ....
3. Their attitude is ....
4. The South Welsh are more ....
5. In the North they are more .... and religious.

II. Understanding

1. What is Neil Kinnock's job in Brussels?
2. Where does he come from?
3. What was Neil's job before he went to Brussels?
4. What major quality is attributed to him?
5. Are there any other MEPs, apart from Glenys Kinnock, who can speak Welsh? If so, how many?
6. What was 'By Faith and Daring'?

III. What do you know about the Kinnocks?

1. Glenys and Neil Kinnock are now living in ....
2. Glenys is an .... and Neil is a European ....
3. Glenys often visits her .... in Wales.

4. She is a former ....
5. During her last visit to Wales she opened the European Information Centre at the .... in Ebbw Vale.
6. In her opening .... she talked about the important role the European Union plays.
7. In Brussels she works on several .... Her work for Third World Countries is a top ....
8. She is in regular contact with Welsh .... in Westminster.
9. She is married to Neil Kinnock, a former leader of the ....
10. Neil resigned after his party had failed to win the .... in 1992.
11. Glenys speaks .... which was her first ....

10 K

The Welsh and their language

One of the European Union's objectives is to support the different languages and cultures of Europe. Welsh is a minority language that gets assistance from the EU. Welsh is a Celtic language, and is therefore *related to* Irish and Scots Gaelic, and also to Cornish and Breton, and to Galician from northern Spain.
It has equal status with English for legal and administrative purposes in Wales, so there are signs in both Welsh and English. Welsh literature has a long and distinguished history, from the time of the Bards - poets who *recited* at the courts of the Welsh princes. And the Royal National Eistedfodd is still an *annual* event for celebrating Welsh literature and music, and for the Crowning of the Bard, the year's prize-winning poet. This contrasts with the decline of spoken Welsh. In the 1880s 80% of the people in Wales could speak Welsh. In the 1990s it is 20%. And only a few people use Welsh regularly. This decline has been *halted*, partly by the increasing use of Welsh in schools and by the media. In fact, the Welsh started the first minority-language television channel in the European Union.

to be related to	verwandt sein mit	annual	jährlich, Jahres-
to recite	vortragen, rezitieren	to halt	zum Stillstand bringen

Summary of vox pops

Helen asked some young people what they thought about their Welsh nationality in relation to other people.
They all agreed that they felt Welsh because they were brought up in Wales and went to Welsh schools. Asked whether he considered himself to be European, a young man who spoke Welsh *fluently* argued that the opening up of the European barriers was a good thing because there were fewer differences between countries,

though he felt that each individual country should retain its own identity. He thought people should be proud of where they were from, but should aim at creating a better relationship with their neighbours.

vox pops	Meinungsumfrage
fluently	fließend

Welsh voices and Welsh rugby

The Welsh have a *vibrant* culture, in which music plays a central role. Their *male voice choirs* were once the *pride* of Wales. Although they are *dwindling* in number and strength, the Welsh try to keep their country's choral tradition alive.
The Welsh sing their hymns and songs to greet their rugby team and as a form of battle-cry against their opponents. In the South of Wales, rugby is a form of religion. The *arch-enemies* are the English. To lose against the English at Cardiff Arms Park is to lose more than a rugby match.

vibrant	dynamisch, pulsierend	to dwindle	abnehmen, schrumpfen
male voice choir	Männerchor	arch-enemy	Erzfeind
pride	Stolz		

Understanding

1. What group languages does Welsh belong to?
2. What is a Bard?
3. What does 'Croeso i Gymru' mean in English?
4. What percentage of the population of Wales can speak Welsh nowadays? 80%, 50% or 20%?
5. What has been largely responsible for halting the decline of spoken Welsh?

The Land of My Fathers

The land of my fathers, the land of my choice,
The land in which poets and minstrels rejoice;
The land whose stern warriors were true to the core,
While bleeding from freedom of yore.

Wales! Wales! fav'rite land of Wales!
While sea her wall, may naught befall
To mar the old language of Wales.

Old mountainous Cambria, the Eden of bards,
Each hill and each valley, excite my regards;
To the ears of her patriots how charming still seems
The music that flows in her streams.

My country tho' crushed by a hostile array,
The language of Cambria lives out to this day;
The muse has eluded the traitors' foul knives,
The harp of my country survives.

(Ebenezer Thomas)

Monmouthshire Canal

10 L

Wales (TV commentary)

Wales is part of Britain, along with England, Scotland and Northern Ireland. Over 60% of its population lives in the south-east corner of Wales, and Cardiff is its capital. Cardiff is to become the seat of a Welsh National Assembly, which will be created as the result of a *favourable* vote in a referendum held in 1997.
Wales has magnificent castles, and Caerphilly Castle in South Wales is the largest, with its *leaning* tower and the remains of an architectural plan based on the castles of the *crusaders*.
The oldest castle is Chepstow. It was the first stone castle built in Norman times, and like the others it was intended to dominate the Welsh, whose princes and people fought the English for several hundred years before being finally *conquered*.
Nowadays the countryside near the border with England is peaceful, and the canals which used to carry coal and iron *ore* are a quiet attraction for visitors.
Tintern Abbey, a *Cistercian* monastery built at the end of the 13th century. The ruins and their *setting* in the Wye valley have a special *air* of mystery and romance.

favourable	positiv	Cistercian	Zisterzienser
leaning	schräg, schief	ore	Erz
crusader	Kreuzritter	setting	Umgebung
to conquer	besiegen, bezwingen	air	*hier*: Note

Tintern Abbey

A PLAYWRIGHT IN DUBLIN

11

11 A

Introduction

Bernard Farrell

This programme is about Bernard Farrell, one of Ireland's leading *playwrights*. Bernard's plays are *performed* throughout Europe and he is now Resident Playwright at the Abbey Theatre in Dublin, the National Theatre of Ireland.
Bernard describes how he started writing plays, and talks about the *subjects* and characters he likes to write about. He shows Helen some of the places *associated with* James Joyce, best known for his *novel* 'Ulysses', which is *set in* Dublin.
Dublin is famous for its *novelists*, poets and playwrights, and Helen visits the Dublin Writers Museum to be reminded of Ireland's immense contribution to literature.

Helen is in Dublin at the time of the annual Theatre Festival. She watches a *rehearsal* of Bernard Farrell's latest play, 'Stella by Starlight'. Later she attends a performance of the play at the Gate Theatre and interviews the theatre's director, Michael Colgan.
The programme ends with an explanation of the Irish language and a look at some of the places in and near Dublin which have been important in the political and cultural history of Ireland.

playwright	Dramatiker(in), Stückeschreiber(in)
to perform	aufführen, darstellen
subject	Thema
to be associated with	verbunden sein mit
novel	Roman
to be set in	angesiedelt sein in
novelist	Romanschriftsteller(in), Romancier
rehearsal	(Theater-)Probe

11 B

Helen interviews Bernard Farrell in the Abbey Theatre

Helen: Bernard, what does your position as Resident Playwright at the Abbey Theatre involve?
Bernard: Well, I suppose it's *three-fold.* The first one is - well, it's a position of *honour*, at the National Theatre, and for that reason I was *delighted* to have it. Secondly, the *remit* of the theatre is to produce Irish plays and the Articles of Association say that there must be a playwright *on the board* - and that's myself. And thirdly it means that the Abbey automatically *commissions* my next play, so the next play I write will be for the Abbey.
Helen: Bernard, how did you become a playwright?
Bernard: I don't think one becomes a playwright. You find that you want to write. When I was about sixteen years of age, at school, I had my first short story published in one of the national newspapers, and I thought then that I was already on my way to Stockholm to collect the Nobel Prize. And it took years of *rejection slips* before I realised that short stories were not the way - were not the form in which I should work, but rather there was a different form, and I moved on to different forms before I came to play-writing.
Helen: What influenced you most of all to write?
Bernard: Well, I don't think you start by influences. It comes from a need inside you to express yourself in a certain way. I often think that people that don't win arguments or that are not very *articulate* are the best writers, because it means that they can move into the writing area, in which they can win all the arguments because they set up the pros and the cons. But my parents were very good theatregoers, and as children we were all brought to the theatre a lot, and the house was always full of books, so my parents probably were the greatest influence in guiding me towards what form of writing I should take.

Helen: How did you earn a living before you became a playwright?
Bernard: I worked for a shipping company. I was a *clerk* in a shipping company for about fourteen years, and at the end of that I did an examination and I became a customs clerk, and I was doing that for two years. And then I left. I was a very bad *customs clerk* because I admired people who smuggled, which is not the best *requirement*. I think there's within me a feeling of anarchy probably which shows itself in the plays. So law and order is *inclined to annoy* me a little bit, and frustrate me a little bit, so I wasn't a good customs clerk.
Helen: What was your first play about?
Bernard: My first play was about *encounter groups*, and it was written mainly because I had lots of very intellectual friends at the time who were *forever* going to encounter groups and group therapy. And all I could think of was, a play about group therapy would make a very interesting and maybe funny play. And when I had finished it, I thought, "Now, who will I send it to?", I thought, "Well, why not send it to the National Theatre?" So I sent it here, and they put it on, and that was the beginning of my career.
Helen: What kind of subjects do you write about in your plays?
Bernard: I'm more inclined to go for characters than subjects. I have a great interest in the *downtrodden*, in people that are not able to make their way in life on their own, and I like to *pit* those people *against* people that seem to know their way around, and who are very *accomplished*, just to see how they come out. So I think I like to write about the 'little man', if you know what that means: man, people who are not so accomplished in life.
People often say - if I'm going to a party or something - "Here comes Bernard Farrell, say nothing, or you'll find yourself on the stage."
I really think, and I keep explaining this to my friends, that in the plays there's much more of me than there is of other people, and anyway, when you *devise* a character in a play, you never devise just one person because they would be quite boring. You devise a *composite* of many people, and you put the *facets* of all these people into one character to make him very interesting. And people who are *offended* that they see themselves suddenly on the stage, what they see is just a little bit of themselves, and if they weren't so sensitive, they would see there's lots of other people in there as well. But I think the characters are mainly me, and people shouldn't be too worried.
Helen: Do you only write for the stage, for the theatre?
Bernard: No. I write for television as well. I spent five years working for BBC Television in London, and RTE Irish Television here. And I also write for the radio. I write radio plays as well. But my first love would be the theatre.
Helen: What is the difference between writing for the theatre, for television, for radio?
Bernard: Quite a big difference. If I can take them the other way round, I think the purest form for a writer is the radio, because you have to describe everything, and therefore you have a great liberty to write everything. That's what writers really

like; they love describing things, and they love showing how clever they are. Now, that's radio. If you move to television, television speaks with the camera, so less words are necessary, so you just have to be able to describe what the camera sees. It's a different art form. The theatre, I think, has an *amalgam* of both of those, but it has the very exciting aspect of having a live *audience* there.
Helen: Can you tell me about the special privileges that writers in Ireland enjoy?
Bernard: I think fifteen or twenty years ago there was a law brought in that Irish writers would be tax-free from their *earnings* as writers. In other words, if they have two jobs, they will still pay tax on the normal job, but from their writings they would be tax-free. Which means - the purpose of the law was to try and keep Irish writers in Ireland, because in the past, like Joyce - which is a shining example - and many more: O'Casey ..., they just left the country. And it was to kind of keep writers in Ireland, and it is wonderful, because it means that people who want to write can concentrate on their writing and not feel they have to take a second job.

three-fold	dreifach
honour	Ehre
to be delighted	erfreut, entzückt sein
remit	Aufgabe, Auftrag
on the board	im Ausschuß, im Aufsichtsrat, im Vorstand
to commission	in Auftrag geben
rejection slip	Absage
to be articulate	sich gut/klar ausdrücken können
clerk	Angestellte(r)
customs clerk	Zollbeamter, -beamtin
requirement	Voraussetzung, Erfordernis
to be inclined to	neigen zu
to annoy	ärgern
encounter	Begegnung, Treffen
encounter group	(*psych.*) Encountergruppe
forever	immer, ständig, ewig
downtrodden	unterdrückt, geknechtet
to pit against	einander gegenüberstellen
accomplished	fähig, vollendet, perfekt
to devise	sich ausdenken
composite	Montage, Mischung
facet	Seite, Aspekt
to offend	beleidigen, kränken
amalgam	Mischung
audience	Publikum
earnings *pl*	Verdienst, Ertrag

I. Vocabulary

a) Put the noun that corresponds to each of the following verbs in a sentence of your own.

1. describe
2. produce
3. require
4. express
5. argue
6. offend

b) Give a word or phrase of similar meaning to

1. to go on the stage
2. character
3. to earn a living
4. the remit of the theatre
5. the pros and the cons

II. Understanding

1. Why did Bernard become a writer?
2. What influenced Bernard most to become a playwright?
3. What did Bernard do before he became a playwright?
4. What does Bernard mean when he says "... there's within me a feeling of anarchy" (page 169, line 6)?
5. What characters does Bernard like to write about?
6. What are the special privileges Irish writers enjoy nowadays?

III. Test your English: relatives

Complete the sentences with a suitable relative word.

1. Bernard was late yesterday, ... was unusual for him.
2. The first time I saw him was ..... he gave us an interview at the Abbey Theatre.
3. To ..... am I speaking?
4. The letter ..... arrived this morning contained good news for Bernard.
5. I don't like the person ..... is sitting next to Bernard.

11 C

James Joyce and Dublin

James Joyce

In the early part of this century, many writers had to leave Ireland in order to make a living. The most famous of these was James Joyce. Before he left, Joyce spent a short time at Sandycove outside Dublin, which he made the *setting* for the opening of his novel 'Ulysses'. Sandycove has a very special significance for Bernard Farrell because he was born there, and in his very early days he read and enjoyed 'Ulysses'.

The first chapter of Ulysses begins in an old *watch-tower*, where one of the characters, Buck Mulligan, has just got out of bed: "*Stately*, plump Mulligan came from the *stairhead*, bearing a *bowl* of *lather* on which a mirror and a razor lay crossed. A yellow *dressing-gown*, *ungirdled*, was *sustained gently* behind him by the mild morning air. He held the bowl *aloft* and *intoned*: - *Introibo ad altare Dei*."

Many fans of 'Ulysses' make a *pilgrimage* to Sandycove and other places in and around Dublin, which are described in great detail by Joyce. In Dublin itself there are *inscriptions* on the *pavements* with *suitable extracts* from the novel, and it is possible to walk through the city, following events and characters *featured* in the story. And, of course, there is a statue of James Joyce himself.

Bernard Farrell said that in Ireland there was a great *celebration* of the dead, and the Irish were inclined to forget the living. Bernard himself would be inclined to remember the living as well, but he admitted that it was very difficult to go around Dublin and not walk into a *relic* of a dead writer. He said: "Throw a stone up in the air in Dublin and you'll probably hit a writer."

setting	Rahmen, Schauplatz	to intone	anstimmen
watch-tower	Wachturm	Introibo ad altare Dei.	(*lat.*) *Anfang der katholischen Messe*
stately	stattlich	pilgrimage	Wall-, Pilgerfahrt
stairhead	oberster Treppenabsatz	inscription	Inschrift
bowl	Schale	pavement	Pflaster
lather	(Seifen-)Schaum	suitable	passend
dressing-gown	Morgen-, Bademantel	extract	Auszug
ungirdled	lose, offen, nicht zugebunden	to feature	vorkommen, (mit)spielen
to sustain	*hier*: tragen	celebration	Verherrlichung
gently	behutsam, sachte	relic	Überbleibsel, Relikt
aloft	empor, nach oben, in die Luft		

Understanding

a) Questions

1. Who wrote the novel 'Ulysses'?
2. What was the setting for the opening of this novel?
3. Where was Bernard Farrell born?

b) Complete the sentences with the correct meaning according to the text above.

1. Many writers had to leave Ireland ....
   a) to avoid paying taxes at home
   b) to make a living
   c) because the climate was unhealthy
2. Buck Mulligan is ....
   a) a character in Ulysses
   b) an old publican
   c) a novel by Bernard Farrell
3. James Joyce was ....
   a) an actor
   b) a figure in Bernard Farrell's latest play
   c) an Irish writer

11 D

A visit to the Dublin Writers Museum

The Dublin Writers Museum is in a restored 18th century town house. It contains a collection of portraits, manuscripts, *first editions*, and other objects celebrating the lives and work of Ireland's greatest writers.
One of the earliest was Jonathan Swift, who *fiercely* attacked political corruption and *exposed* the miserable conditions of the poor in 18th century Ireland.
However, Swift is best known as the author of 'Gulliver's Travels', the greatest satire in the English language.

Four Irish writers have been *awarded* the Nobel Prize for Literature. The first was the poet and playwright W B Yeats in 1923.
He was followed by George Bernard Shaw in 1935. Shaw wrote on every kind of subject from music to politics, but he is best known as a playwright.
Samuel Beckett, who won the Nobel Prize in 1969, spent much of his life in France and wrote novels and plays, such as 'Waiting for Godot', in both French and English.
Seamus Heaney, the 1995 Prize winner, is considered to be the most important Irish poet since W B Yeats.
Several Irish writers have chosen to live and work abroad. One of them was Oscar Wilde, who entertained London audiences in the 1890s with his brilliant satirical comedies. And the writer whose work is most closely associated with Dublin, James Joyce, wrote about the city while living in various other parts of Europe.

first edition	Erstausgabe
fiercely	schonungslos, scharf, heftig
to expose	aufdecken, darlegen, offenbaren
to award	zusprechen, auszeichnen mit

What do you know about Irish literature?

Complete the sentences with the following words. Use each of them only once.

play • satire • novel • comedies • poet and playwright • poet • poems • playwright

1. Seamus Heaney is famous for his .... He's considered to be the most important .... since W B Yeats.
2. George Bernard Shaw was a well-known .... 'Pygmalion' is one of his best known ....
3. Joyce's most famous .... is probably 'Ulysses'.
4. 'Gulliver's Travels' is a .... written by Jonathan Swift.
5. W B Yeats, an Irish-born .... was awarded the Nobel Prize for Literature in 1923.
6. 'Waiting for Godot' is a .... written by Samuel Beckett.

11 E

What a young Dubliner thinks of his literary heritage

Helen talked to several Dubliners about Irish literature. Here is what one of them said.

I do like Irish literature, yes. I kind of got into it basically when I was in school. There's a very good curriculum at secondary school, and a lot of the Irish writers, the best Irish writers are on the curriculum, such as Joyce and Yeats. Beckett not so much because it's a little bit more *obscure*, but certainly Yeats and Joyce.
My favourite book by Joyce would probably be 'Dubliners'. It's an awful lot more *accessible* than his other works, but for kind of getting your head exercised, 'Ulysses' is very, very good, and 'Finnegan's Wake' is pretty much *unmanageable* really, for anybody.
I've read 'Ulysses' a number of times, and it's completely different every time you read it. I mean, you *pick up on* different *nuances* on each occasion that you read it.

heritage	Erbe, Erbschaft	unmanageable	*hier*: schwer verständlich
obscure	*hier*: schwer verständlich	to pick up on	entdecken
accessible	zugänglich	nuance	Schattierung, Nuance

What about you?

1. Do you read a lot in your leisure time or do you prefer watching television? Give reasons for your preference. (50 to 100 words)
2. What's your favourite book and why? (50 to 100 words)

11 F

Helen interviews Michael Colgan, Director of the Gate Theatre

The Gate Theatre was established in 1928 to provide a more international repertoire than the Abbey Theatre, which had been founded in 1904.

Helen: What is your philosophy behind the plays you put on?
Michael: Well, I'm glad you asked me that. Our *policy* is to do that which we can do, that which we can afford to do, and do it with the least possible bad taste. And the other part of it is obviously that there's a *rivalry* between the Abbey and the Gate that has been going on for years. It's a healthy rivalry - we get on very well, despite what they say - and that's beginning to change a little bit. I mean, in the past, the Gate would do all the plays with *frocks* and very beautiful dresses and everything like that, and the Abbey did all the *kitchen-sink plays*, *peasant plays* - you know, and also we were doing plays by Oscar Wilde, you know. So I think our

policy will be to do the classics, and to do them as well as we can. Recent plays have been - we do Shakespeare, we have recently gone into, as I said, Oscar Wilde, and of course these Becketts.
That's an area that I suppose traditionally people would have said belonged to the Abbey, in some way, but I got to know Samuel Beckett and we did 'Waiting for Godot' at his request. And then I had the *notion* that maybe we should do all of his plays, and I asked him and he said yes. So we've all of those here since 1991.
Helen: And what about the play you have on at the moment?
Michael: 'Stella by Starlight'? Well, that's very much a *departure* for us. And again, you know, Bernard Farrell would be traditionally - most of his plays were done at the Abbey, and there was a period when they weren't being done. And I think he's a great writer, and we decided to commission a play from Bernard. And he was very happy to do it. And this play has been a success.

policy	Grundsatz
rivalry	Rivalität
frock	Gehrock
kitchen-sink play	Alltags-, Wohnküchen-drama
peasant play	Bauernstück
notion	Vorstellung, Idee, Gedanke
departure	*hier*: Abweichen, Ausnahme

I. Vocabulary

Give the opposite of the following words.

1. international
2. past
3. rivalry
4. success
5. happy

II. What about you?

What sort of plays would you expect to see at a theatre in your own country that concentrates on the classics? (about 50 words)

11 G

'Stella by Starlight'

Bernard's recent play 'Stella by Starlight' was performed at the Gate Theatre. The leading players were Gemma Craven as Geraldine and Marion O'Dwyer as Stella. Here's an extract from the play.

Geraldine: I'm terribly sorry about that. I did warn Janice, all right? There's worse things than that happening to me these days.
Stella: Oh, is this what you wanted to tell me?
Geraldine: It is. And Stella, if ever I needed your help in this life I need it now.
Stella: Why? What's wrong?
Geraldine: Well, first I *put off* going to the doctor.
Stella: To the doctor?
Geraldine: For tests.
Stella: Tests?
Geraldine: But eventually I went. And when he rang me at *half one* today I knew instinctively that the news was bad.
Stella: Was bad?
Geraldine: Stella, will you stop *winking* at me like that.
Stella: Sorry. There's something in my eye.
Geraldine: It makes me think I'm going to tell you a joke. But in actual fact it's the worst possible thing that could happen.
Stella: What? Geraldine, you don't mean that you've got ...
Geraldine: Yes. *Pregnant*.

Stella: What?
Geraldine: You heard me.
Stella: *Gee*, that's great.
Geraldine: As if I was going to die or something.
Stella: But we're all dying of something. But you've always wanted a baby for years.
Geraldine: Will you *keep your voice down*?
Stella: He doesn't know?
Geraldine: It's not his.
Stella: It's not his?
Geraldine: You're at it again. It should never have *bloody* happened. But you know Dave I told you about, the new *counter clerk* from Galway?
Stella: Oh, the very young fellow with the dark, *curly* hair that you said must have a lovely body?
Geraldine: That's him, yes. Well he has.
Stella: God!
Geraldine: And all because I, as his *supervisor*, stupidly went back to his flat to look at a *banking system* he said he'd devised and would like to show me.
Stella: Ah, say no more. I mean, go on.
Geraldine: Well, there I was, sitting with this *gorgeous* fellow young enough to be my son looking at a stupid banking system. And suddenly - and he was absolutely *cold sober* - suddenly he began to say that while I was with him he was finding it very difficult to control himself.
Stella: God!
Geraldine: And so eventually he - well, to put it *bluntly*, he ...
Stella: Yes?
Geraldine: ... he didn't.
Stella: He didn't? So how are you pregnant?
Geraldine: He didn't control himself.
Stella: Oh!
Geraldine: So now, after years of nothing ever happening, that young fellow only has to look at me and I'm pregnant.

to put off	aufschieben
half one	halb zwei (Uhr)
to wink	zwinkern, blinzeln
pregnant	schwanger
gee	(*slang*) Mensch, Mann
bloody	(*slang*) verdammt
keep your voice down	sprich bitte leiser
counter clerk	Schalterbeamter, -beamtin
curly	lockig, kraus
supervisor	Aufsicht; Leiter(in)
banking system	Computersystem (für Banken)
gorgeous	großartig, hinreißend
(cold) sober	(stock)nüchtern
bluntly	geradeheraus, unverblümt

I. Vocabulary

Use the noun that corresponds to each of the following verbs and adjectives in a sentence of your own.

1. to die
2. to live
3. pregnant
4. stupid
5. sober
6. difficult

II. Understanding

Summarise the subject of the extract above in one or two sentences.

III. Grammar revision: gerunds

The gerund stands in place of a noun. It is often used instead of the infinitive, especially as the subject of a sentence (eg 'Falling in love is wonderful' rather than 'It's wonderful to fall in love'). In the following sentences replace the infinitive with a gerund and make the gerund the subject of the sentence.

1. It is easy to criticise other people.
2. It was a wonderful experience for Bernard to direct actors.
3. It was a great pleasure to meet such delightful people in Ireland.
4. It is better to work hard than being idle.
5. It will be a useful experience for her to live on her own.

11 H

Helen talks to Bernard about 'Stella by Starlight' and about the Irish language

Helen started by asking about the ending of the play.

Helen: Does it have a happy ending?
Bernard: Sort of. But I can't give too much away. Yes, but it's a bit like life in many ways. We find happiness occasionally but, like life, it's not forever.
Helen: How do you feel that your recent play 'Stella by Starlight' was received?
Bernard: I think it's - it's been received very well indeed. I mean, the reviews for it have been in the main very good, and we're delighted with that.
Helen: Are you influenced by the reviews?
Bernard: I'm not influenced at all by them. I can be either *elated* by them or depressed by them. But a very good friend of mine gave me a piece of advice one time. And he said, "Give yourself four days - just four days. Four days to really enjoy good reviews, and four days to be depressed by bad reviews. And after four days, forget them, and move on and write your next play." I think it's great advice.
Helen: Do you ever use the Irish language in your plays?

Bernard: I think that all Irish people try to use a little bit of Irish ever so often, because I think there's very deep inside us - we feel that we're a little less Irish because we speak English. But the fact of the matter is that most people who've gone through the education system that I went through can't speak Irish, except just a little. So if I'm using ordinary conversation for the characters in the plays, it's inevitable that somebody would use Irish at some stage.
Helen: Can you give me a few examples?
Bernard: People often say 'Fáilte romhat' for you know - 'You are welcome' or when they're leaving they may say 'slán' which is 'goodbye'. And there's a lovely Irish word that is part of the English language. When somebody is very generous, particularly with their money, Irish people say he is very 'flaithiúil' which means 'generous' and that's actually worked itself into the Irish language as Irish people speak it.

to elate	begeistern, in Hochstimmung versetzen

I. Understanding

1. How was Bernard's play received?
2. What does Bernard think about happy endings?
3. What did Bernard's friend advise him to do?

II. Comment

What are the advantages and disadvantages of a theatre performance of a play compared with a performance of the same play on television? (less than 100 words)

11 I

The Irish language

Irish is a Celtic language, with its own *script*, *derived* from the writing of the Irish monks more than a thousand years ago. After nearly dying out in the 19th century, it has been *revived* and is an official language of the Republic. Road signs, for example, are in both Irish and English.
Names of people are often written with their Irish *spelling*, even when they are pronounced more or less the same as in English, like Patrick (Irish: Pádraig) and Mary (Irish: Máire) for example.
Many places have been given Irish names to replace the names *imposed* under English rule. Some, like Dublin, still use the English name for most purposes, in contrast to Dun Laoghaire, the port south of Dublin, which is no longer called Kingstown, the name given to it by the English.

The names of political parties, such as Fine Gael and Fianna Fáil, are never translated into English. The Irish Parliament is always called the Dáil and the Prime Minister is *referred to* as the Taoiseach. But the language of Parliament is English. Officially, Irish is spoken by more than a million people in the Republic, and it is taught at school. But in fact, less than a hundred thousand now speak Irish as their first language in every-day situations.

script	Schrift	to impose	auferlegen, aufdrängen, verhängen
to derive	her-, ableiten	to refer to	sich beziehen auf, verweisen auf
to revive	wiederbeleben		
spelling	Schreibweise		

I. Vocabulary

Give the nouns corresponding to the following verbs.

1. revive
2. pronounce
3. use
4. translate
5. refer
6. spell

II. Understanding

Complete the sentences.

1. Irish is a .... language.
2. It has been .... and is now an official .... in Ireland.
3. The Irish .... is always called the Dáil.

4. Taoiseach is the Irish name for ....
5. The language of the Irish Parliament is ....
6. More than a million people in the Irish .... speak Irish.

11 J

Dublin and its surroundings

The doors of Dublin

Dublin is the capital of the Irish Republic. Ireland was *partitioned* in 1921, when Northern Ireland remained part of the United Kingdom and the Republic of Ireland became an independent country. The Republic has a population of less than four million.

Dublin is a mixture of the old and the new. Previously *run-down* districts, like Temple Bar, have become centres for the city's lively youth culture.

This is in sharp contrast to the 18th century elegance of the Georgian houses in other parts of Dublin. The architecture of these town houses reflects a time of prosperity and achievement, *typified* by Merrion Square, the home of many famous Irish men and women.

Another magnificent example of Georgian architecture is the Custom House.

But Irish history also had a darker side. In the great *famine* of the mid-19th century over a million people died, and many more were forced to emigrate to America, mainland Britain and other parts of the world.

In politics, the cause of the Irish Catholics was *championed* by Daniel O'Connell, known as the Liberator. The 19th century campaign for *Home Rule*, the independence of Ireland from the rest of Britain, was led in the British Parliament by Charles Stewart Parnell. Parnell failed, and it was time for a more violent *approach* to independence.

In the *Easter Rising* of April 1916 armed Republicans occupied the General Post Office. But they were defeated and many of their leaders were executed by the British. Their rebellion is now commemorated by a statue of the mythical Irish hero Cúchulainn.

Below the statue is the text of the first *Proclamation* of the Irish Republic. And five years after the Easter Rising the Irish flag was flying again over the Post Office building.

Another Dublin *landmark* is Trinity College. Outside is the statue of Oliver Goldsmith, the 18th century playwright who was a student there. Trinity is Ireland's oldest university, and is famous for its library, which was built in the early 18th century.

The main hall of the Old Library is nearly 65 metres long. It's a copyright library, so it is meant to receive a copy of every Irish and British publication. There's room for less than 10% of them in the Old Library itself, but the most important and *valuable* books are kept on the shelves there.

The library's most *treasured* possession is the Book of Kells, an *illuminated* manuscript of *the Gospels*, which was produced by monks in the 8th or 9th century.

South of Dublin the ruined monastery of Glendalough is another reminder of the early years of Christianity in Ireland.

Glendalough

to partition	teilen	approach	Vorstoß, Ansatz, Methode
run-down	heruntergekommen	Easter Rising	Osteraufstand
to typify	verkörpern	proclamation	Verkündung, Ausrufung
district	Bezirk, Gebiet	landmark	Wahrzeichen
famine	Hungersnot	valuable	wertvoll
to champion	eintreten, sich engagieren für	treasured	geschätzt, in Ehren gehalten
Home Rule	Selbstbestimmung, -verwaltung	illuminated	*hier*: verziert
		the Gospels	das Evangelium

Questions

1. Is Ireland part of the UK?
2. What is the elegant architecture of the 18th century usually called?
3. Why did so many people have to leave Ireland in the mid-19th century?
4. Who was known as the Liberator?
5. What is the Book of Kells?

MUSSEL FARMERS IN BANTRY

12

12 A

Introduction

Mussel farming

This programme is about John and Maria Murphy. They live in Bantry in West Cork which is in the South-West of the Irish Republic, and their main *source of income* is *mussel farming*, now a major industry in the *fishing community* of Bantry Bay.

Helen meets John and Maria with their family. She learns how the mussel farming industry in the area has grown and how mussels are farmed, and she is told about a new process for freezing mussles. She also interviews the Director of the Marine Research Institute in Cork to find out about *food poisoning* in *shellfish*.

Many people in this part of Ireland have more than one job, and the Murphys run a fashion business, with shops in Bantry, Cork and Dublin.

We learn about the history of Bantry Bay, and since the South-West of Ireland attracts many tourists, we finish the programme with a look at the beautiful countryside of the neighbouring county of Kerry.

Accents:
John Murphy has a fairly strong Irish accent. Particularly noticeable is the way in which he pronounces 'th' as 't'.
Much of what he says in the programme is included in the book, and you are advised to read the interviews 12 B, 12 E and 12 G before watching the programme.

source of income	Einnahmequelle	fishing community	Fischerdorf
mussel	(Mies-)Muschel	food poisoning	Lebensmittelvergiftung
mussel farming	Muschelzucht	shellfish	Schalen-, Krustentier(e)

12 B

Helen interviews John and Maria Murphy (1st part)

Helen asked how the people of West Cork had made a living over the years.

John: It's difficult in West Cork, here, to *survive*, because of the rural community. But the main income is through small farming, fishing and tourist-related activities. Most people are involved in a combination of both to survive here. The tourism business has been very, very good here in Ireland because of our scenery and the nice green country we have - if we could *get rid of* some of the rain we'd probably be much better off - but small farming has been very difficult.

John explained that the produce from farming, supplemented *by fishing, had to provide an income and feed the farmers' families, which were traditionally quite large, with between six and twelve or thirteen children. It was quite a difficult task to feed all these children.*
Helen then asked what type of fishing went on around Bantry.

John: We are involved in shellfish farming. We grow mussels.
Helen: And tell me a little about the tradition of mussel farming.
John: Mussel farming started here in 1982 and the company I have was the first company to get involved. We grow the mussels on the *ropes* - it's rope culture. In the Bantry area this was the first introduction of mussel farming. In areas like Cromane, which is in County Kerry, they have wild beds of mussels which are *dredged*; they also have them in Wexford and in Carlingford Lock. They are the main beds in Ireland.
Maria: What he means by 'wild mussels' is that they are not grown from a rope. They are on the *bottom* of the sea bed.
Helen: So whose idea was it to introduce growing mussels on a rope?
John: In Ireland most of the good ideas and *conceptions* of industry are created in the pub. So, having a few drinks, a friend of mine, Vincent Rowntree, had seen the idea of growing mussels on a *raft* in Connemara up in Galway. And this had been introduced to Connemara from Spain. In our first year we produced eight tons of mussels, which was a *sizeable feat* at the time because it was all done by hand. We then discovered that the system of growing mussels was better on a long line as opposed to a raft. The *feed cycle* was much better on the long line, therefore our production grew, and from eight tons we now produce approximately 700 tons *per annum*.

to survive	überleben	conception	Vorstellung(svermögen)
to get rid of	loswerden	raft	Floß
to supplement	ergänzen	sizeable	beträchtlich, ansehnlich
rope	Schnur, Seil, Leine	feat	Leistung
to dredge	ausbaggern	feed cycle	Ernährungszyklus
bottom	Grund, Boden	per annum	pro, im Jahr

I. Vocabulary

Find words or phrases in the text which could replace the following.

1. countryside
2. to lose
3. generally
4. hard work
5. sort
6. began
7. idea
8. originated
9. considerable
10. output
11. in contrast to

II. Understanding

1. What are the main sources of income in the South-West of Ireland?
2. In what type of business is John involved?
3. Where do the Irish discuss and create new ideas?

4. From which country did the Irish fish farmers introduce the growing of mussels on rafts?
5. How big was the production of mussels when John started his business?
6. Why did it increase?
7. How big is the yearly output at present?

12 C

The process of mussel farming

Mussels on ropes

John explained the process of mussel farming:
The *seed*, or baby mussels, is bought off *guys* who go out on the strand during the months of January and February, when the tides are very low, and pick the young mussels off the rocks. Then the seed is collected from the *shore* and taken to the fish factory.
The seed is packed into long, nylon *stockings* and placed into the *purification tanks* until the sea is *calm* enough for the boats to go out on the bay. The stockings are hung onto long lines. Two head ropes *stretch* from one *buoyant barrel* to the next. Each head rope has *approximately* eight stockings hanging off it into the sea. The mussels will stay on the long lines for approximately 18 months.
In the summer, the mussels have to be *thinned out* in order to grow. Each nylon stocking is raised out of the water. The mussels have grown through the stockings and hang on the ropes in *clusters*. *Casual workers strip off* the smaller mussels and we *repack* to achieve market size. This has to be done at a specific time during July

and August, to prevent *coral settlement* on the *shell*. There is usually no *harvesting* during these months as the mussels can be affected by *red tide*. Red tide causes food poisoning.

After the stockings have been taken out of the water, they are pulled onto the boat with a crane, and the mussels are harvested. Back in the harbour, they are transported in large sacks to the fish factory. The mussels are washed and *depurated* in large tanks. Thirty-six hours is the recommended time to place the mussels in depuration, but it really depends on the *contamination*.

They are *graded* according to size, and then *debearded* and *weighed*. Finally, they are transported all over Ireland, Belgium, France, Germany and England.

seed	Samen
guy	Typ, Kerl, Bursche
guys	*hier*: Leute
shore	Strand
stockings	Strümpfe; *hier:* längliche Netze
purification	Reinigung
tank	Kessel, Behälter
calm	ruhig
to stretch	(sich) spannen
buoyant	schwimmend
barrel	Faß
approximately	annähernd
to thin out	ausdünnen
cluster	Büschel, Gruppe
casual worker	Gelegenheits-, Saisonarbeiter(in)
to strip off	entfernen
to repack	umsetzen
coral settlement	Korallenansiedlung
shell	Schale
(to) harvest	Ernte; ernten
red tide	giftige Algenpest
to depurate	reinigen
contamination	Verunreinigung, Verschmutzung
to grade	klassifizieren
to debeard	(Muschel-)Bart abnehmen, Haftfäden (bei Muscheln) abnehmen
to weigh	wiegen

I. Vocabulary

a) Give the opposites of the following words and phrases from the text above.

1. employment
2. bought
3. low
4. calm
5. raised out of (the water)
6. large

b) Give the noun corresponding to each of the following words from the text and use it in a sentence of your own.

1. successful
2. to establish
3. to grow
4. to recommend
5. to weigh

II. Understanding

Complete the sentences, using the information from the text above.

1. There are three methods of mussel farming. The mussels can be left to grow wild, on the sea bed; or they can be grown on rafts; or they can be grown on ....
2. This last method, also known as rope culture, produces the largest number of .... The process starts in winter.
3. The .... - as the baby mussels are called - is collected off the rocks and taken to the fish factory.
4. Then, the mussels are packed into ....
5. They are kept in .... tanks until the weather is favourable.
6. Then the stockings are hung on ropes between floating ....
7. In summer the mussels have to be .... out. The smaller ones are removed so that the larger ones can grow to the right size for eating.
8. After growing on the ropes for a total of 18 months, the mussels are .... and taken back to the fish factory.
9. For the next 36 hours, the mussels are ...., which means that impurities are removed.
10. After that they are .... into different sizes and .... before being sold.

12 D

Helen interviews Kevin James, Director of the Marine Research Institute in Cork

Helen: John Murphy told me about the problems of red tide in mussel farming. Can you explain to me what red tide means?
Kevin James: Well, red tide is a common name given to *marine algae*. And if they are *harmful* they get named red tide, and they are harmful because shellfish *consume* these materials, and some of these algae contain *toxic* materials which end up in the shellfish.
Helen: So how can you prevent this *toxicity* from getting into the *food chain*?
Kevin James: Since it's a natural occurring event, the shellfish have very good mechanisms for removing the *toxins* by natural means, and the only thing that has to be done is to take care that the shellfish are tested for these toxins *prior to* harvesting.
Helen: How often is the shellfish tested?
Kevin James: The shellfish from here is tested at least once a week - chemical testing and biological testing.
Helen: Is there any other kind of pollution in Bantry Bay that could affect the mussels?

Kevin James: Not really. The main pollution from this area would be simply *nutrients* from farm land, and obviously that goes into rivers and the rivers end up in this bay. That could *contribute* to the algal growth, but this area never had heavy industry, so there's no heavy metal pollution, no *pesticide* pollution, so from those aspects the shellfish are very, very good.

marine	Meeres-, See-	toxin	Giftstoff
algae	Algen	prior to	vor
harmful	schädlich	nutrient	Nährstoff
to consume	aufnehmen, verzehren	to contribute	beitragen
toxic	giftig, Gift-	pesticide	Schädlings-bekämpfungsmittel
toxicity	Giftgehalt		
food chain	Nahrungskette		

I. Vocabulary

Give a synonym for each of the following words from the text above.

1. to test
2. pollution
3. to prevent
4. to remove
5. prior to

II. Understanding

1. In what way can red tide be harmful?
2. What is the main pollution problem in Bantry Bay?

12 E

Helen interviews John and Maria (2nd part)

Helen: How can you keep your supply of mussels constant if you're not harvesting around the year

John: Our involvement has been totally in the fresh side over the last number of years. But market demands that have changed now demand continuous supply, and this was a problem for us because of the fresh mussel life cycle after processing is approximately five to maximum of six days, seven days *at the outside*. Therefore we had to *come up with* a process of supplying the market that required mussels on a 52-week basis. So we put our heads together and have come up with a new process for freezing mussels, *encapsulating* the juice and the meat within the shell. The mussel has to be cooked or *blanched* before being frozen. We have patented the process which we have undertaken, and this enables us to retain a closed shell holding in the juice and the meat, and when the customer or the *end user* places this mussel on the restaurant table or on the family table, it will open up again.

Helen: And will it taste exactly the same as a fresh mussel?
John: I believe the taste is exactly the same as the fresh mussel.
Helen: So to what extent is mussel farming supporting the community?
John: I would say to a very large extent. At the moment, there are - we have a German *pharmaceutical* company here. We have a fairly large building company which is based in Bantry, and I would say that there aren't too many industries around here. So the mussel farming is at the moment the industry that's keeping the younger people here.
Helen: And the importance of mussel farming here in Bantry is also reflected in a special kind of festival. Can you tell me a little about it?
Maria: This festival takes place in May every year. It's a four-day festival which was *conceived* about nine years ago when the mussel industry was just growing here in Bantry. The *onus* is on mussels, where free mussels are happily given out by all the producers here in Bantry. Last year we had over 30,000 people visiting Bantry on the four-day festival. There's mussels *galore* in pubs and hotels, and we've international *acts* and music and it's a family-based festivity.

at the outside	im äußersten Fall
to come up with	kommen auf, sich ausdenken
to encapsulate	in der Schale lassen, umhüllen
to blanch	blanchieren
end user	Endverbraucher
pharmaceutical	pharmazeutisch
to conceive	sich ausdenken
onus	Last, Pflicht
galore	in Hülle und Fülle
festivity	Feier, Festlichkeit
act	Veranstaltung

I. Vocabulary

*Explain the expressions in **bold** letters.*

1. **to come up with** a new process
2. mussels **galore**
3. a building company **based** in Bantry
4. **end user**

II. Understanding

1. The market demands a continuous supply of mussels all the year round. How did John solve this problem?
2. How important is mussel farming for Bantry?
3. What do people in Bantry celebrate in May every year?

III. Grammar revision: adjective or adverb?

Complete the sentences.

1. From an .... (economic) point of view, this problem is .... (extreme) difficult to solve.
2. .... (economic) speaking, the mussels industry keeps the youth in the Bantry area.
3. The mussels tasted .... (delicious).
4. Prices for shellfish are .... (tremendous, high)
5. People .... (willing) accepted the free offer of mussels.
6. He was .... (unbelievable) generous.

12 F

Some information about shellfish

The most popular shellfish in the restaurants around Bantry Bay are *oysters*, *scallops*, *clams* and mussels. Oysters are usually served in their shells. They're the most exclusive and the most expensive shellfish.
Scallops and clams can be prepared in many ways. They're often cooked with sauces in their open shells. Mussels are the cheapest and the most popular shellfish. The *flesh* of the mussel *differs* in colour: the white mussel is male, the red mussel is female.
It is sometimes said that in the past people in Bantry did not eat mussels. John thought that was an old wives' tale and that in the famine of the 1850s and 1860s, when the potato *crop failed*, people survived by eating shellfish. He admitted that mussels used to be considered the food of poorer people and were therefore unfash-

ionable. But in recent years the taste, the flavour and the freshness of mussels had begun to be *appreciated*, and so there was a whole new market for them.

oyster	Auster	crop	Ernte
scallop	Jakobsmuschel	to fail	scheitern, *hier*: schlecht ausfallen
clam	Venusmuschel		
flesh	(Muschel-)Fleisch	to appreciate	zu schätzen wissen
to differ	sich unterscheiden		

I. Grammar revision: prepositions

Complete the sentences.

1. The Irish are dependent ..... fish.
2. Ireland cannot do ..... fish and chip shops.
3. Fish and chips is a dish Ireland shares ..... the United Kingdom.
4. If you want to enjoy fish and chips ..... their very best, you should take them straight out ..... the shop and eat them ..... the street.
5. Some ..... the fish which has arrived ..... Bantry this morning will be consumed ..... tonight.

II. What about you?

Answer one of the following questions and give reasons for your answer.

1. Do you like fast food?
2. Do you like eating shellfish?
3. Have you ever eaten fish and chips? If you have, what did you think of them? If you haven't, do you think you would like them or not?

12 G

Helen interviews John (3rd part)

Mussels from Bantry Bay are exported all over Europe. Ireland's membership of the European Union means that the whole Irish fishing industry is affected by agreements *covering member states.*

Helen: Do you think the fishermen here in Ireland are in favour of the EU?
John: I think that, on the *aquaculture* side of the business, because seed funding is required to develop the infrastructure and the capital investment, the EU funds have been appreciated. There is a problem from the *whitefish* side, whereas our fishing *fleets*, who have been established over a number of years, are *restricted* by *quotas*, and these quotas come from within the EC. And because Ireland is surrounded by water, the *catches* of the Irish fleet are very restricted. And we have now got reduced to a six-mile limit.

Helen: Is your love of the sea so great that you can see yourself farming mussels for the rest of your life, or would you sometimes like to try something completely different?

John: When I met and married Maria, I think she tried very hard to get me to Dublin, but I felt my love for the sea - I just couldn't move. My mother came from Whiddy Island here in Bantry, so as a young boy in my school holidays I spent the time with my grandparents on the island, and I think this is where I got the love for the sea. We fished *mackerel*, we walked the shores and picked shells, and it's just beautiful.

Helen: Are you investing in the future of Bantry?

John: I think that *goes without saying*. Once we are living here - we have four children - I think - I believe - I hope my children will further develop what we have got involved in. And I believe the industry, through the stability of having processing available here in Bantry, will go from strength to strength. And the people that are involved in the *processing* sector - er, onshore jobs, - these jobs have to be *sustained* by the supply of the product. Which means you have the sea jobs. So you have every day a number of people going to sea to produce the mussels, and onshore you have the processing.

agreement	Vereinbarung, Abmachung
aquaculture	Fischzucht
whitefish	Weißfisch
fleet	Flotte
to restrict	begrenzen, beschränken
quota	Quote
catch	Fang
mackerel	Makrele
to go without saying	sich von selbst verstehen
processing	(Weiter-)Verarbeitung
to sustain	erhalten

I. Vocabulary

a) Give a synonym or synonymous expression for each of the following from the interview above.

1. be in favour of
2. restricted
3. completely
4. involved (in)
5. onshore job
6. be sustained
7. a number of

b) Give the opposite of the following words.

1. beautiful
2. stability
3. available
4. to reduce

II. Understanding

1. Is Ireland's membership of the EU an advantage or a disadvantage for Irish fishermen?
2. What would happen if countries were allowed to catch as many fish as they wanted?
3. Where would John like to live?
4. In what way does John invest in the future of Bantry?

III. Translation: auxiliary verbs used in special ways

1. Wenn es ihm hier nicht gefällt, dann soll er woanders arbeiten.
2. Was soll das bedeuten?
3. Er soll vier Kinder haben.
4. Die Kinder sind alle ausgewandert. Jetzt muß er sein mühselig (*painstaking*) aufgebautes Unternehmen verkaufen.
5. Das sollte ein Angebot sein.
6. Ich möchte nicht, daß er noch mehr Geld in die Firma steckt (investiert).

12 H

More about the Murphy family

John's mussel-farming company is called Fastnet Ltd and is based in the town of Gearhies. But like many people in West Cork, the Murphys run several businesses. One of them is a fashion business, with a boutique in the centre of Bantry. When Helen asked which of the two businesses the Murphys preferred to concentrate on, mussel farming or fashion, John answered that because the fashion business was well established, with shops in Bantry, Cork and Dublin, and because it was a family business, he could concentrate his time on the mussel farming.
When Maria was asked how she and John had met, she said that it was eleven years ago at a fashion show in Paris. Maria was selling clothes, and John was buying them.
The Murphys do not have much spare time. They spend what spare time they have with their four young children who keep them very busy.

I. What do you know about John and Maria Murphy?

1. John and Maria Murphy run several ....
2. They have .... shops in Bantry, Cork and ....
3. John concentrates on ....
4. He established a .... called Fastnet at Gearhies, County Cork.
5. John was brought up in ....
6. In his school holidays he spent much time with his .... on Whiddy Island.
7. John and Maria met .... ago at a .... in Paris where Maria was selling ....
8. The Murphys have four ....

II. Translation

Fastnet - a company profile

Fastnet Mussels Ltd is based at Gearhies, County Cork, Ireland. The company has its origins in sea farming and is considered one of the pioneers of suspended cultured mussel farming in Ireland. For the past twelve years Fastnet has supplied prestige markets throughout Europe with the highest possible quality produce. To ensure continued quality Fastnet installed an enclosed system of U.V. (ultra violet) treated seawater raceways. This was followed by the construction of a processing facility which would become the main production unit for the newly developed Frozen-in-Shell product of which the company is so rightly proud.

(*'Fishtrader', the news magazine of the seafood business, September, 1997*)

III. Comment

John and Maria have a large and happy family, but they are both busy professional people. In your opinion, what are the main challenges they face as a family? (at least 100 words)

12 I

Bantry and the South-West of Ireland (TV commentary)

The calm and peaceful landscape contrasts with the often stormy history of Bantry Bay. The coastline of West Cork has had its *fair* share of *shipwrecks*. And there have been invasions, too.
In 1689 the French landed in an attempt to help the exiled King James regain the English throne.
They failed, but they were back again in 1796, this time to help Wolfe Tone, an Irish leader inspired by the ideals of the French Revolution.
The invaders never came *ashore*. They were stopped through the efforts of a local landowner, Richard White, who was made Baron Bantry by King George III as a reward for his *loyalty* to the English.
The White family still live here in Bantry House, which is full of works of art and *furnishings* collected by the family during their travels in Europe. The house is typical of the *stately* homes of the English *aristrocracy* who *settled* in Ireland from the 17th to the 19th century.
The beautiful gardens of the house look north over Bantry Bay, in the direction of the *neighbouring* county, Kerry.
The Ring of Kerry is one of the most popular tourist attractions in Ireland. This is an area where the government has done much to encourage the revival of the Irish language.
Kerry is famous for its dramatic skies and its beautiful scenery. You can see the remains of several pre-historic settlements in this part of Kerry. They were often guarded by forts like Staigue Fort, which is about three thousand years old.

fair	*hier*: ganz ordentlich, ziemlich viel	furnishings	Mobiliar, Einrichtung
		stately	herrschaftlich
shipwreck	Schiffbruch	aristocracy	Adel
ashore	an Land	to settle	sich niederlassen
loyalty	Treue	neighbouring	benachbart

Helen in Ireland

Understanding

1. Why was Richard White made Baron Bantry?
2. What is a stately home?
3. What is the Ring of Kerry famous for?

AN ADVERTISING EXECUTIVE IN LONDON 13

13 A

Introduction

This programme is about advertising and about Simon Binns, an advertising executive at Ogilvy & Mather, one of Britain's largest *advertising agencies*, which is based in Canary Wharf, the centre of London's newest business district.
Simon talks to Helen about his work as an *account director* with the agency, and explains how an advertising campaign to *launch* a new product moves from the first discussions with the *client* to the production of a *television commercial*. Helen also interviews Simon's boss, who tells her about British advertising and shows her two of the agency's prize-winning commercials. And we hear what people think about advertising and whether they are influenced by advertisements.
We see Simon getting ready for the cricket season, shopping with his girlfriend, and visiting an *antiques market*.
The programme, and our series, ends with a short trip down the River Thames.

advertising agency	Werbeagentur	client	Kunde, Kundin
account director	(*Werbung*) Kundenberater, Etatdirektor	(television) commercial	Werbespot
to launch	(*Produkt*) auf den Markt bringen, einführen	antiques market	Antiquitätenmarkt

13 B

Helen interviews Simon Binns (1st part)

Helen: How did you start your career in advertising?
Simon: I had always been interested in *the media*. When I was at university I was the editor of the student newspaper. I wanted to do a job that was related to the media, and so I applied to an advertising agency, to their graduate trainee scheme and I applied to this agency, which was Ogilvy & Mather, and got a place on their training programme.
Helen: What does your job in the company involve?
Simon: My job really is to look after a specific *account* for a client. Currently, my big project this year is working on the launch advertising for the new Ford Mondeo,

which will be launched in the UK in October. That's quite a big project, because it's a very big *undertaking* for Ford when they launch a new model, and it's very important that we get the advertising as *accurate* as possible and as effective as possible.

(the) media	(die) Medien	undertaking	Projekt, Unternehmen
account	(*Werbung*) Etat	accurate	genau, sorgfältig

Simon Binns

I. Vocabulary

What is meant by the following words from the text above?

1. the media
2. advertising
3. launch
4. undertaking

II. Understanding

1. What is an account director?
2. What project is Simon working on at the moment?

13 C

The work of the Account Director

Simon is an Account Director in the Account Management Department, the part of the agency which coordinates work on the advertising accounts of its clients. The client gives Simon the information he needs about the product to be advertised. He takes this information to the Planning Department, which then finds out what *consumers* think about the kind of product involved. Simon also goes to the Media Department to choose the most suitable media: press, television, cinema, etc.
Finally, he *briefs* the Creative Team, the people in the agency who actually write the advertisements.

consumer	Verbraucher(in)
to brief	instruieren, beauftragen

13 D

Advertising a new product

The process starts with the client giving the agency as much information as possible about the new product and the kind of consumers it is aimed at. For example, is it an *up-market* product, designed to *appeal to* consumers who are looking for superior quality? The agency is asked to come back to the client with a *creative brief*, which will form the basis of all the advertisements in the campaign to launch the product.
The next step is to get some opinions from consumers. The agency puts together some *positioning research* groups and shows them some *visuals*, in order to get consumers talking about the kind of product to be advertised and telling the agency what makes them buy that kind of product.
After the consumers have indicated what appeals to them, there is a meeting of the *account planners*. They *assimilate* the information that both the client and consumers have given them, and turn that into a creative brief, the document which is given to the creative team of designers and *copywriters*. It is their job to design and write scripts for TV commercials, press advertisements, posters, etc.
To start work on a TV commercial, for example, the creative team writes a script which is presented to the client. When the script has been approved, a storyboard with pictures illustrating key parts of the commercial is shown to a group of consumers. Provided the consumers' reactions are favourable, the agency can go ahead and choose a TV director. When the director has been chosen, the actual production of the commercial begins.

up-market	anspruchsvoll, exklusiv
to appeal to	ansprechen, Anklang finden bei
creative brief	(*Werbung*) Vorgabe, Instruktion für die Produktion eines Werbespots
positioning research	Verbraucherforschung
visual	grafischer Entwurf
account planners	Planungsabteilung
to assimilate	aufnehmen, integrieren
copywriter	Werbetexter(in)

I. Vocabulary

Give a synonym or a synonymous expression for each of the following words from the text above.

1. consumer
2. visual
3. commercial
4. approved
5. actual

II. Understanding

1. What is a creative brief?
2. What does a copywriter do?

13 E

The TV commercial for the new Mondeo

The ideas of the creative team have to be translated by the TV director into less than a minute of television screen time.

The commercial shows a man driving his new Ford Mondeo through the rain in a remote part of the Scottish Highlands to return to his girlfriend.

'Mondeo *sharpens your senses.*' This was the *proposition*, or message, in the creative brief, and the TV commercial follows it: the new Mondeo *makes* you more *aware of* what is happening when you drive. But the finished commercial actually ends with: 'It *brings you to your senses*.' There's an extra message here. The man in the car goes back to his girlfriend. Driving the new Mondeo has made him change his mind, so that he now knows he's got the right girlfriend, and of course, the right car, too.

sharpens your senses	schärft Ihre Sinne
proposition	Vorschlag
to make aware of	bewußtmachen
brings you to your senses	bringt Sie zur Vernunft

Questions

1. Do you think that the TV commercial will be a success? Give reasons for your answer.
2. Why do you think some TV commercials spend so little time dealing with the product itself?
3. Why is the job of the director of a TV commercial especially difficult?

13 F

Helen interviews Eddie Bowman, Simon's boss

Helen: British advertising is for ever winning awards worldwide. Can you name some of your *award-winning* adverts?
Eddie: Well, there are lots, and I could talk about them for hours. I guess I'll just mention one, which is for a client of mine called BUPA, and in case - for those of you that don't know, BUPA is the largest private health *insurer* in the country. And we've produced a *stunning* campaign for BUPA. Most health companies have marketed themselves on a platform of - if you like - making people better, and what the BUPA campaign does is talk about how wonderful your body is, and that BUPA can help you stay wonderful, so the line is 'You're amazing. We want you to stay that way.'
Helen: Do you think there's an explanation for why British advertising is so creative?
Eddie: Well, I have to say to start with, I think, that there are many countries now that are producing advertising that's just as creative as ours. But we do have a heritage that places creativity right at the very centre of our business.
Helen: Apart from the BUPA ads, can you think of another one that has been creatively so successful?
Eddie: A charming campaign for Nestlé that we did for a *peculiarly* English product which is *jelly*, which is a sort of *wobbly dessert* that you eat, which was so incredibly simple and visually interesting that it *swept the board* of many awards. It's lovely advertising, very simple.

Note:
Eddie Bowman shows Helen a TV commercial for Rowntree's jelly, which ends 'If it's not Rowntree's jelly, throw a wobbly.' ***To throw a wobbly*** is to lose control, to shake or wobble with anger or fear. Rowntree's is one of a group of companies owned by Nestlé.

award-winning	preisgekrönt
insurer	Versicherer
stunning	überwältigend, großartig
line	*hier*: Werbespruch
peculiar	seltsam, eigenartig
jelly	Gelee, Götterspeise
wobbly	wacklig
wobbly dessert	Wackelpudding, Götterspeise
to sweep the board	alle Preise gewinnen, abräumen

I. Vocabulary

a) Find words in the interview that could replace the following words.

1. prize
2. splendid
3. imaginative
4. delightful
5. particularly

b) Complete each sentence with one of the words. Use each word only once.

copywriters • advertising • campaign • advertisement • ads • advertisers • market

1. Without a good advertising .... it is difficult to launch a new product.
2. Our company finds it difficult to .... products in that part of the world.
3. The writer of this .... did not follow the creative brief he was given.
4. For charities and special interest groups with a limited .... budget, being mentioned in the media is often more effective than spending money on a series of ....
5. These days, ... in the US are very careful not to offend consumers.
6. Creative .... and art directors are paid a lot of money, but their work can help to increase a client's sales enormously.

II. Understanding

1. Why are British advertisements so successful?
2. Name one award-winning Ogilvy & Mather TV commercial.
3. What makes BUPA ads different from their rivals?

13 G

Advertising media

Television, radio, newspapers, magazines and *billboards* are the media that carry advertising. The media buyers in the advertising agencies buy *space* such as *air-time* from a broadcaster or magazine pages from a publisher.

Different advertising media work in different ways. For example, TV advertisements use sound and *vision* to make a powerful impact on people at home in a short space of time, maybe just half a minute.

A poster can create a strong *visual* impression and support it with a memorable *slogan* to *catch the eye*. And press advertisements can provide detailed product information, which would be too much to be shown on a poster or to be included in a short TV commercial.

billboard	Reklametafel	visual	Seh-, optisch
space	Platz, Raum, Fläche	slogan	Werbespruch
airtime	Sendezeit	to catch the eye	(die) Aufmerksamkeit gewinnen
vision	*hier*: Bild		

I. Vocabulary

Match each word with one of the descriptions below.

1. proposition
2. airtime
3. billboard
4. launch
5. media buyer
6. slogan
7. commercial

a) A person who buys airtime from a broadcaster or space on the pages from a publisher.
b) Short advertisements inserted into TV or radio broadcasts.
c) Time during which programmes are broadcast.
d) The introduction of a new product onto the market.
e) A short phrase about a product used in an advertisement.
f) A board on which posters are displayed.
g) A message which is intended to persuade people to buy a product.

II. Questions

1. TV, radio, newspapers and magazines are media that carry advertising. Name at least two other media suitable for advertising.
2. What are the possible disadvantages of using a well-known or successful personality to advertise a product?

III. Grammar revision: Get your tenses right

1. "When commercial television .... (start) here, people .... (think) that viewers would resent advertising breaking into programmes, so they .... (try) to make commercials that .... (be) entertaining. We .... (never, look back)." (Winston Fletcher)
2. The novelist Fay Weldon .... (invent) the slogan 'Go to work on an egg.'
3. National newspaper advertising in Britain .... (lose) ground against television for the past years.
4. Some scenes .... (have to, cut) from this commercial so that it could .... (show) on television.
5. If advertising .... (disappear) from television and radio, it .... (would, go) to other media.

13 H

Helen interviews Simon (2nd part)

Simon and his colleague from the Media Department

Helen: In what way do you believe that advertising could be used to influence people to consume less?
Simon: It sounds quite odd, doesn't it, advertising to make someone do something less. But actually it's quite common. We, for instance, have a number of clients where we do actually do exactly that - encourage people to do something less. For instance, we do some work for the government for their anti-drugs campaign. We try and persuade people to contact the *drugs help line* to find out a bit more about the harm that using drugs might be doing to them. We also did a campaign *targeted at* teenagers, which was trying to encourage them to spend less time *sniffing glue* and remind them of the negative effects of that. We also do work for the Samaritans, and again we try and encourage people to share their problems and use a help line and solve their problems that way.
Helen: What was the most *tricky* moment that ever happened to you with a client?
Simon: Probably the most difficult experience I've had so far was when we had to borrow a number of vehicles from a client. In this case they were small *vans*, to appear in a commerical, and when I returned to the agency I got a call from my client, whom we'd borrowed the vans from, and he said, "Simon, I've got the vans back, but I've only got half of them." I didn't understand what he was talking about. He said that they had been delivered back to him, but the roofs of the vans had been completely removed. So he was completely *flabbergasted* by this, and it turned out

that when they were being transported on the back of a lorry, they had gone under a low bridge and the roofs of all the vans had been removed. And they had just been delivered back to the client, and the guy who was driving the *lorry* hadn't told anyone - had just left them there and driven off. So that was quite a difficult problem to sort out.

Helen: Rather an *embarrassing* moment, I should think.

Simon: Quite embarrassing, and it did take a while to sort out.

Helen: But you kept the client.

Simon: We kept the client, yes - after quite a lot of work.

Helen: Do you think you're influenced by advertising when you go shopping?

Simon: Who knows, who knows? Sometimes, I guess, if there's a particular offer on. But advertising is supposed to work at a much more sort of *subconscious* level. So you're not actually supposed to be consciously aware that the advertising is affecting you.

(drugs) help line	Notrufstelle (für Drogenabhängige)	tricky	schwierig, knifflig
		van	Lieferwagen, Transporter
to target at	(ab)zielen auf, als Zielgruppe haben	to flabbergast	verblüffen
		lorry	Lastwagen
to sniff	schnüffeln	embarrassing	peinlich
glue	Klebstoff	subconscious	unterbewußt

I. Vocabulary

a) Use the noun for each of the following words from the text in a sentence of your own.

1. to believe
2. to encourage
3. to persuade
4. to appear
5. to deliver
6. to remove
7. embarrassing

b) Choose the word which best completes the sentence.

1. It sounds odd influencing people to consume less, but .... it is quite common.
   a) eventually b) currently c) actually d) presently
2. We .... young people of the negative effects of sniffing glue.
   a) remind b) remember c) recollect d) recall
3. The advertisements encourage people to .... their problems and use a help line to do so.
   a) share b) divide c) separate d) part

4. The agency had to .... vehicles from a client.
 a) lend b) give c) loan d) borrow
5. The guy who was .... the lorry hadn't told anyone about the accident.
 a) riding b) running c) driving d) moving
6. You should not be aware that advertising is .... you.
 a) affecting b) concerning c) moving d) touching

II. Understanding

1. Give an example of ways in which Ogilvy & Mather have encouraged people not to consume things or to consume less.
2. What was wrong with the vans Simon had borrowed from a client?

13 I

What people think of advertising and the ways it affects them

Helen asked several people about the ways advertising affected them and what they thought about advertising.
Simon's girlfriend Anna thought that she must be influenced by something when she chose to buy a particular kind of beer since most beers tasted the same.
Two women *admitted* being influenced by television advertising, one of them saying that she bought cornflakes because she really liked the cornflakes commercial. Both of them added that they were satisfied with the products which they chose as a result of advertising.
Another woman bought a particular washing powder because she had used a *trial packet* and found it satisfactory. But she said she had not been influenced by television advertising for the product.
A young man who was asked what he thought about advertising claimed that everyone was influenced by advertisements whether or not they were conscious of them. He thought that advertising made people believe what the advertisers wanted them to believe.
Another man admitted that he was influenced by advertising on television, but not on billboards because he was usually too busy driving his car to notice them.
Finally, a young woman said that advertisements were important in persuading people to make certain choices. In her case, they affected her choice of *running shoes* since she was a runner.

to admit	zugeben, eingestehen
trial packet	Probepackung
running shoes	Joggingschuhe

What about you?

1. Do you like to watch advertisements on TV? If so, why? If not, why not?
2. Have you ever been influenced by a commercial on TV? If so, give an example. If not, why not?
3. Which has the strongest, which has the least influence on people - advertising on TV, on the radio, in a newspaper or by posters? Give reasons why.

13 J

Simon talks about his private life

Simon playing cricket

I do work long hours, although I quite enjoy the environment and the *buzz* in it. There are a lot of young people who work in our company here. The average age is probably about twenty-eight, so I quite enjoy the job. I do quite a lot in my spare time. We're just coming up to the summer now, so we're just training for the cricket season. I play cricket for a team made up of people I was at university with. Although cricket is not as popular as it was fifty years ago, it's still considered to be the typically English summer sport. I do normal things that everyone else does in his spare time, like going shopping with my girlfriend Anna, looking for antiques, buying things in ***Islington*** possibly, and obviously going to the supermarket.

Note: ***Islington*** is a district of North London, known for its antique shops.

buzz *hier*: Aufregung

What do you know about Simon?

1. Simon works for an .... in London's Docklands.
2. He's an .... in the Account Management Department.
3. His big project this year is working on the .... advertising for the new Ford Mondeo.
4. He works long .... but he enjoys the job because he likes the buzz in it.
5. In his spare time he plays .... with friends he was at university with.
6. On Saturdays he likes going .... with his girlfriend Anna and looking for .... in Islington.

13 K

A trip down the Thames

The Docklands area

London was once the busiest port in the world. From the 17th to the 19th century docks were built on both sides of the River Thames to handle the increasing number of ships and their *cargoes*. But by the 1970s the docks were *in decline* and now only a few *moorings* are left.

Down river from Tower Bridge, old *wharves* where ships used to unload their cargoes have been *converted* into offices, restaurants and apartments. They have been joined by newer buildings both for living in and for business purposes such as the Canary Wharf Tower, designed by the Argentine-born architect Cesar Pelli, which is Europe's second largest commercial building. It is part of the Docklands development on the north bank of the Thames, which has transformed this area of the old London docks.

Further down the river is the Cutty Sark, a 19th century sailing ship. It is next to the Royal Palace at Greenwich, which was designed by Sir Christopher Wren for King Charles II. Until recently the palace housed the Royal Naval College.

Beyond Greenwich is the Thames Barrier, which was built to prevent *flooding* by controlling the amount of water which flows from the sea at high tide.

cargo (*pl* -oes)	Ladung	wharf (*pl* -ves)	Kai
to be in decline	verfallen	to convert	umwandeln, umbauen
mooring	Anlegesteg	flooding	Überfluten
down river	flußabwärts		

Canary Wharf Tower, the new landmark in London

Thames Barrier

"We've come to the end of our series about life and work in different parts of the British Isles. I hope that you enjoyed yourselves with us and that we have encouraged you to practise your English and maybe even visit our country some time. Thank you for joining us. Good bye and good luck."

Key to the exercises

A journalist in London

1

1 B

I. Vocabulary

a) 1. serving - **2.** a review - **3.** headlines - **4.** issue - **5.** vocations - **6.** felicity

b) 1. ambition - **2.** decision - **3.** consideration - **4.** combination - **5.** establishment - **6.** satisfaction - **7.** publishing/publication

II. Understanding

1. Ruth Gledhill covers news on the religious as well as on the charity front, she is the Religion Correspondent of The Times. - **2.** She started as a journalist on the Birmingham Post & Mail, a provincial newspaper. - **3.** Her father influenced her in choosing her career. - **4.** Ruth went to Rwanda to report about the refugee disaster.

III. Test your English

1. She is thinking of going to Africa. - **2.** I apologised for not warning him. - **3.** She asked for her article to be printed at once. - **4.** Haven't you finished your article yet? - **5.** You'd better not go to the meeting tomorrow.

1 C

Questions

1. *Quality papers* - often called broadsheets - contain serious news, eg political, industrial and cultural news and devote pages to finance matters and international news. They have an undramatic layout with lengthy articles. *Tabloids* contain sensational stories and aim to excite the reader visually, using techniques such as large headlines and photographs. The tabloids are half the size of a broadsheet paper. - **2.** National papers in Britain are: The Times, The Independent, The Guardian, The Daily Telegraph, The Financial Times. Provincial papers are the Yorkshire Post and the Birmingham Post & Mail. - **3.** A supplement is an extra and separate addition to a newspaper, a magazine.

1 D

Vocabulary

1. not influenced by sth or sb/uncommitted - **2.** part - **3.** reports - **4.** to acquire - **5.** a report which assesses the merits of a film, play or book

1 E

I. Vocabulary

1. surprisingly - **2.** main stories - **3.** timetable (for work) - **4.** to follow - **5.** meeting - **6.** fixed (*or*: final) time for finishing sth - **7.** to make a story worth publishing - **8.** slow in doing sth - **9.** mistake - **10.** special

II. Test your English

1. until - **2.** by - **3.** until ... by - **4.** until - **5.** by - **6.** by

1 F

I. Questions

1. A newspaper gets its information from many sources: from staff reporters, local correspondents, foreign correspondents and news agencies. - **2.** The Times was founded by a printer who invented a new printing method. - **3.** Newspaper owners have introduced cheaper printing methods which require less labour.

II. Understanding

1. a printer - **2.** expanding - **3.** news coverage - **4.** huge readership - **5.** copies - **6.** moved

III. Test your English
1. opened - **2.** has been printed - **3.** was launched - **4.** has had ... has won - **5.** had taken place - **6.** took place - **7.** will meet

1 G

I. Vocabulary
a) 1. average number of papers, magazines, etc, sold each day, month or year - **2.** news reporting - **3.** local freelance journalist - **4.** tribute to a prominent person who has recently died - **5.** two meanings: a) division of a printed page, b) regular contribution by a particular writer - **6.** two meanings: a) one example of a newspaper, b) text written by a journalist
b) 1. editor - **2.** foreign correspondent - **3.** stringer - **4.** sub-editor - **5.** freelance writer (*or*: journalist)

II. Translation (*Suggestion*)
Wenn die sensationellsten Nachrichten bekannt werden, neigen Journalisten instinktiv dazu, zuerst als Nachrichtenredakteure zu reagieren und erst dann als Menschen. Das mag ungerecht sein: Vielleicht machen wir ja im Gegensatz zu anderen Leuten beides gleichzeitig, wir reagieren mit Schock und Trauer, aber wir überlegen auch sofort, was wir in der Zeitung bringen. Diese Erfahrung hat sicherlich jeder Journalist gemacht, als uns die Nachricht in den frühen Morgenstunden des 31. August erreichte. Keine Geschichte in diesem Jahrhundert hat seither so viel Platz in den britischen Zeitungen oder in den Zeitungen weltweit in Anspruch genommen. Allein in dieser Hinsicht war der Tod von Diana, der Prinzessin von Wales, ohne Zweifel das größte Nachrichtenereignis des Jahrhunderts - einmal ganz abgesehen von der emotionalen und tragischen Auswirkung oder der Fähigkeit, in Großbritannien eine ganze Nation gegen die Monarchie aufzurütteln, die offenbar mit ihren Untertanen nicht mehr im Einklang ist.
Aber war es auch die bedeutendste Nachricht? In den Redaktionen hat das eine Diskussion darüber entfacht, welche Nachrichten die gleiche Wirkung auf Redakteure und Leser gehabt haben.

1 H

Ruth Gledhill
1. Correspondent - **2.** provincial newspaper - **3.** tabloids - **4.** covers ... news - **5.** refugee disaster - **6.** favourite ... food review - **7.** pastime (*or*: hobby) - **8.** couple ... blessing ... newspapers - **9.** shopping ... meeting ... fashionable

1 I

I. Understanding
1. licence - **2.** satellite ... for their services - **3.** local ... stations

II. Comment (*Suggestion*)
Newspapers have several advantages over television. They give you much more detailed news and comment than television, and they have useful supplements and special interest sections. You don't have to be at home near a TV set to get your news from them. You can read a newspaper when you want to, and you can decide how much time to spend reading it. You can also choose which (bits of) news or comment to read, and you can choose the newspaper which suits your opinions, your politics and your lifestyle.
But newspapers do have disadvantages. Unlike television, they cannot report events on the spot (*sofort*) or immediately after they have happened. Newspapers may take up too much of your time, they are quite bulky (*dick*) and they have to be disposed of. And, of course, you have to buy them.

1 J

I. Vocabulary
1. denomination - **2.** broadly similar to - **3.** rise - **4.** initiative

II. Understanding
1. The Queen (*or*: The Monarch) is the Head of the Church of England. - **2.** He lives at Lambeth Palace. - **3.** It does not follow the practices of the Established Church. - **4.** The Bishop calls the reports pessimistic because he considers them wrong. In fact, the churches' membership is rising again.

Teachers in Cambridge 2

2 B

I. Vocabulary
1. examinations at the end of the last year at school - **2.** a school that provides secondary education to all students whatever their abilities are - **3.** to make a careful study - **4.** research done in the field - **5.** necessary

II. Understanding
1. He teaches sixth-form students in their final year at school. - **2.** She teaches chemistry. - **3.** He is the Deputy Head (Teacher) of the Netherhall School, a comprehensive school in Cambridge. - **4.** He is a teacher of geography and he is Head of the Sixth Form.

2 C

I. Vocabulary
a) 1. accommodate - **2.** require - **3.** recommend - **4.** choose - **5.** combine - **6.** opt - **7.** enter - **8.** need
b) 1. to be in charge of - **2.** to mention - **3.** we would demand - **4.** relatively - **5.** careers - **6.** invariably - **7.** to gain access

II. Test your English
1. Helen wanted to know what the sixth form was. - **2.** Helen asked me if I had heard what Nick had done the night before. - **3.** Helen asked Nick if he would be seeing Phil that afternoon. - **4.** Helen asked him if he was aware that smoking caused cancer. - **5.** Helen asked the student why he had painted his bike black. - **6.** Helen asked Anne when she was going to take her A-levels.

2 D

Understanding
1. A sixth-former is a student who is in his final two years secondary education. - **2.** They take GCSE examinations at the age of 16. - **3.** They usually take GCSEs in eight or nine subjects. - **4.** Students who have successfully passed their GCSEs - **5.** They should have three grade passes at A-level for entrance to Oxford or Cambridge.

2 E

I. Understanding
1. A game of pool and an informal game of football - **2.** They have time for practising during the lunch break. - **3.** A typical meal in the school canteen would be fish and chips or simply sandwiches. - **4.** A large room where students can relax during the school breaks

II. Test your English
1. bear/tolerate - **2.** consider - **3.** inquired about - **4.** rely on - **5.** Come and see me/us (*or*: Pay a visit) - **6.** finished - **7.** find a solution to/deal with - **8.** test - **9.** met - **10.** delayed - **11.** progressing/making progress - **12.** happened

III. What about you?
(*no suggestion*)

2 F

Understanding
1. Pupils or students have different levels and types of ability and some are more talented than others. - **2.** Compulsory school years last from age five to age 16. (*or*: Compulsory school lasts for eleven years.) - **3.** Further education is full-time and part-time education for those over school-leaving age as well as voluntary spare-time occupation and training for those over school-leaving age. - **4.** Education which trains the mind, in contrast to vocational education which is more practical

2 G

I. Understanding
1. They charge fees. They offer students a different environment. They usually have better facilities. They have freedom to control the curriculum and the management of the school. Many of them are boarding schools. Many of them require students to pass an entrance exam. - **2.** They have more money than state schools and can spend more on facilities. - **3.** They were educated privately at home.

II. Say it in English
1. That is too difficult a task. - **2.** That was too good an opportunity. - **3.** I'm going to stay at home and study all evening. - **4.** We'll see each other tomorrow. - **5.** They like each other a lot. - **6.** What do you think about the new teacher? - **7.** Three weeks ago today he passed his A-levels. - **8.** The party was to be a surprise. - **9.** A few/Some people were still here/there at midnight. - **10.** Our school is near the station.

III. Comment (*Suggestion*)
Yes. They have come from families which already have money to help their children in all kinds of ways. They are provided with better facilities for both work and leisure activities. And at boarding schools they can concentrate on their education, free from the interruptions of family life at home.
No. Although they may enjoy better facilities at private boarding schools, they are cut off from everyday life and from their families.

2 H

I. Vocabulary
1. different - **2.** opportunity - **3.** to conceive - **4.** to consult sb - **5.** to receive - **6.** career - **7.** frankly - **8.** antidote (to)

II. Understanding
1. Cambridge - **2.** teacher - **3.** difficult ... imagine - **4.** advice ... careers - **5.** leisure ... with his children, feeding ... daughter

III. Test your English
1. Hearing this news ... - **2.** Having passed his GCSEs ... - **3.** Arriving in the pub ... - **4.** Being very poor ... - **5.** There being nothing to do ... - **6.** The weather being fine ...

2 I

I. Translation
1. Ich finde, heute sollten den Frauen alle Berufe offenstehen. - **2.** Er sollte einer der hervorragendsten Naturwissenschaftler seiner Zeit werden. - **3.** Er kommt eventuell morgen. - **4.** Sie arbeitete so hart/schwer, daß sie schließlich den Test/die Prüfung bestand.

II. The language of education
1. assembly - **2.** sixth-formers - **3.** A-levels - **4.** GCSEs - **5.** geography - **6.** breather/break - **7.** chemistry - **8.** comprehensive - **9.** red-brick - **10.** fieldwork - **11.** canteen - **12.** nursery - **13.** fees - **14.** boarding

III. Comment (*Suggestion*)
A: I think school uniform is a good idea. Wearing uniform makes sure that everyone in the school looks tidy.
B: I disagree. Students at schools where they wear uniform just look different from other children and teenagers. They look less natural.
A: But wearing uniform gives them a sense of belonging to a particular school community, a sense of identity as part of that community.
B: Students who don't have to wear uniform can have a sense of their own identity. They can choose what they wear, and wear clothes that they feel comfortable in.
A: A lot of parents like their children to wear uniform.
B: The parents don't have to wear the uniform. They might have a different opinion if they did. And you don't see children in school uniform at the weekend, do you?

A: Uniform gives a good impression of the school. (*or*: Students in uniform help to give the school a good appearance.)
B: Then why don't the teachers wear uniform?

2 J

I. Understanding
1. b) - **2.** a) - **3.** c) - **4.** b)

II. Translation (*Suggestion*)
Sind Sie auf das Leben als Student vorbereitet?
Obwohl heute mehr junge Leute als je zuvor den Zugang zur Universität erlangen, wird immer deutlicher, daß viele auf das Leben fort von zu Hause nicht vorbereitet sind. Universitätsberater berichten, daß Studenten ihre Kurse innerhalb der ersten Wochen nach ihrer Ankunft wieder aufgeben möchten, weil sie Heimweh haben. Andere (wiederum) haben keine Ahnung, wie man einen Arbeitsplan aufstellt und sind daher schnell im Rückstand. Georgina Newson, die das Studentenberatungszentrum an der Universität Reading leitet, ist verwundert, daß so viele Studenten die elementarsten Dinge des Lebens nicht beherrschen.

A publican in the New Forest 3

3 B

I. Vocabulary
a) 1. poor - **2.** near/not far - **3.** single - **4.** female - **5.** general/average
b) 1. suppose - **2.** in vogue - **3.** consider - **4.** The majority of - **5.** demanded

II. Understanding
1. He runs a pub. - **2.** The laws which regulate the sale of alcoholic drinks and the opening hours of pubs, restaurants, etc - **3.** People are critical. - **4.** Going to a pub or restaurant is not so expensive as it was. Nowadays, people have more money to spend. - **5.** It means to provide guests with food and drink. - **6.** Pubs are supposed to be the favourite meeting place where people can get together and relax with friends over a pint of beer. - **7.** Nowadays, it caters for women and families with children as well. There is a play area where children can play while their parents have a drink or a meal. And there is often entertainment for both adults and children.

III. Test your English
1. are served - **2.** is still being prepared - **3.** had not been sold - **4.** has not been delivered - **5.** has been asked - **6.** has been made - **7.** is being delivered ... has not been damaged

3 C

I. Understanding
1. Ordinary pubs generally have to order their beers from a single brewery whereas a Free House can order its beers from any brewery. - **2.** It's a big slice of bread, a wedge (*Ecke*) of cheese, some pickle and an onion. - **3.** It's a potato baked in its skin with a filling on top.

II. Test your English
1. On ... for ... at - **2.** to - **3.** at - **4.** from - **5.** of - **6.** with - **7.** into ... over ... by

III. What about you?
(*no suggestion*)

3 D

I. Vocabulary
1. characteristic; sth which attracts interest or attention; sth which looks interesting - **2.** horse-drawn vehicle (formerly) carrying passengers along a regular route, with stops or stage posts at regular intervals - **3.** sb who takes goods illegally into or out of a country - **4.** selection - **5.** in the same way - **6.** people living in the neighbourhood, in this case in the village of Wooton

II. Understanding
1. The landlord owns the pub whereas the publican leases the property from a brewery. - **2.** He offers a children's menu, he has a climbing frame in his garden where children can play, and he organises entertainment for children. There's also a little zoo and the children can ride on ponies.

III. Comment (*Suggestion*)
A: What are you having?
B: I'm not very hungry. I don't want a lot to eat. I'm going to have a jacket potato with cheese on top.
A: Are you having anything with it, like a salad?
B: No. Just on its own.
A: I want more than a snack. I want something that's hot, like steak and kidney pie. I'll have it with chips and peas. And then I'll have an ice-cream.
B: What are you having to drink? I know you like wine.
A: Yes, I do. But with steak and kidney pie I'd prefer beer. I'd like a pint of beer. What about you? What would you like to drink?
B: I'm driving, so I'll just have water, and a coffee later.

3 E

I. Vocabulary
1. supplier - **2.** promotion - **3.** tasting/taste - **4.** entertainment - **5.** service/servant

II. Understanding
1. He feeds the animals. - **2.** VAT means value added tax. - **3.** He goes for a ride on his pony. - **4.** He puts shoes on the ponies. - **5.** It means that the publican has to look after his guests.

III. Test your English
1. goes/will go ... has counted - **2.** has ... been - **3.** knew - **4.** were ... doing ... phoned - **5.** was - **6.** has he been running

3 F

I. Vocabulary
a) 1. production - **2.** mixture/mix - **3.** fermentation - **4.** brewery/brew - **5.** popularity - **6.** remains/remainder
b) 1. taste - **2.** cask

II. Understanding
1. It's a beer drawn or pulled from a barrel. - **2.** Stout traditionally comes from Ireland. - **3.** A pint is a little bit more than half a litre (*or*: 0.57 of a litre).

3 G

I. Vocabulary
a) 1. dangerous - **2.** influential - **3.** cultural - **4.** traditional - **5.** residential - **6.** selective
b) 1. getting or collecting money for a special purpose - **2.** not drinking any alcohol - **3.** young people

II. Understanding
1. He supports disabled children and adults who are mentally handicapped. - **2.** No, he moved to the New Forest ten years ago. Before that, he had three pubs in London. - **3.** His favourite drink is coffee.

III. Questions
1. She interviewed a local who was a friend of Steve as well as the landlord and the landlady who ran the pub before Steve. - **2.** Steve organised some entertainment for the evening.

IV. What do you know about Steve? (*Suggestion*)
Steve has a busy time running his pub. He starts the day by feeding the animals. Then he does his office work, keeping the accounts up to date, dealing with the wages, etc. He also organises entertainment for the children and for special evenings. He plans the menu with the pub's chef, and orders supplies, either on the phone or by visiting suppliers, especially the breweries which provide beer for 'The Rising Sun'. During the pub's opening hours Steve looks after the guests and keeps them happy. Sometimes he serves behind the bar.
Steve does charity work with the Fortune Centre of Riding for handicapped children, and with a group which helps mentally handicapped adults. His favourite leisure pastime is riding one of his ponies.

3 H

I. Understanding
1. William the Conqueror - **2.** They were used for shipbuilding. - **3.** It was founded in the 13th century. - **4.** King Henry VIII - **5.** The National Motor Museum - **6.** It's famous for its ponies who have the right of way on the roads and paths and it's a beautiful recreation area.

II. Letter-writing (*Suggestion*)

...
13 Tile Lane
Wyford
OP3 4HY
Tel: 01663 456

New Forest
Tourist Information Centre
High Street Car Park
Lyndhurst, Hampshire
SO43 7NY

Dear Sir/Madam,

I would be grateful for information about accommodation in the New Forest. I am thinking of spending a week in the area with my family in the first half of June.
I would like to have information about hotels and bed-and-breakfast accommodation for two adults sharing a room, and three children. The eldest child would require a single room, but the two younger ones could share a twin room.
I would appreciate details of separate charges for meals, and for full board and half board accommodation.

I look forward to hearing from you.

Yours faithfully,

...

An apprentice in Cornwall

4

4 B

I. Vocabulary
1. to put together - **2.** place where metal is melted and moulded or shaped - **3.** worker who makes and repairs wooden parts - **4.** room in which things are made or repaired

II. Understanding
1. An apprentice is sb who learns a trade and has agreed to work for a certain number of years in return for being taught. - **2.** He services and repairs pumps at Svedala Ltd.

4 C

I. Vocabulary
a) 1. recognition - **2.** decision - **3.** preference - **4.** imagination - **5.** thought
b) 1. to make up one's mind - **2.** choice - **3.** in other/foreign countries - **4.** to stay - **5.** award/certificate/degree
c) 1. Arbeitsplatz - **2.** Lehrlingsausbildung/Lehre - **3.** Anzeige - **4.** Berufsausbildung

II. Understanding
1. He is being paid while he is training for a qualification and he likes the work. - **2.** It will last for five years. - **3.** He saw an advertisement in the paper and sent an application to Svedala.

4 D

I. Understanding
1. He goes to college once a week, every Monday. - **2.** His favourite subject is CAD which means computer-aided design. - **3.** He learns how to operate heavy machinery.

II. Test your English
1. must pay - **2.** needn't check - **3.** mustn't use - **4.** must leave - **5.** must attend - **6.** need to take up - **7.** must go

4 E

I. Understanding
1. apprenticeship - **2.** A-levels - **3.** graduate - **4.** practical - **5.** engineering - **6.** college - **7.** National Vocational Qualification - **8.** vocation/work - **9.** levels - **10.** qualified

II. Comment (*Suggestion*)
Gavin will spend five years as an apprentice at Svedala. During this time, he will attend college once a week and gain a National Vocational Qualification. This will enable him to become an Engineering Technician.
A student aiming for an engineering degree will need to pass A-levels and take a university course before joining an engineering company. He will eventually become a Chartered Engineer.
Gavin thinks he is better off because he is gaining practical experience and being paid, and he likes the practical subjects he studies at college. In the short term he may have advantages over a graduate, but later on a graduate would probably find it easier to get a senior post than Gavin.

4 F

I. Vocabulary
1. wonderful/excellent - **2.** to finish - **3.** rather - **4.** leisure time/free time

II. Understanding
1. Truro in Cornwall - **2.** Gavin's friends who didn't get a job continued going to school or college. - **3.** He borrows his mother's car from time to time. - **4.** He means going to a nightclub where he and his friends get together and dance. - **5.** Going to the beach, playing football, riding his motorbike, playing snooker and going clubbing

III. What about you?
(*no suggestion*)

4 G

I. Vocabulary
1. to start/to begin - **2.** uncertain - **3.** unhappy - **4.** theoretical - **5.** old - **6.** bad

II. Say it in English
1. I'm hoping that Svedala Ltd is going to offer me a full-time position/job when I've finished my apprenticeship. - **2.** Gavin's girlfriend works in the invoice department of the company. She deals with incoming invoices. - **3.** After Chris had finished his studies at Cambridge University he moved back to Cornwall. He decided to apply for an apprenticeship at Svedala.

4 H

What do you know about Gavin?
1. apprentice ... Cornwall - **2.** College ... theoretical - **3.** Vocational - **4.** brother - **5.** countryside ... motor-cycle - **6.** clubbing - **7.** beach

4 I

Understanding
1. It is influenced by the Gulf Stream. - **2.** Tin mining - **3.** China clay is mainly used for making pottery. - **4.** St Ives is a beautiful and picturesque seaside resort on the Cornish coast, and it is also a centre for the arts. - **5.** Land's End

4 J

Translation (*Suggestion*)
Das Geheimnis einer guten Ausbildung
Ein Jahrhundert oder länger hatte Großbritannien den Ruf, ziemlich gut in der akademischen Ausbildung (zumindest der gesellschaftlichen und intellektuellen Elite) zu sein, aber erschreckend schlecht in der (praktischen) Berufsausbildung.
Das scheint sich zu ändern, da Vertreter von 56 Staaten sich heute zu einer Konferenz in London versammeln, um die Vorzüge der NVQs zu sondieren (diskutieren) - der National Vocational Qualifications (der Staatlichen Zeugnisse über den Abschluß einer Berufsausbildung), die 1986 zur Verbesserung der beruflichen Bildung eingeführt worden waren.

A tourist executive in Jersey 5

5 B

I. Vocabulary
a) 1. department - **2.** task - **3.** (a good) time - **4.** to be present at - **5.** show
b) 1. arrival - **2.** inclusion - **3.** greeting - **4.** attraction - **5.** attendance - **6.** discussion - **7.** arrangement

II. What about you? (*Suggestion*)
In favour: meeting people, meeting journalists, etc, helping tourists
Against: long working hours, having to be nice to people

5 C

I. Vocabulary
1. to retire - **2.** to explore - **3.** precious - **4.** adventurous - **5.** in particular - **6.** to tend to - **7.** popular - **8.** as a rule

II. Understanding
1. All sorts of water sports, like swimming, surfing, windsurfing, diving, sailing. On land you can cycle round the island, walk, play golf, tennis or cricket, go horse-riding. - **2.** It's a town on the coast often with many hotels, where people go to spend their holidays.

III. Letter-writing (*Suggestion*)

Dear Sir/Madam,

I will be attending a language course in Jersey this summer. I would be grateful if you could find a single room (with shower) in a small guest house or with a family in St Helier.
I expect to arrive on 8th June and I shall be staying for three weeks.
Would you please let me know whether you have a room available and how much my stay is likely to cost?
I look forward to hearing from you soon.

Yours faithfully,

5 D

I. Understanding
Jersey is visited by British people as well as by tourists from all over Europe. While the younger tourists intend to do some sort of activities like water sports, tourists with families and even older people prefer going to the beach, walking or cycling around the island. Young people also come to Jersey to attend a language course.

II. Comment (*Suggestion*)
Many people want something completely different from their daily routine and are looking for excitement or adventure without taking too many risks. Some of them have discovered that trying to relax on holiday is more tiring than being active and energetic. And they also have the chance of making new friendships among people they would not expect to meet in their usual surroundings. Finally, they like to have something special to tell their workmates and friends when they get home.

5 E

I. Vocabulary
1. the people employed in a company or organisation - **2.** to put right/correct - **3.** to be useful - **4.** recognised/praised - **5.** range - **6.** owner - **7.** support - **8.** to ask for

II. Test your English
1. in ... on - **2.** at - **3.** on ... until/till - **4.** At ... with - **5.** from ... to ... to ... of

III. Comment (*Suggestion*)
A crowded beach: I prefer a crowded beach because I come on holiday to be with people and to make friends. On a crowded beach there's a chance to play games like football or volleyball, to talk to people you've never met before, even to meet a new girl/boyfriend. If I go onto a deserted beach, I think that there must be something wrong. I think "Where is everybody?"
A deserted beach: I hate crowded beaches with people treading (*treten*) on you or getting in your way when you try to move. They even get in the way when you're in the sea. I come to the seaside to get away from people, to enjoy a good book, maybe to fall asleep. I come on holiday for peace and quiet, so I like deserted beaches.

5 F

I. Understanding
1. tourism - **2.** trippers - **3.** stay - **4.** choice ... guest houses

II. Comment (*Suggestion*)
If you go to another country as a tourist, you may begin to understand how other people live, what their problems are and in what ways they are the same as yourself or different. This is also true when tourists visit your own country. In both cases, you have to make an effort to get on with each other, and this helps nations as well as ordinary people come closer to one another. Unfortunately, a lot of tourists go on organised tours which encourage them to be with people from their own country so that, apart from the sunshine, the scenery and the food, it is like staying at home.

5 G

I. Vocabulary
1. decide - **2.** argue - **3.** book - **4.** complain - **5.** think

II. Understanding
1. She went to France to work at Nice airport. - **2.** She went into teaching.

III. Say it in English
1. Sue has been working in tourism for seven years. - **2.** We hope the weather will be fine tomorrow. - **3.** Sue's colleague is getting married in October. - **4.** He's always coming late.

5 H

I. Test your English
1. enthusiastically - **2.** good - **3.** fascinating - **4.** probably - **5.** carefully

II. What about you?
(*no suggestion*)

III. What do you know about Sue?
1. shopping ... potatoes - **2.** cycling - **3.** cyclists ... speed - **4.** protect - **5.** pubs - **6.** like going

5 I

Understanding
1. c) - **2.** a) - **3.** b) - **4.** a)

5 J

I. Understanding
1. income tax ... inheritance - **2.** resident ... wealthy - **3.** GDP (Gross Domestic Product)

II. Test your English
1. has proved ... has employed - **2.** has been strengthened - **3.** has been produced - **4.** was announced ... had become - **5.** has been established

A student in Birmingham 6

6 B

I. Vocabulary
1. decide - **2.** choose - **3.** graduate - **4.** enter - **5.** recruit

II. Understanding
1. He's a student of Law and French at the University of Birmingham. - **2.** He wants to pass his final degree examinations and become a Bachelor of Laws. - **3.** He speaks three languages: English, French

and a bit of German. - **4.** No, he doesn't want to enter the law profession. He wants to work in industry or in commerce.

III. Test your English

1. If I went to a university, I would study Business Administration. - **2.** If I had intended to study Law, I would have gone to the London School of Economics. - **3.** If you have done well in your final degree examinations, you will not need to fear (*or*: you need not fear) unemployment. **4.** If she had been a good student, she would not have failed her examinations. - **5.** If you had lived in France, you would have learned French rapidly.

6 C

I. Understanding

1. Solicitors advise clients on all questions of law and prepare cases for barristers. - **2.** Bar Examinations have to be taken in order to be called to the Bar, to speak in law courts. - **3.** 'QÇ' means 'Queen's Counsel'. It's an honorary title which successful barristers can apply for.

II. Test your English

1. Ein Rechtsanwalt kann einen Mandanten in Bagatellfällen vor Gericht vertreten. - **2.** Darf ich Ihre/deine Bilder anschauen? - **3.** Er bemüht sich sehr und hat vielleicht Erfolg. - **4.** Darf ich hereinkommen? - **5.** Die Produktion kann sich als sehr teurer Mißerfolg erweisen. - **6.** Er mag ein netter Kerl sein, aber er ist sehr häßlich.

6 D

I. Vocabulary

a) 1. grounds of the university - **2.** companion who shares the same house as yourself - **3.** talk - **4.** hall where you can do gymnastics and indoor sports
b) 1. late - **2.** often - **3.** few - **4.** near

II. Understanding

1. A student district in Birmingham - **2.** He goes to the gym. - **3.** Since he doesn't live far from the university campus he spends it at home with his housemates. - **4.** He likes watching greyhound races with his friends or going out for a meal to a Balti restaurant with his girlfriend Adele. - **5.** It's a restaurant where Indian food is served.

6 E

I. Vocabulary

1. a) - **2.** c) - **3.** b) - **4.** d)

II. What about you?

(*no suggestion*)

6 F

I. Vocabulary

1. consideration - **2.** difficulty - **3.** organisation - **4.** difference - **5.** importance

II. Understanding

1. He went to Limoges, where he studied French. - **2.** Activities which are not part of the curriculum of a school or university

6 G

How to write a CV

1. by ... for - **2.** of - **3.** at ... at - **4.** by - **5.** with ... of - **6.** at - **7.** of - **8.** about ... about

David's CV

(*no suggestion*)

6 H

Understanding
1. A civic university, usually founded in the 19th century. 'Red-brick' refers to the use of bricks and the style of architecture popular in the 19th century. - **2.** They go to get information about jobs and contacts with potential employers. - **3.** A temporary job with a company in which a student can get experience of work and of the company concerned

6 I

I. Vocabulary
1. studies which a student undertakes after getting a degree - **2.** places which are far away, in a distant part of the world - **3.** a job for which there is a lasting contract with an employer - **4.** expectations and likelihood of employment

II. Say it in English
1. He has been living in Birmingham for several years. - **2.** She has had a new bike for a week. - **3.** I have known David for more than a year, and he has always been very reliable. - **4.** We haven't heard from him for ages. - **5.** The lecture has already lasted for more than an hour now.

6 J

Applying for a job (*Suggestion*)

Dear Ms Simpson,

Awards Team Assistant - Reference 1564/98

I wish to apply for the advertised vacancy for an Awards Team Assistant. I enclose a full CV.
I am interested in working in the charity field. I have always liked being part of a team and enjoy contact both with people in other organisations and with the general public. I am also used to working independently and on my own initiative.
I am happy working for my present employers, but after four years of useful experience with them I feel it is time for a change. I would be free to take up a new position at two months' notice.
I look forward to hearing from you and enclose a stamped addressed envelope.

Yours sincerely,

Note: This is a typical of the kind of letter that might be written by someone in their twenties who was looking for a change of career.

6 K

Summary
Each year the Rover Group recruits 300 to 400 young people as trainees from the age of 16 upwards. Of these, 80 to 90 are graduates. They spend up to twelve weeks with the company in the year before they graduate, as part of Rover's Student Placement Scheme. If both the student and the company are satisfied with the experience gained, they are offered employment for the year after they graduate.

Note: In the TV programme David has his interview just before graduation and would have to spend his twelve weeks with the company later than is normal for graduate trainees.

6 L

I. Vocabulary
1. information - **2.** statement about one's abilities - **3.** result - **4.** information taken from newspapers and kept for future reference - **5.** proof

II. Understanding
1. David is a strong believer in further European integration. - **2.** He would like to work on projects which would be successful and to come up with ideas which would be used effectively by others.

III. What do you know about David?
1. Law and French ... examinations ... law - **2.** Birmingham ... students - **3.** early ... lectures - **4.** lunchtime - **5.** Balti ... greyhound

6 M

Understanding
1. At the end of the 18th century and in the early 19th century - **2.** It was used to transport materials and finished goods. - **3.** It's famous for the City of Birmingham Symphony Orchestra. - **4.** The invention and production of all kinds of machinery - **5.** Various kinds of engines and machines needed for the production of goods in the Industrial Revolution

A senior conductor in York 7

7 B

I. Vocabulary
1. person who travels regularly between their work in a town and their home in another town or in the country - **2.** carriage for a baby - **3.** demand - **4.** chair for the use of disabled persons

II. Understanding
1. First, he joined the army, and later he got a job on the railway as a porter. - **2.** It lasts about eight hours. - **3.** He likes the London route most. - **4.** People often take the wrong seats and sometimes travel in the wrong direction (*or*: take the wrong train).

III. Say it in English
1. John has been living in Newcastle for several years. - **2.** The strike of the railway workers has already lasted (for) three weeks now. - **3.** I have been waiting for the Edinburgh train (*or*: the train to Edinburgh) for an hour. - **4.** I have known John for more than two years and he has always been very reliable. - **5.** I haven't seen him since last week.

7 C

I. Vocabulary
1. c) - **2.** a) - **3.** b) - **4.** d) - **5.** d) - **6.** b)

II. Comment (*Suggestion*)
(All things can happen during the conductor's tour on duty ...).
A senior conductor's shift lasts eight hours. When he reports for duty, he is given the schedule for his journey. Then he collects his equipment and goes to the train. He may take over from another conductor and there may also be a change of catering crew. During the journey, he makes announcements and checks tickets. He also looks after the needs of passengers and deals with their problems. He has to look after disabled passengers and others with special needs. And sometimes passengers board the wrong train, or sit in the wrong seats, or lose their luggage and other possessions.

7 D

I. Vocabulary
1. place to which a person is going - **2.** reduced price - **3.** times when there are few passengers - **4.** older people

II. Test your English
to ... for ... with ... from ... to ... by ... in ... between ... of ... for ... . to ... from

7 E

I. Vocabulary
a) 1. ownership - **2.** utilities - **3.** companies
b) 1. nationalisation - **2.** subsidy - **3.** investment/investor

II. Understanding
1. The last Conservative government - **2.** The state/taxpayers

7 F

I. Understanding
1. privatised ... companies - **2.** owns - **3.** rolling stock - **4.** leased ... operates - **5.** franchises

II. Questions
1. GNER now gives better service to passengers than they would get with other forms of transport, and it has increased efficiency. There are now more trains, they are more reliable and they are cleaner. - **2.** Aggressive marketing means doing more than just making trains available. It means selling more tickets, selling tickets in advance at discounted prices, and persuading people that travelling by train is actually better than using other means of transport. - **3.** The railways and their operations are paid for by the people who use them rather than by all taxpayers. Competition between operating companies leads to rivalry in providing better service and lower prices. And dividing responsibility for different parts of the rail system (infrastructure, rolling stock and operations) results in each part being financed and run by those who specialise in their own particular field. Finally, staff are happier, which should make them do their work more effectively.

7 G

I. Vocabulary
1. to be in charge of - **2.** security - **3.** to transmit - **4.** to develop

II. Understanding
1. Railtrack owns York station. - **2.** Nigel is responsible for 80 people. - **3.** He was a train driver.

III. Test your English
1. considered - **2.** was in charge - **3.** started - **4.** moved - **5.** would love

7 H

Understanding
conductor ... arriving ... staff ... travelling ... welcoming

7 I

I. Questions
1. It began in the 1820s or 1830s. - **2.** It is fast and convenient and there are a lot of trains every day.

II. Test your English
1. will you be - **2.** was ... was listening - **3.** 'll be seeing - **4.** has already asked - **5.** lived ... was - **6.** hasn't written - **7.** have we been talking

III. Comment (*Suggestion*)
A good railway system has several advantages. First, it can carry large numbers of passengers and large quantities of freight on existing rail tracks which are relatively simple to maintain. So it reduces the amount of traffic on a road network which would otherwise require extension to meet increased demand and which is likely to be more difficult and expensive to maintain. There are other advantages, too. Rail travel is generally faster than travel by road, both in crowded cities and over long distances. Rail travel is generally safer than road travel. Railways are the best means of transporting heavy loads, especially over long distances. Rail traffic causes less pollution than road traffic. Railways are less liable to disruption because of bad weather.

7 J

Question
(*no suggestion*)

An electronics engineer in Silicon Glen 8

8 B

I. Vocabulary

a) 1. marriage - **2.** decision - **3.** thought - **4.** security - **5.** employment
b) 1. scenery/landscape - **2.** to see - **3.** in fact - **4.** position/employment - **5.** drive - **6.** to look for - **7.** expert - **8.** likely to become successful

II. Understanding

1. She works as a specialist in eye diseases. - **2.** Because Charlie got a job in Glasgow and Clackmannon is half-way between Glenrothes and Glasgow, so John and Charlie have about the same distance to travel to their work. - **3.** They've been living there for three years. - **4.** When John left school a career in the field of electronics looked promising due to the establishment of new companies in Scotland.

III. Grammar revision

1. I'd like you to meet John whose parents are old friends of mine. - **2.** Charlie works in a hospital which is part of the University of Glasgow. - **3.** They live in Clackmannan which is a small village in the Scottish Lowlands. - **4.** John has a colleague called Jim Hain, who is an excellent golfer.

8 C

I. Vocabulary

1. factory - **2.** monitor - **3.** desk - **4.** some/a number of - **5.** to carry out/to have - **6.** part

II. Understanding

1. The mouse enables computer users to find their way around the screen and to give instructions to the computer's programs. - **2.** A mouse moves on a pad, a remote control is held in the hand. - **3.** An organisation uses a server when several people in the organisation need to share the same computer functions and information.

8 D

I. Understanding

1. False - **2.** True - **3.** False - **4.** False - **5.** False - **6.** True

II. Say it in English

1. We need an expert to supervise (*or*: to oversee) the project. - **2.** The computers are assembled in the Glenrothes manufacturing plant. - **3.** John spends most of his money on computer games. - **4.** Much of the computer market is controlled by Japanese companies. **5.** Cost-effectiveness must be ensured.

III. Comment (*Suggestion*)

Few industrial processes or commercial operations nowadays depend on the talents and efforts of a single person working on his/her own. People work together in teams and effective team-work is essential. Here are three important aspects of team-work.
Communication. Facts, opinions and decisions need to be available and accessible to everyone working together on a particular task or in a particular field of work.
Consultation. People work better if they know that their views matter, are asked for, and are taken seriously.
Participation. There needs to be a common sense of purpose, and a sense of sharing the work, the achievement and, if possible, the rewards resulting from it.

8 E

I. Vocabulary

1. published - **2.** isolation - **3.** employees ... productivity ... reducing - **4.** connected - **5.** creative - **6.** technological

II. Understanding
1. It goes through several stages or revisions before manufacture. - **2.** The processor gives the computer its power and operating speed. - **3.** They vary because different customers have different requirements. - **4.** Defects in computer components usually lead to failure early in their product lifetime.

III. Comment (*Suggestion*)
In the past, little thought was given to the welfare of workers. Now it is recognised that healthy and contented workers are more productive. Most large companies make efforts to provide sufficient rest periods, encourage social contact between workers, and offer facilities to help workers improve their lives and remain fit and healthy.

8 F

Understanding
1. She is a test engineer. She tests the prototype of a new computer. - **2.** She says that it's not rare (*or*: it's quite common) to find women in the computer industry as a whole, but that there are very few women in jobs that are closely involved with hardware. - **3.** She studied Information Technology. - **4.** Industrial placement means practical training within a company. - **5.** No, she isn't. She's from Yorkshire.

8 G

Vocabulary
1. easy for the user to understand and operate - **2.** items of information organised and held in the computer so that they can be accessed in various ways - **3.** illustrations/pictures - **4.** use of computers to produce store and edit written documents

8 H

I. Vocabulary
a) 1. distribute - **2.** innovate - **3.** create - **4.** employ - **5.** invest - **6.** communicate
b) 1. firm - **2.** to think - **3.** to make great efforts - **4.** start - **5.** expectations - **6.** strong - **7.** secure position - **8.** to go on - **9.** it will be completely changed

II. Understanding
1. These large companies are dominating the marketplace and dictating future developments. - **2.** He thinks the standard (*or*: calibre) is very high. - **3.** The money largely comes from America and the Far East.

III. Grammar revision
1. lived ... has been called - **2.** have been largely forgotten - **3.** spent - **4.** graduating ... dreamt - **5.** won - **6.** was finished ... works - **7.** devoted - **8.** remained ... seeing - **9.** died - **10.** live ... is recognised ... celebrated

8 I

What do you know about John?
1. electronics engineer - **2.** personal computers - **3.** test engineer - **4.** has been married - **5.** eye diseases ... Glasgow - **6.** Edinburgh - **7.** Master of Business Administration ... part-time - **8.** golf ... St Andrews - **9.** mountain biking

8 J

Understanding
1. to know how to use a computer - **2.** electronic mail - mail sent from one computer to another - **3.** fundamental knowledge - **4.** café where over a cup of coffee people can surf the Internet or play games on computers or communicate with people and databases across the world

8 K

Comment
(*no suggestion*)

8 L

How much do you know about Scotland?
1. Edinburgh ... Athens - **2.** Presbyterian - **3.** parliament - **4.** reformer - **5.** bagpipes - **6.** clan - **7.** Holyroodhouse

An environmental official in the Highlands 9

9 B

I. Vocabulary
a) 1. unfortunate - **2.** rarely - **3.** slow - **4.** minor - **5.** to enter
b) 1. protective - **2.** environmental - **3.** fortunate - **4.** agricultural - **5.** industrial

II. Understanding
1. The main environmental concerns in the Highlands are forestry, agriculture, fish farming and waste disposal problems. - **2.** She worked in the North of England. - **3.** Since water is needed for cooling the system, the nuclear power plants are built on river banks or along the coast.

9 C

I. Vocabulary
1. to regulate - **2.** job/function - **3.** to burn - **4.** emission - **5.** levels/amounts

II. Understanding
1. a) - **2.** b) - **3.** c) - **4.** b) - **5.** a)

9 D

I. Vocabulary
1. fly-tipping - **2.** various firms - **3.** the stage of impurity - **4.** a decisive role - **5.** likely to damage the environment - **6.** examined

II. Comment (*Suggestion*)
My main objective would be to encourage people to help in the fight against pollution rather than to make laws that would punish them after they had caused pollution. So I would make a law which rewarded people in big cities for using public transport instead of their own cars and in this way reduce pollution from fuel emissions.
Every owner or regular user of a private car would be given a pass that would give them a discount when they travelled by public transport. At the same time there would be additional public transport into and within cities, which would be financed by introducing payments for bringing private cars into cities.

9 E

I. Vocabulary
a) 1. satisfaction - **2.** discussion - **3.** comfort - **4.** negotiation - **5.** tendency - **6.** inspection
b) 1. place - **2.** often - **3.** appeared - **4.** indications - **5.** evidently - **6.** lucky - **7.** two

II. Grammar revision
1. Our air is polluted, but/yet industry still continues ... - **2.** Although/Even though there is a shortage of paper, we throw away ... - **3.** Although/Even though scientists tell us that nuclear power stations are dangerous, the government has decided ... - **4.** Environmental agencies enforce strict regulations for the discharge of substances into the air and water, but/yet factories still dispose of ... - **5.** Whereas/While thousands of children in the Third World are suffering from malnutrition, we live ... - **6.** Empty bottles could be recycled, but/yet most people throw ...

9 F

Understanding
1. It is mixed with hot water (to make a liquid which is fermented with yeast). - **2.** It's in the Highlands near the royal castle of Balmoral. - **3.** It has to be kept at least eight years in oak casks. - **4.** Single malt whisky is the product of one distillery, whereas blended whisky is mixed with the products from several distilleries. - **5.** A wee dram is a small quantity (*or*: measure) of whisky.

9 G

I. Vocabulary
a) 1. place where fish (*or*: plants) are hatched - **2.** place where whisky is produced - **3.** the most important region of a country - **4.** gas present in the air and necessary to the existence of life - **5.** person with a special knowledge of sth - **6.** quantity (of sth) produced
b) 1. Household *waste* is increasing all over the world. - **2.** Cars release less *pollutants* with lead free petrol. - **3.** Kent is a *fertile* county in the South of England. - **4.** He is particularly *sensitive to* criticism.

II. Understanding
Hundreds of small distilleries have been built on the banks of rivers and streams which are very sensitive to pollution. These distilleries release organic waste which can bring down the oxygen levels in the water. They also release hot water which changes the rate of growth of young fish so that they leave for the sea earlier than they should.

9 H

I. Understanding
1. We should think about how we used water, and what we did about waste disposal. - **2.** We should think about recycling waste products, change the way we used cars and make more use of public transport.

II. Grammar revision
1. trying to catch - **2.** to persuade ... to care - **3.** her studying to be - **4.** to allow us to enter ... putting on - **5.** to escape being ... to think up - **6.** playing ... them walking

III. Say it in English
1. Very little has been done so far for the protection of the environment. - **2.** The Green Party have brought environmental issues to the public's attention. - **3.** Many household products contain chemicals which are harmful to the environment. - **4.** We have to change our lifestyles and think of recycling methods.

9 I

I. Vocabulary
1. damage - **2.** litter - **3.** to urge/to influence - **4.** to re-use - **5.** countryside

II. Comment (*Suggestion*)
Most major threats to the environment at the end of the 20th century are the result of the increasing number of people in the world, the demands they make on the world's resources, and the ways in which these demands are satisfied.
We have not yet learnt how to generate sufficient power for our needs without also producing excessive waste which poisons (*vergiftet*) the air, contaminates (*verunreinigt*) the water and destroys trees, plants and animals. We transport people and goods all over the world at high speeds, yet many methods of transport create problems which directly affect the environment. We are producing more food, but we are also increasing the risks of food poisoning. The pesticides we use make agriculture more reliable but have harmful results of their own. And very often the poorer of the world's countries have to pollute the environment in order to survive in a world dominated by richer countries which have found ways of dealing with some of our environmental problems.
So perhaps the greatest threat to the environment is what used to be called progress.

9 J

What do you know about Karen?
1. environmental - **2.** protection - **3.** waste ... pollution - **4.** meetings - **5.** water ... analysed - **6.** pressure groups ... environment - **7.** climbing (*or*: hill walking) ... mountain

9 K

Understanding
1. At Culloden - **2.** Prince Charles Edward Stuart, the grandson of the last Stuart king of England, James II - **3.** Isle of Skye - **4.** For its monster

A European politician in Wales 10

10 B

I. Vocabulary
a) 1. important - **2.** time-consuming - **3.** decline - **4.** closed - **5.** disadvantage
b) 1. Third World countries - **2.** The European Union spends more money on aid to the Third World than is spent by countries outside the EU. - **3.** to work without payment - **4.** a poor region

II. Understanding
1. Glenys Kinnock is on two committees. The main one deals with relations between the EU and the Third World. - **2.** Because coal mining has stopped and the iron and steel industry has contracted.

10 C

I. Vocabulary
1. involvement - **2.** application - **3.** discovery - **4.** insurance - **5.** familiarity - **6.** explanation

II. Understanding
1. It's an area or district which elects a representative to a parliament. - **2.** She is Glenys Kinnock's Personal Assistant. She organises visits for Glenys in Wales. - **3.** She wanted to talk to the people who were affected by a gas explosion that had happened there. - **4.** She was a school teacher. - **5.** She opened a European Information Centre.

10 D

I. Vocabulary
1. disagree - **2.** misinformation - **3.** uninhabited - **4.** inexpensive - **5.** re-elected

II. Grammar revision
1. for - **2.** about ... of - **3.** in ... of - **4.** for ... between ... for ... on

III. Translation (*Suggestion*)
Vielen Dank, daß Sie mich eingeladen haben, hierher zu kommen. Es ist für mich eine einmalige Gelegenheit, denn was Europa angeht, so glaube ich, daß wir mehr mit Fehlinformationen als mit Informationen zu tun haben. Ich halte es deshalb für sehr wichtig, daß wir hier oben den sichtbaren Beweis dafür haben, welch sinnvolle Rolle die Europäische Union spielt.
Wir gehören alle unserem europäischen Kontinent an (*oder*: Wir sind alle Europäer) und haben eine gemeinsame Zukunft vor uns. Deshalb entwickeln wir gemeinsame Ziele.
Ich glaube, daß wir - mehr als alles andere - dieses Ideal erreichen müssen. Als Europäer haben wir uns bekämpft, wir haben unsere Länder in zwei schrecklichen Kriegen in diesem Jahrhundert zerstört. Der allerwichtigste Grund, die europäische Einigung positiv zu sehen - die europäische Vision, die wir haben - ist, daß wir uns nie mehr auf irgendeinem europäischen Schlachtfeld bekämpfen; und den Frieden zu erhalten, deshalb wurde die Europäische Union gegründet.

Ich danke Ihnen sehr, es ist eine große Ehre, hier zu sein. Ich gratuliere Ihnen sehr zu der vielen Arbeit, die Sie (ganz) offenbar investiert haben, um dies hier möglich zu machen. Mit großer Freude schneide ich also das Band durch und erkläre das Europäische Informationszentrum für eröffnet.

10 E

Understanding
1. House of Commons - **2.** Plaid Cymru - **3.** constituencies - **4.** Opposition - **5.** general election - **6.** Labour - **7.** Parliament - **8.** MPs - **9.** House of Lords

10 F

I. Vocabulary
1. confrontation - **2.** achievement - **3.** scrutiny - **4.** preparation - **5.** nationality/nation - **6.** truth - **7.** relation/relative

II. Understanding
1. The European parliament works through committees. EU legislation is scrutinised by committees before going to the full Parliament. The way of working is not adversarial. It's less confrontational. The aim is to get results by consensus and cooperation rather than by defeating political opponents. **2.** European pension rights and buying houses or flats in Europe are treated.

III. Comment (*Suggestion*)
a) *I would like to be an MEP* because I think that many of the laws which affect us as Europeans are going to become more important than the laws which are passed in our own countries. I would like to be part of the process which makes those laws. I would enjoy working with politicians from other countries and cooperating with them in order to make Europe a better place to live in. Maybe we could influence our local politicians to cooperate with each other more than they do at present.
b) *I would not like to be an MEP* because the work would take me away from my home town too often. Also, I am not really interested in politics and I find that politicians are not really interested in people, only in having power and influence for themselves. In any case, I would not like to be a member of a parliament that has done so little to control the European Commissioners, who succeed in producing regulations which make our lives more complicated and restricted.

10 G

Understanding
1. The member states - **2.** There are 626 MEPs. - **3.** They are held in Strasbourg and in Brussels.

10 H

I. Understanding
1. She is a Welsh Member of the European Parliament representing Mid and West Wales. - **2.** They discussed a report on BSE or mad cow disease.

II. Grammar revision
1. became - **2.** could - **3.** was earning - **4.** had planned ... had bought ... took - **5.** feels ... is doing ... believes

10 I

I. Understanding
1. Environmental issues and unemployment are important European concerns. - **2.** It's optimistic and she is in favour of an extension of the European Union.

II. Say it in English
1. We have to reduce the high level of unemployment. - **2.** Many people will have to be re-trained. - **3.** What is Glenys going to talk about at the next Plenary session? - **4.** What are the coal miners living on if their Social Security benefits are insufficient? - **5.** Even though we speak different languages, we have to try to live together.

10 J

I. Vocabulary
1. different - **2.** rural - **3.** self-contained - **4.** outward-looking - **5.** earnest

II. Understanding
1. He is the European Commissioner responsible for Transport. - **2.** He's from South Wales, from the valleys, from Tredegar. - **3.** He was a leader of the Labour Party. - **4.** He's a master of speech (*or*: rhetoric). - **5.** There are two other Welsh-speaking MEPs. - **6.** It's a collection of interviews with British women, published in 1993.

III. What do you know about the Kinnocks?
1. Brussels - **2.** MEP ... Commissioner - **3.** constituency - **4.** school teacher - **5.** library - **6.** speech - **7.** committees ... priority - **8.** MPs - **9.** Labour Party - **10.** election - **11.** Welsh ... language

10 K

Understanding
1. It's Celtic. - **2.** A poet - **3.** It means 'Welcome to Wales'. - **4.** 20% can speak Welsh. - **5.** The media and the use of Welsh in schools

A playwright in Dublin 11

11 B

I. Vocabulary
a) 1. Can you give me a *description* of the play? - **2.** This play is one of the best *productions* in this year's Theatre Festival. - **3.** Can you fulfil the *requirements* of college entrance? - **4.** The *expression* on his face showed that he was happy. - **5.** I listened to his *arguments* for and against the European single currency. - **6.** I was angry, but I did not mean to cause *offence*.
b) 1. to become an actor/actress - **2.** person in a play/figure - **3.** to earn enough to live/what is needed for life - **4.** the task of the theatre/what the theatre is expected (*or*: commissioned) to produce - **5.** the arguments for and against

II. Understanding
1. He felt a need to express himself, to describe characters. - **2.** Probably his family background. His parents had a lot of books at home and they often took Bernard to the theatre when he was a child. - **3.** He was a clerk in a shipping company. - **4.** He admires people who break the rules, who take no notice of regulations. - **5.** He likes to write about people who are not getting on so well in life, about the down-trodden. - **6.** They do not have to pay taxes on their earnings as writers.

III. Test your English
1. which - **2.** when - **3.** whom - **4.** that/which - **5.** who

11 C

Understanding
a) 1. James Joyce - **2.** It was an old watch-tower in Sandycove. - **3.** He was born in Sandycove, near Dublin.
b) 1. b) - **2.** a) - **3.** c)

11 D

What do you know about Irish literature?
1. poems ... poet - **2.** playwright ... comedies - **3.** novel - **4.** satire - **5.** poet and playwright - **6.** play

11 E

What about you?
(*no suggestion*)

11 F

I. Vocabulary
1. national - **2.** future - **3.** harmony - **4.** failure - **5.** unhappy

II. What about you?
(*no suggestion*)

11 G

I. Vocabulary
1. We were sorry to hear about the *death* of his friend. - **2.** She lost her *life* in a car accident. - **3.** During her *pregnancy* she suffered from morning sickness. - **4.** His *stupidity* prevented her from marrying him. - **5.** He sometimes drank a little, but he was well-known for his *sobriety*. - **6.** Do you have any *difficulty* in understanding the lesson?

II. Understanding
Geraldine wants to give Stella some news about herself, but finds it difficult to say what has happened to her. Eventually she reveals that she has been made pregnant by a young colleague at work.

III. Grammar revision
1. Criticising other people is easy. - **2.** Directing actors was a wonderful experience for Bernard. - **3.** Meeting such delightful people in Ireland was a great pleasure. - **4.** Working hard is better than being idle. - **5.** Living on her own will be a useful experience for her.

11 H

I. Understanding
1. It was well received. Most of the reviews were good. - **2.** He thinks they ought to be like life. Happiness is not forever. - **3.** He advised Bernard to take four days to enjoy good reviews and four days to recover from bad reviews. Then he should forget the reviews and start to write his next play.

II. Comment
Advantages: There is a sense of occasion. You get rewarded for leaving home and making the effort to go to the theatre. You are part of an audience of real people taking part in a live event. There is also a sense of reality in a stage performance. You are watching people perform the play in the same place as the audience. Actors and audience can react to one another. For example, if the audience laughs, the actors can react to the laughter and make their performances fit the mood of the audience. You can choose details of the action and the characters which you want to concentrate on.
Disadvantages: You can't see or hear some of the details as clearly as on TV. There are no close-ups (*Nahaufnahmen*). You may go to the theatre on a bad night, when the actors are not at their best or when one of them is ill. There are lots of distractions in the theatre. Other members of the audience get in the way so that you can't see what is happening, or they cough so that you can't hear everything that is said. Theatrical performances cannot take the drama out of the theatre and set it in the world outside.

11 I

I. Vocabulary
1. revival - **2.** pronunciation - **3.** use - **4.** translation - **5.** reference - **6.** spelling

II. Understanding
1. Celtic - **2.** revived ... language - **3.** Parliament - **4.** Prime Minister - **5.** English - **6.** Republic

11 J

Questions
1. No. It's a separate state, the Republic of Ireland. - **2.** Georgian - **3.** Because there was a terrible famine. - **4.** Daniel O'Connell - **5.** An illuminated manuscript of the Gospels

Mussel farmers in Bantry

12

12 B

I. Vocabulary
1. scenery - **2.** to get rid of - **3.** usually - **4.** a difficult task - **5.** type - **6.** started - **7.** conception - **8.** created - **9.** sizeable - **10.** production - **11.** as opposed to

II. Understanding
1. Farming, fishing and tourism - **2.** John is involved in fish farming, in growing mussels. - **3.** They discuss it over a few pints in a pub. - **4.** From Spain - **5.** Eight tons in the first year - **6.** Because they introduced rope culture which meant that the feed cycle was better. - **7.** 700 tons

12 C

I. Vocabulary
a) 1. unemployment - **2.** sold - **3.** high - **4.** rough - **5.** put down into (the water) - **6.** small
b) 1. John's business is a *success*. - **2.** The *establishment* of new companies brought employment to the people of West Cork. - **3.** The steady *growth* of towns means increased demands for water. - **4.** Following the *recommendation* of the committee, prices will be raised next year. - **5.** The mussels in this bag are two kilos in *weight*.

II. Understanding
1. ropes - **2.** mussels - **3.** seed - **4.** stockings - **5.** purification - **6.** barrels - **7.** thinned - **8.** harvested - **9.** depurated - **10.** graded ... weighed

12 D

I. Vocabulary
1. to examine - **2.** contamination/infection - **3.** to stop/to hinder - **4.** to take off/to take away - **5.** before

II. Understanding
1. Red tide can be harmful if shellfish consume toxic materials from the algae, which then enter the food chain. - **2.** The main pollution problem is that nutrients from farm land go into rivers and then into the bay where they can add to the growth of algae.

Note: There is also the risk of pollution from oil tankers in the bay, but this was not mentioned by Kevin James.

12 E

I. Vocabulary
1. to find - **2.** plenty of (mussels) - **3.** which has its headquarters - **4.** customer

II. Understanding
1. He invented a new method of freezing mussels which preserves all the natural juices within the shell. - **2.** It is very important for the economy and encourages young people to stay in Bantry. - **3.** There is a festival, where the producers give mussels away.

III. Grammar revision
1. economic ... extremely - **2.** Economically - **3.** delicious - **4.** tremendously high - **5.** willingly - **6.** unbelievably

12 F

I. Grammar revision
1. on - **2.** without - **3.** with - **4.** at ... of ... in - **5.** of ... at ... by

II. What about you?
(*no suggestion*)

12 G

I. Vocabulary

a) 1. approve of - **2.** limited - **3.** absolutely - **4.** occupied (with) - **5.** work/employment on land - **6.** be supported - **7.** several

b) 1. ugly - **2.** instability - **3.** unobtainable/unavailable - **4.** to increase

II. Understanding

1. It's an advantage for fish farmers such as John, because fish farming is funded by the EU. It's a disadvantage for the people who go out into the sea and catch whitefish, because the quotas have been restricted. - **2.** There would not be many fish left in the sea in a few years. - **3.** He would like to live in the Bantry area. He was brought up there (*or*: He has his roots there) and he loves the sea. - **4.** He has four children and his hope is that they will continue his business.

III. Translation

1. If he doesn't like it here, then let him work elsewhere. - **2.** What is that supposed to mean? - **3.** He is said to have four children. - **4.** The children have all emigrated. Now he will have to sell his business which he has so painstakingly built up. - **5.** That was meant to be an offer. - **6.** I don't want him to invest more money in the company.

12 H

I. What do you know about John and Maria Murphy?

1. businesses - **2.** fashion ... Dublin - **3.** mussel farming - **4.** company - **5.** Bantry - **6.** grandparents - **7.** eleven years ... fashion show ... clothes - **8.** children

II. Translation (*Suggestion*)

Fastnet Mussels Ltd befindet sich in Gearhies, in der Grafschaft Cork in Irland. Die Ursprünge des Unternehmens liegen in der gewerblichen Nutzung des Meeres, und es gilt als eines der Pioniere der Muschelzucht an Seilen (Strängen) in Irland. In den letzten zwölf Jahren belieferte Fastnet renommierte Märkte in ganz Europa mit einem Produkt der absoluten Spitzenklasse. Um eine gleichbleibende Qualität zu gewährleisten, legte Fastnet ein geschlossenes System von Rinnen an, die mit UV-behandeltem Seewasser gefüllt sind. Danach erfolgte der Bau einer Verarbeitungsanlage. Sie sollte die wichtigste Produktionseinheit für die damals gerade neu entwickelte, in der Schale gefrorene Muschel werden, auf die die Firma mit Recht stolz ist.

III. Comment (*Suggestion*)

Perhaps the main challenge is sorting out priorities. If John and Maria had no children, or if only one of them was working, the priorities might be easier to deal with. But in their circumstances, they have to keep asking themselves 'What is best for the family?' not just 'What would we like to do?' or 'What will earn us the most money?' There will be times when they have to put family interests before business interests, for example, when one of the children is ill, or even when it's just a question of a child having a birthday on the same day as an important business meeting in another part of the country. Or it might be the opposite, if, for instance, there is a crisis at work and the children's interests have to suffer.

John and Maria also face the challenge of organising their busy lives so that each one can take the right share of professional and domestic responsibilities. They may also need to get additional help at home to look after the children. Such help will have to be paid for if it comes from outside the family. If it comes from relatives, it could lead to pressures and problems with the family members involved.

12 I

Understanding

1. It was a reward for his loyalty to the English king. - **2.** It's a large home usually in the country belonging to the aristocracy or a rich family. - **3.** It's famous for the magnificent scenery and for its dramatic skies.

An advertising executive in London

13

13 B

I. Vocabulary

1. Mass communications such as the press (newspapers, magazines), broadcasting stations (television, radio), posters, etc - **2.** The use of media to inform consumers about products and to persuade them to buy the products concerned - **3.** The introduction of a new product onto the market - **4.** Project/Work that one has agreed to do

II. Understanding

1. An executive in an advertising agency who is in charge of a team responsible for one or more clients and their accounts - **2.** He's working on a campaign to launch the new Ford Mondeo.

13 D

I. Vocabulary

1. purchaser/sb who buys sth - **2.** picture/illustration - **3.** TV or radio advertisement - **4.** accepted - **5.** real

II. Understanding

1. A document produced by the agency's account planners, which gives the creative team the necessary guidance for designing and writing advertisements for a particular product - **2.** A copywriter works with other members of the creative team on the content of advertisements for a product, and also writes the words of the advertisements.

13 E

Questions

1. *Yes*. It will appeal to people looking for an up-market car which makes them more aware of what is happening when they drive it. The car is good-looking and also gives the impression of being reliable and able to deal with difficult roads. - *No*. The car is not very exciting and it is being driven by someone who seems unpleasant. He has already left his girlfriend once and looks as if he might do so again. Who would want to buy a car that appeals to people like that? - **2.** Advertisers have to appeal to people's feelings about themselves and about the world around them. So TV commercials often look at the kind of people who use the product advertised, and at their lives, rather than just at the product itself. - **3.** The director has to turn a lot of ideas into an attractive film lasting less than a minute. And the commercial he directs has to be better than all the other commercials for the same kind of product.

13 F

I. Vocabulary

a) 1. award - **2.** stunning - **3.** creative - **4.** charming - **5.** peculiarly

b) 1. campaign - **2.** market - **3.** advertisement - **4.** advertising ... ads - **5.** advertisers - **6.** copywriters

II. Understanding

1. British advertisers put creativity at the heart of their business. - **2.** A commercial which was part of an advertising campaign for Rowntree's jelly. A commercial for BUPA, a private health insurance company - **3.** Advertisements for most health insurance companies concentrate on people being cured when they have become ill, but the BUPA campaign does not mention illness. It tells consumers that BUPA wants them to stay healthy.

13 G

I. Vocabulary

1. g) - **2.** c) - **3.** f) - **4.** d) - **5.** a) - **6.** e) - **7.** b)

II. Questions
1. Posters, telephone, mail, Internet - **2.** The personality becomes associated with the product, and might damage his/her career. If the personality becomes less successful, the product suffers because it is associated with failure rather than success.

III. Grammar revision
1. started ... thought ... tried ... were ... 've never looked back - **2.** invented - **3.** has been losing - **4.** had to be cut ... be shown - **5.** disappeared ... would go

13 H

I. Vocabulary
a) 1. He had lost his *belief* in God. - **2.** His letter contained words of *encouragement*. - **3.** *Persuasion* is better than force in international relations. - **4.** The actor made his first *appearance* in a TV commercial. - **5.** The young driver was responsible for the *delivery* of the vans. - **6.** The furniture is ready for *removal* from the house. - **7.** He said his girlfriend was an *embarrassment* for his family.
b) 1. c) - **2.** a) - **3.** a) - **4.** d) - **5.** d) - **6.** a)

II. Understanding
1. They have advertised in support of the government's anti-drugs campaign, by drawing attention to the harm drugs can cause. They started a campaign aimed at young people convincing them not to sniff glue. - **2.** The vans were delivered back to the client without their roofs. The driver of the lorry carrying the vans had to pass under a bridge which was so low that all the roofs had been removed from the vans.

13 I

What about you?
(*no suggestion*)

13 J

What do you know about Simon?
1. advertising agency - **2.** Account Director - **3.** launch - **4.** hours - **5.** cricket - **6.** shopping ... antiques

Crossword puzzle (*page 264*)

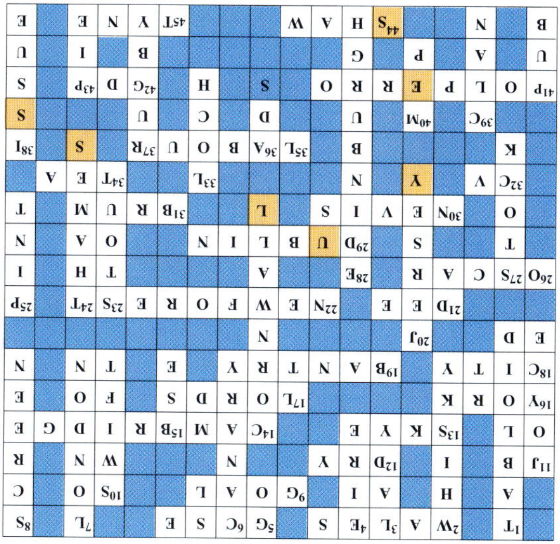

Wordlist

a

access 8 A	zugreifen auf
accessible 11 E	zugänglich
acclaim 5 E	anerkennen
accommodation 5 B	Unterkunft, Quartier
accomplished 11 B	fähig, vollendet, perfekt
account 13 B	(*Werbung*) Etat
account director 13 A	(*Werbung*) Kundenberater, Etatdirektor
account for 5 J	ausmachen, der Grund sein für
account planners 13 D	Planungsabteilung
accountancy 2 C	Rechnungswesen, Buchhaltung; Steuerberatung
accounts 3 E	Einnahmen und Ausgaben
accurate 13 B	genau, sorgfältig
achievement 6 G	Leistung
act 12 E	Veranstaltung
admit 13 I	zugeben, eingestehen
adopt 10 G	annehmen
adult 1 G	Erwachsene(r)
adventurous 5 C	abenteuerlustig
adversarial 10 F	gegnerisch
advertising agency 13 A	Werbeagentur
affect 1 J	sich auswirken, beeinflussen
affected by 10 C	betroffen von
affordable 3 B	erschwinglich
agency 9 A	Geschäftsstelle, Behörde
aggressive 7 F	hart, aufdringlich
agreement 12 G	Vereinbarung, Abmachung
agriculture 9 B	Landwirtschaft
air 1 G	*hier*: (eine Meinung) verbreiten, darlegen
air 10 L	*hier*: Note
airtime 13 G	Sendezeit
algae 12 D	Algen
aloft 11 C	empor, nach oben, in die Luft
amalgam 11 B	Mischung
ambition 1 B	Ziel, Ehrgeiz
amend 10 G	ändern
an awful lot 3 G	ziemlich viel
annoy 11 B	ärgern
annual 10 K	jährlich, Jahres-
antidote 2 H	*hier*: Ausgleich, Gegenmittel
antiques market 13 A	Antiquitätenmarkt
appallingly 10 I	entsetzlich
appeal to 13 D	ansprechen, Anklang finden bei
apple pie 3 C	Apfelkuchen
application 6 F	Bewerbung
application 9 D	*hier*: Antrag, Anmeldung
apply for 6 F	sich bewerben um
appoint 5 I	ernennen
appreciate 12 F	zu schätzen wissen
apprentice 4 A	Lehrling, Auszubildende(r)

apprenticeship 4 A	Lehre, Lehrzeit
approach 1 C	*hier*: Aufmachung
approach 11 J	Vorstoß, Ansatz, Methode
approximately 12 C	annähernd
aquaculture 12 G	Fischzucht
arbiter 1 E	Herr, Gebieter
arched 7 G	gewölbt
arch-enemy 10 K	Erzfeind
archery 5 E	Bogenschießen
area of policy 5 I	Fachgebiet
aristocracy 12 I	Adel
articulate 6 L	*hier*: gut
as a rule 5 C	in der Regel
ashore 12 I	an Land
assassination 1 G	Ermordung
assemble 4 B	zusammensetzen, -bauen, montieren
assembly 2 E	Versammlung; Morgenandacht
assembly area 4 B	Montagehalle, Montagebereich
assembly line 8 E	Fließband
assimilate 13 D	aufnehmen, integrieren
assist 7 B	helfen
association 5 E	Vereinigung, Verein
at a professional level 9 I	in beruflicher Hinsicht
at first hand 2 B	aus erster Hand
at the outside 12 E	im äußersten Fall
atrocious 2 J	grauenhaft, widerwärtig
attempt 9 K	Versuch
attend 2 J	besuchen
attitude 10 J	Einstellung, Haltung
audience 11 B	Publikum
authority 1 F	*hier*: Kompetenz
award 11 D	zusprechen, auszeichnen mit
award-winning 13 F	preisgekrönt

b

Bachelor of Laws 6 A	*etwa*: Magister der rechtswissenschaftlichen Fakultät
backup 5 E	Unterstützung
backwater 6 M	Stauwasser
bailiff 5 I	Verwalter, Minister
banking system 11 G	Computersystem (für Banken)
Bar 6 C	Anwaltschaft
bargain 7 D	*hier*: Sonderpreis
barley 3 F	Gerste
barrel 12 C	Faß
barrier 6 C	Schranke, Sperre
barrister 6 B	Rechtsanwalt, -anwältin *bei Gericht*
basics 8 J	Grundbegriffe, Grundlagen
battlefield 10 D	Schlachtfeld
be articulate 11 B	sich gut/klar ausdrücken können
be associated with 11 A	verbunden sein mit
be based at 5 B	seinen Sitz (*hier*: Büro) haben in
be computer-literate 8 B	einen Computer bedienen können, sich auskennen

be delighted 11 B	erfreut, entzückt sein
be detached from 1 B	losgelöst, abgetrennt sein von
be dilatory in 1 E	sich Zeit lassen mit
be due to 5 E	aufgrund, zurückzuführen sein auf
be fortunate 9 B	Glück haben
be in charge of 7 A	verantwortlich sein für
be in decline 13 K	verfallen
be inclined to 11 B	neigen zu
be involved in sth 1 B	mit etw. zu tun haben
be out of step 1 G	nicht im Gleichklang sein
be related to 10 K	verwandt sein mit
be set in 11 A	angesiedelt sein in
be subject to 5 I	unterworfen sein
be tied 3 D	gebunden, verpflichtet sein
bear in mind 6 F	im Auge behalten, nicht vergessen
benefactor 2 J	Wohltäter(in), Gönner(in)
benefit 5 E	Nutzen
billboard 13 G	Reklametafel
bio-degradable 9 I	biologisch abbaubar
blanch 12 E	blanchieren
blended 9 F	(mit anderen Sorten) vermischt
bloody 11 G	(*slang*) verdammt
bluntly 11 G	geradeheraus, unverblümt
board 7 B	einsteigen
boarding school 2 G	Internat(sschule)
bolt 2 J	Bolzen
booking 5 B	Buchung, Bestellung
books 3 E	Einnahmen und Ausgaben
bottom 12 B	Grund, Boden
bowl 11 C	Schale
break 2 E	Pause, Unterbrechung
breather 2 E	Verschnaufpause
brief 13 C	instruieren, beauftragen; Instruktion, Auftrag
brief 6 C	Unterlagen zu einem Fall; Auftrag an einen Anwalt
broad-based 4 D	breitgefächert
broadcast 10 J	im Hörfunk sprechen
broadsheets 1 C	*seriöse Presse*
BSE 10 H	BSE, Rinderwahn(sinn)
buoyant 12 C	schwimmend
burial ground 5 H	Begräbnisstätte
bury 9 C	begraben, eingraben
business administration 8 I	*etwa*: Betriebswirtschaft
buzz 13 J	*hier*: Aufregung
by virtue of that 3 D	aufgrund dessen, deshalb

C

cage 9 D	Käfig
calculation 2 J	Berechnung
calibre 8 H	Format
calm 12 C	ruhig
campus 6 D	Universitätsgelände
carbon 9 D	Kohle(nstoff)

career path 6 B	Laufbahn, Karriereweg
career prospects 6 A	Berufsaussichten
carer 9 I	im Sozialbereich Tätige(r)
cargo (*pl* -oes) 13 L	Ladung
carpenter 4 B	Schreiner, Tischler
cask 9 F	Faß
cast 6 M	*hier*: gießen
casting 4 B	Abguß
casual worker 12 C	Gelegenheits-, Saisonarbeiter(in)
catch 12 G	Fang
catch the eye 13 G	(die) Aufmerksamkeit gewinnen
cater for 3 B	mit Speisen und Getränken versorgen
catering college 5 E	Hotelfachschule
catering crew 7 C	für Speisen und Getränke zuständiges Zugpersonal
cattle 9 K	Vieh
cede 9 K	abtreten
celebrate 6 A	feiern
celebration 11 C	Verherrlichung
censor in (a mistake) 1 F	absichtlich (einen Fehler) machen
chair 10 A	den Vorsitz führen
challenge 8 F	Herausforderung
chamber 10 F	(Parlaments-)Kammer
chambers *pl* 6 C	(Anwalts-)Kanzlei
champion 11 J	eintreten, sich engagieren für
chassis 8 E	Gehäuse
chat 6 D	plaudern
china clay 4 B	Porzellanerde, Kaolin
circuit 8 E	Schaltung, Schaltsystem
circulation 1 C	Auflage
Cistercian 10 L	Zisterzienser
citizen 5 I	(Staats-)Bürger(in)
civil service 6 B	Staatsdienst
claim 6 L	Aussage
claim 8 K	beanspruchen, behaupten
clam 12 F	Venusmuschel
clergyman 1 B	Geistlicher, Pfarrer, Seelsorger
clerk 11 B	Angestellte(r)
client 13 A	Kunde, Kundin
climbing frame 3 D	Klettergerüst
cloisters 2 J	(Kloster-)Kreuzgang
cloth 8 K	Tuch, Stoff
cluster 12 C	Büschel, Gruppe
coal-mining community 10 C	Bergarbeiter-Siedlung
coating 4 B	Überzug, Schicht; Anstrich
cobbled street 3 H	Straße mit Kopfsteinpflaster
cod 3 C	Kabeljau
collect 3 C	*hier*: einziehen, kassieren
collide 10 J	zusammenprallen, -stoßen
column 1 B	Kolumne, Spalte
come to grief 5 H	zu Schaden kommen
come up with 12 E	kommen auf, sich ausdenken

commemorate 5 D	gedenken
commercial 1 I	Werbefilm, Werbespot
commercial (television) 13 A	Werbespot
commercial premise 9 H	Gewerbegebiet
commission 11 B	in Auftrag geben
commit 10 G	verpflichten
committee 10 B	Ausschuß
common 10 F	gemeinsam
common room 2 E	Gemeinschaftsraum
communicate 5 I	in Verbindung stehen, sich verständigen
communicator 6 L	Redner
commuter 7 B	Pendler(in)
compensation 10 C	Entschädigung
competition 7 F	Wettbewerb, Konkurrenz
complaint 5 G	Beschwerde
complement 10 J	ergänzen
component 4 B	(Maschinen-)Teil
composite 11 B	Montage, Mischung
compulsory 2 F	verpflichtend
conceive 2 H	denken, vorstellen
conceive 12 E	sich ausdenken
conception 12 B	Vorstellung(svermögen)
concern 9 B	Anliegen, Sorge
concrete 5 H	Beton
conditional 10 J	bedingt
conductor 7 A	Zugführer; Schaffner
confectionery 7 J	Konfekt, Süßwaren
confine to 9 H	beschränken auf
connoisseur 9 G	Kenner
conquer 10 L	besiegen, bezwingen
consensus 10 F	Übereinstimmung
constituency 10 A	Wahlkreis
constituent 10 F	Wähler(in)
constraint 9 B	Ein-, Beschränkung; Zwang
consult 2 H	zu Rate ziehen
consume 12 D	aufnehmen, verzehren
consumer 13 C	Verbraucher(in)
contamination 12 C	Verunreinigung,Verschmutzung
contemplate 2 H	nachdenken über
contract 10 B	schrumpfen
contradiction 1 E	Widerspruch
contribute 12 D	beitragen
contribution 9 I	Beitrag
convenient 8 C	zweckmäßig, praktisch, vorteilhaft
convert 13 K	umwandeln, umbauen
convert into 5 D	umwandeln in
cope with 9 E	fertigwerden, zurechtkommen mit, vertragen
copper 4 I	Kupfer
copy 1 B	Exemplar; Text
copy 1 E	*hier*: Artikel
copywriter 13 D	Werbetexter(in)
coral settlement 12 C	Korallenansiedlung
coronation 1 G	Krönung

cost-effectiveness 8 D Rentabilität, Preis-Leistungsverhältnis
counsel 6 C Ratgeber
counter clerk 11 G Schalterbeamter, -beamtin
county 4 I Grafschaft
couple 5 D Paar
courier 5 B Reiseleiter(in)
court circular 1 G Hofnachrichten
courtyard 2 J (Innen-)Hof
cover 1 B (*Presse*) berichten über
coverage of 1 B Berichterstattung über
craft 4 D Handwerk, Gewerbe
creative brief 13 D (*Werbung*) Vorgabe, Instruktion für die Produktion eines Werbespots
crop 12 F Ernte
cross-functional 8 D multipel
crucial 1 B entscheidend, äußerst wichtig
crusader 10 L Kreuzritter
curly 11 G lockig, kraus
currency 5 J Währung
curriculum 2 G Lehrplan
curriculum vitae (CV) 6 A Lebenslauf
custard 3 C Vanillesoße
customs clerk 11 B Zollbeamter, -beamtin
cut back 1 F sich einschränken
cyanide 9 D Zyanid, Blausäuresalz

d

daring 10 J Kühnheit
database 8 B Datenbank
deadline 1 E letzter Termin, *hier*: Redaktionsschluß
debeard 12 C (Muschel-)Bart abnehmen, Haftfäden (bei Muscheln) abnehmen
decline 10 B Rückgang, Niedergang
decline 7 I abnehmen
deem sth to be 2 I etw. erachten, halten für
demanding 2 C anspruchsvoll
denomination 1 J Konfession, Bekenntnis
departure 11 F *hier*: Abweichen, Ausnahme
deposit 5 J Guthaben
depurate 12 C reinigen
deputy head teacher 2 A stellvertretende(r) Schulleiter(in)
derive 11 I her-, ableiten
design 8 D Entwurf
desktop 8 C Schreibtisch, Desktop (liegendes Computergehäuse)
destination 7 D Ziel
devise 11 B sich ausdenken
devote 1 G widmen
diary 1 E *hier*: Terminkalender
dictate 8 H vorgeben, diktieren
differ 12 F sich unterscheiden
directive 9 C Weisung
disabled *pl* 3 G Behinderte
discerning 3 B anspruchsvoll, kritisch

discharge 9 C	Ausströmen, Ausstoß
discounted 7 D	ermäßigt
dispatch 7 G	*hier*: Abfahrt
dispatch 8 E	Versand
dispose of 9 D	beseitigen
dissolve 2 J	auflösen
distillery 9 A	(Branntwein-)Brennerei, Destillerie
distinctive 3 C	unverkennbar, unverwechselbar
distinguished 10 E	ausgezeichnet, herausragend
distribution 8 H	Vertrieb, Verbreitung
district 11 J	Bezirk, Gebiet
diving 5 C	Tauchen
do jet-skiing 5 D	Wasserski fahren
do up 3 D	herrichten, renovieren
domestic politics 1 F	Innenpolitik
dominate 8 H	beherrschen
donkey 3 D	Esel
donor 10 B	Spender(in), Stifter(in)
down river 13 K	flußabwärts
downtrodden 11 B	unterdrückt, geknechtet
dram 9 F	Schluck Whisky
draught beer 3 F	Faßbier
dredge 12 B	ausbaggern
dressing-gown 11 C	Morgen-, Bademantel
dumping 9 B	(Schutt-, Müll-)Abladen
duty 5 A	Pflicht, Aufgabe
dwindle 10 K	abnehmen, schrumpfen

e

earnestness 10 J	Ernst(haftigkeit)
earnings *pl* 11 B	Verdienst, Ertrag
Easter Rising 11 J	Osteraufstand
economics 1 F	*hier*: Wirtschaft
edition 1 E	Ausgabe (*einer Zeitung*)
editor 1 A	Chefredakteur(in)
editorial 1 G	redaktionell, Redaktions-
efficient 7 F	leistungsfähig
effort 6 I	Mühe, Anstrengung
elate 11 H	begeistern, in Hochstimmung versetzen
electronics engineer 8 A	Elektroingenieur(in)
Eleven-Plus (examination) 2 F	*Aufnahmeprüfung ins Gymnasium*
e-mail (short for *electronic mail*) 8 I	E-Mail (*elektronische Post*)
embarrassing 13 H	peinlich
embassy 6 F	Botschaft
emergency 9 C	Notfall, Notlage
emit 9 D	ausstoßen
emphasis 2 F	Betonung, (Schwer-)Gewicht
employer 6 G	Arbeitgeber(in)
encapsulate 12 E	in der Schale lassen, umhüllen
encounter 11 B	Begegnung, Treffen
encounter group 11 B	(*psych.*) Encountergruppe
encouraging 6 I	ermutigend
end user 12 E	Endverbraucher
endowment 2 J	Stiftung, Schenkung

enforce 9 C durchführen, geltend machen, sorgen für
engineering 2 C Ingenieurwesen, Maschinenbau, Technik
enlarge 10 I erweitern
enquirer 5 E (Nach-)Fragende(r)
ensure 5 B sicherstellen, sichergehen
entail 2 C mit sich bringen, erfordern
enter up 3 E eintragen
enterprise 7 E Unternehmen
entrance exam 2 G Aufnahmeprüfung
environment 2 B Umwelt; Umfeld, Umgebung
environment protection 9 A Umweltschutz
environmental regulator 9 B Umweltschützer(in)
environmentalist 9 B Umweltschützer(in)
equipment 7 C Ausrüstung, Ausstattung
era 2 H *hier*: Generation
establish oneself 1 B sich etablieren, anerkannt werden
Established Church 1 B Staatskirche
evidence 10 D Beweis
executive 5 A leitende(r) Angestellte(r), Manager(in)
executive body 10 G ausführendes Organ
exhibition 5 B Ausstellung
explore 5 C erkunden, erforschen, entdecken
expose 11 D aufdecken, darlegen, offenbaren
extract 11 C Auszug
extra-curricular 6 F nicht zum Lehrplan gehörend
extravert 10 J extrovertiert, nach außen gekehrt

f

facet 11 B Seite, Aspekt
facilities 2 G Einrichtungen
factual account 1 D Tatsachenbericht
faculty 6 D Fakultät, Fachbereich
fail 12 F scheitern, *hier*: schlecht ausfallen
fair 12 I *hier*: ganz ordentlich, ziemlich viel
fairly 1 C recht
faith 1 J Glaube
fall back on 4 G zurückgreifen auf
famine 11 J Hungersnot
fare 7 D Fahrpreis
far-flung 6 I abgelegen
farmhouse 5 E Bauernhof, -haus
farrier 3 E Hufschmied
favourable 10 L positiv
feat 12 B Leistung
feature 11 C vorkommen, (mit)spielen
feature 3 D Merkmal, Besonderheit
feed cycle 12 B Ernährungszyklus
felicity of the music 1 B Musikauswahl
fellow 2 J *hier*: Mitglied der Universität, des akademischen Lehrkörpers
ferment 3 F gären, zur Gärung bringen
fertile 9 G fruchtbar
festivity 12 E Feier, Festlichkeit
fibre 9 D Faser

fiercely 11 D	schonungslos, scharf, heftig
figures 3 E	Zahlen
file 6 L	Akte
final product 8 D	Endprodukt
first edition 11 D	Erstausgabe
fish farm 9 A	Fischzucht(anlage)
fishing community 12 A	Fischerdorf
fit 4 B	*hier*: montieren, einbauen
flabbergast 13 H	verblüffen
flavour 9 F	Geschmack, Aroma
fleet 12 G	Flotte
flesh 12 F	(Muschel-)Fleisch
flooding 13 K	Überfluten
fluently 10 K	fließend
fly-tipping 9 B	illegales Müllabladen
focal point 3 B	Mittelpunkt, Brennpunkt
focus on 7 B	sich konzentrieren auf
food chain 12 D	Nahrungskette
food poisoning 12 A	Lebensmittelvergiftung
foothold 8 H	Stand, Halt, sichere Ausgangsposition
footpath 9 I	Fußweg
for pleasure 7 H	zum Vergnügen
foreign affairs 1 F	Außenpolitik
forestry 9 B	Forstwirtschaft
forever 11 B	immer, ständig, ewig
form tutor 2 E	Klassenlehrer
found 2 J	(be)gründen
founder 8 K	(Be-)Gründer(in)
foundry 4 B	Gießerei
franchise 7 F	Lizenz
franchisee 7 F	Lizenznehmer
frankly 2 C	offen gestanden, ehrlich gesagt
freelance 1 G	freiberuflich, freischaffend
freight 7 G	Fracht
frock 11 F	Gehrock
full-scale 8 E	großangelegt, umfassend
fully licensed 3 C	mit voller Schankkonzession, -erlaubnis
funding 10 C	Geldbeschaffung
fund-raising 3 G	Geldbeschaffung
funds *pl* 3 G	Mittel, Gelder
funeral 1 G	Trauerfeier, Begräbnis
furnishings 12 I	Mobiliar, Einrichtung
further education 2 F	*hier*: Weiterbildung, schulische Fortbildung
further education college 4 A	Berufsschule, Schule für Weiterbildung

galore 12 E	in Hülle und Fülle
gather 9 K	sich versammeln
gathering 2 E	Versammlung, Zusammenkunft
GCSE examinations (= General Certificate of Secondary Education) 2 C	*entspricht etwa der Mittleren Reife*
gee 11 G	(*slang*) Mensch, Mann
general election 10 E	allgemeine Wahlen (*Unterhauswahlen*)
gently 11 C	behutsam, sachte

get rid of 12 B	loswerden
glamour 7 G	Glanz
glue 13 H	Klebstoff
go on the swings 2 H	schaukeln (gehen)
go without saying 12 G	sich von selbst verstehen
goal 9 H	Ziel
gorgeous 11 G	großartig, hinreißend
the Gospels 11 J	das Evangelium
gossip 2 E	Klatsch, Tratsch; Schwatz
grade 12 C	klassifizieren
graduate 6 B	Hochschulabsolvent(in); graduieren, die Abschlußprüfung bestehen
graduation day 6 A	Abschlußfeier (*an der Universität*)
grain 3 F	Korn, Getreide
graph 8 B	Schaubild, Diagramm
graze 3 H	weiden, grasen
greyhound racing 6 D	Windhundrennen
grief 1 G	Trauer
Gross Domestic Product (GDP) 5 J	Bruttosozialprodukt (BSP)
grounding 4 G	Grundwissen, Grundlagen
guard 7 B	Schaffner(in), Zugbegleiter(in)
guidance 4 D	Führung, (An-)Leitung
guild 5 E	Gilde, Verein
guy 12 C	Typ, Kerl, Bursche
guys 12 C	*hier*: Leute
gym(nasium) 6 D	Sporthalle, Fitnessraum

h

habit 7 H	Gewohnheit
half one 11 G	halb zwei (Uhr)
halt 10 K	zum Stillstand bringen
hands-on 4 D	praktisch, aktiv
handy 10 J	geschickt, praktisch
harm 9 I	schaden, verletzen
harmful 12 D	schädlich
harvest 12 C	Ernte; ernten
hatch 9 D	(aus)brüten
have dealings with 6 C	zu tun haben mit
head of state 10 G	Staatsoberhaupt
headline 1 B	Schlagzeile
headquarters 9 A	Hauptsitz
heartland 9 G	Kernland
help line 13 H	Notrufstelle
hemicycle 10 I	Halbkreis
hence 9 G	also
heritage 11 E	Erbe, Erbschaft
high tide 5 H	Flut
hill 8 K	Hügel
Home Rule 11 J	Selbstbestimmung, -verwaltung
honeymoon 5 D	Flitterwochen
honour 11 B	Ehre
honour 9 G	ehren, respektieren
hops 3 F	Hopfen

horseradish 3 C Meerrettich
hospitality 5 E Gastfreundschaft
hotel staff 5 E Hotelpersonal
House of Commons 10 E (britisches) Unterhaus
House of Lords 10 E (britisches) Oberhaus
housemate 6 D Mitbewohner(in)
humanity subjects 2 C Geisteswissenschaften
hurdle 6 E Hindernis, Hürde

i

illuminated 11 J *hier*: verziert
imminent 8 H unmittelbar bevorstehend
impact 1 G (Aus-)Wirkung
impose 11 I auferlegen, aufdrängen, verhängen
impose 5 J (*Steuern*) erheben
in court 6 C vor Gericht
in dread of 3 E in (ständiger) Angst vor
in power 10 E an der Macht
in terms of 3 A betreffend
in the course 1 J während, im Laufe
in the long run 10 F auf (die) Dauer
in turn 5 I wiederum
in vogue 3 B in Mode
inception 8 H Beginn, Anfang
incinerate 9 C verbrennen, einäschern
income tax 5 J Einkommensteuer
incredibly 1 E unglaublich, unwahrscheinlich
inevitably 2 C zwangsläufig, unweigerlich
infant 2 F (Klein-)Kind
influencing opinion 10 F meinungsbildend
Information Technology 8 F Informatik
inhabit 9 K bewohnen
inherit 10 E erben
inheritance tax 5 J Erbschaftsteuer
initiate 6 L anstoßen, initiieren
injection 8 H Spritze, *hier*: Schub
innovation 8 H Neuerung
Inns of Court 6 C *die vier englischen* Juristenverbände
inscription 11 C Inschrift
insight 10 J Einblick
insured 10 C versichert
insurer 13 F Versicherer
intentional 7 B absichtlich
internal 5 I innere, Innen-
into the forefront 9 H an die Spitze, *hier*: ins Blickfeld
intone 11 C anstimmen
invariably 2 C unweigerlich
investigate 2 B untersuchen
investment 5 J Investition
invoice 4 G (Waren-)Rechnung
inward-looking 10 J introvertiert, in sich gekehrt; beschaulich
iron 6 M Eisen
issue 1 B Frage, Angelegenheit, Problem

j

jacket potato 3 C	in der Schale gebackene Kartoffel
jelly 13 F	Gelee, Götterspeise
justify 2 I	rechtfertigen

k

keep ahead of 8 E	einen Vorsprung sichern vor, einen Schritt voraus sein
keep up with 8 J	Schritt halten, mithalten mit
keep your voice down 11 G	sprich bitte leiser
keyboard 8 C	Tastatur
kitchen-sink play 11 F	Alltags-, Wohnküchendrama
knit 5 H	stricken
know the ropes 4 E	sich auskennen

l

landfill (site) 9 C	Mülldeponie, -halde
landlord 3 D	Gastwirt (*gleichzeitig Eigentümer des Pubs*)
landmark 11 J	Wahrzeichen
large-scale 8 D	großangelegt
lather 11 C	(Seifen-)Schaum
launch 13 A	(*Produkt*) auf den Markt bringen, einführen
law 2 C	Recht
lawyer 6 B	Anwalt, Anwältin
leader 1 G	Leitartikel
leading article 1 G	Leitartikel
leaning 10 L	schräg, schief
lease 3 D	Pacht(vertrag)
leasing 7 F	Pacht
lecture 6 D	Vorlesung
lecturer 4 A	Dozent(in)
legislation 9 C	Gesetzgebung
let 7 F	vergeben, vermieten
Letter to the Editor 1 G	Leserbrief
level 9 D	Grad, Stufe
licence fee 1 I	*hier*: Fernsehgebühr
license 9 A	eine Lizenz, Konzession vergeben an
licensing laws 3 B	Schankgesetze (*Gesetz über den Ausschank und Verkauf alkoholischer Getränke*)
lifestyle 9 H	Lebensstil, -weise
light-hearted 1 G	unbekümmert, vergnüglich
lighthouse 5 H	Leuchtturm
limit oneself 6 E	sich beschränken
limitation 5 F	Beschränkung, Einschränkung
Limited liability company (Ltd) 4 A	Gesellschaft mit beschränkter Haftung (GmbH)
line 13 F	*hier*: Werbespruch
linen 8 K	Leinen
litter 9 I	Abfälle
location 8 K	Lage
loch (*in Scotland*) 9 C	See
locker 3 D	Schließfach, *hier*: Safe
lodging house 3 C	Pension
log 7 B	Aufzeichnungen

lonely 9 J einsam
long-distance train 7 G Fernverkehrszug
lorry 13 H Lastwagen
low tide 5 H Ebbe
loyalty 12 I Treue

m

mackerel 12 G Makrele
mad cow disease 10 H Rinderwahn(sinn)
mainland Europe 5 C das europäische Festland
maintenance 4 E Wartung, Instandhaltung
make aware of 13 E bewußtmachen
male voice choir 10 K Männerchor
male-orientated 3 B für Männer bestimmt
malt 3 F Malz
manor house 5 E Herrenhaus
Manufacturing Process Proving 8 E *etwa*: Herstellungskontrolle
marine 12 D Meeres-, See-
markedly 10 J merklich, wesentlich
marketplace 8 H *hier*: Markt
mature 9 F reifen, reif werden
measure 7 E Maßnahme
media 13 B Medien
media tycoon 1 B Medienmagnat, -zar
medieval 5 H mittelalterlich
Member of the European Parliament (MEP) 10 B Europaabgeordnete(r)
memorable 10 J denkwürdig, unvergeßlich
mentally handicapped 3 G geistig behindert
merchant 6 F Handels-
millenium 1 J Jahrtausend
Mine Host 3 E Herr Wirt
minor 6 C unbedeutend, geringer
minority 10 E Minderheit
misinformation 10 D Fehlinformation
misread 7 B falsch lesen, nicht richtig verstehen
missile 1 G Rakete
molten 4 B geschmolzen
monastery 2 J Kloster
monitor 8 D überwachen, kontrollieren
monk 3 H Mönch
mood 10 J Stimmung
mooring 13 K Anlegesteg
mosque 1 B Moschee
motherboard 8 E Hauptplatine
mould 4 B (Guß-)Form
mound 5 H Hügel
mount 8 E montieren
move 8 B Schritt
munroe (*in Scotland*) 9 J Berg
mussel 12 A (Mies-)Muschel
mussel farming 12 A Muschelzucht

n

National Assembly 10 A Nationalversammlung
National Vocational Qualification (NVQ) 4 A *etwa*: Staatliches Zeugnis über den Abschluß einer Berufsausbildung

nationalise 7 E verstaatlichen
nationwide 9 I landesweit
negotiate 9 E ver-, aushandeln
neighbouring 12 I benachbart
network 8 C Netz(werk)
news desk 1 E Nachrichtenredaktion
news editor 1 E Nachrichtenredakteur
newspaper cutting 6 L Zeitungsausschnitt
noble 9 G edel
notion 11 F Vorstellung, Idee, Gedanke
novel 11 A Roman
novelist 11 A Romanschriftsteller(in), Romancier
novelty value 3 D Neuheitswert, Reiz des Neuen
nuance 11 E Schattierung, Nuance
nuclear processing plant 9 B Atomkraftwerk
nursery ground 9 G Brutstätte
nutrient 12 D Nährstoff

o

oak 3 H Eiche
obituary 1 F Nachruf
objective 10 D Ziel
obscure 11 E *hier*: schwer verständlich
occasion 7 B Gelegenheit, *hier*: Ereignis
occupation 5 D Besatzung
odd 5 G merkwürdig, sonderbar, komisch
offend 11 B beleidigen, kränken
off-peak times 7 D außerhalb der Stoßzeit(en)
on business 7 H geschäftlich
on that count 1 G (*fig.*) in diesem Punkt
on the board 11 B im Ausschuß, im Aufsichtsrat, im Vorstand
onus 12 E Last, Pflicht
operate 7 F betreiben
operating speed 8 E Rechengeschwindigkeit
opt to 2 C sich entscheiden für
ordination 1 B Priesterweihe
ore 10 L Erz
organic 9 G biologisch
orthoptist 8 B Augenarzt, -ärztin
outcome 6 L Ergebnis
output 4 E *hier*: Leistung
output 9 G Produktion, Ausstoß
outweigh 2 H überwiegen
overall 10 G allgemein, umfassend
overlooking 8 K mit Blick, Aussicht auf
ownership 7 A Besitz, Eigentum
oxygen 9 G Sauerstoff
oyster 12 F Auster

p

package up 1 F	zusammenstellen, präsentieren
pad 8 C	Unterlage, Pad
painstaking 12 G	mühselig
palatable 1 F	schmackhaft, genießbar; (*fig.*) attraktiv
partition 11 J	teilen
pass a law 5 I	ein Gesetz verabschieden
pass grade 2 C	Abschluß-, Prüfungsnote
pastime 6 G	Freizeitbeschäftigung, Zeitvertreib
pattern 4 B	Muster, Vorlage, *hier*: Gußmodell
pavement 11 C	Pflaster
peasant play 11 F	Bauernstück
peat 9 F	Torf
peculiar 13 F	seltsam, eigenartig
peer 10 E	*Angehöriger des hohen Adels*
peninsula 4 I	Halbinsel
per annum 12 B	pro, im Jahr
perform 11 A	aufführen, darstellen
performance 2 F	*hier*: schulische Leistung
perpendicular 2 J	senkrecht, perpendikular
pesticide 12 D	Schädlingsbekämpfungsmittel
pharmaceutical 12 E	pharmazeutisch
pick a quarrel 10 F	einen Streit vom Zaun brechen
pick up on 11 E	entdecken
picket 1 F	Streikposten
pickle 3 C	(in Essig) eingelegtes Gemüse
picturesque 3 H	malerisch, pittoresk
pilgrimage 11 C	Wall-, Pilgerfahrt
pillar 7 G	Pfeiler, Säule
pit 4 B	Grube, Zeche
pit against 11 B	einander gegenüberstellen
placement 8 F	Praktikum
plaice 3 C	Scholle (*Fisch*)
plant 1 F	Werk(sgelände), Produktionsanlage
plant 8 A	Fabrik
player 1 F	Anbieter
playwright 11 A	Dramatiker(in), Stückeschreiber(in)
Plenary 10 F	Plenum, Vollversammlung
plough 3 C	pflügen
polarised 10 F	polarisiert, in (gegnerische) Lager geteilt
policy 11 F	Grundsatz
pollutant 9 G	Schadstoff
pollution 9 A	Verschmutzung
(a game of) pool 2 E	Billardspiel
pop in(to) 3 C	(auf einen Sprung) vorbeikommen, hineingehen in
porter 7 B	Gepäckträger
positioning research 13 D	Verbraucherforschung
possession 5 J	Besitz
postgraduate 6 I	Postgraduierte(r) (*führt seine/ihre Studien nach dem ersten Abschlußexamen weiter*)
postgraduate study 6 I	Anschlußstudium
pour (in) 4 B	*hier*: (*in die Form*) gießen

powerful 8 H	*hier*: günstig
pram 7 B	Kinderwagen
preach 8 K	predigen
precious 5 C	kostbar
predicted 6 F	vorhersehbar
pre-eminent 1 F	herausragend
preference 7 H	Vorliebe
pregnant 11 G	schwanger
premises *pl* 2 G	Gelände
prepare a brief 6 C	einen Fall vorbereiten
preserve 5 A	erhalten, bewahren
preside (over) 5 I	leiten
press release 1 E	Pressemitteilung
pressure 10 E	Druck
pressure group 9 H	Interessengruppe, -verband
prevent 9 C	verhindern
pride 10 K	Stolz
pride oneself on sth 5 E	sich einer Sache rühmen (können)
primarily 2 F	*hier*: höchstwahrscheinlich
primarily 9 H	hauptsächlich, in erster Linie
primary school 2 F	Grundschule
prior to 12 D	vor
processing 12 G	(Weiter-)Verarbeitung
proclamation 11 J	Verkündung, Ausrufung
progress 2 C	weiterkommen, Fortschritte machen, sich entwickeln
promote 5 A	werben für
promotion 3 E	Sonderangebot
proper 9 G	eigentlich, richtig
proportional representation 10 E	Verhältniswahlsystem
proposal 10 G	Antrag, Vorschlag
proposition 13 E	Vorschlag
proprietor 5 E	Eigentümer, Besitzer
prospects 2 D	Aussichten
prosperity 10 H	Wohlstand
public holiday 7 D	Feiertag
public services 7 E	öffentlicher Dienst
publican 3 A	Gastwirt (*und Pächter des Pubs*)
pull up 3 D	anhalten
purification 12 C	Reinigung
purpose 10 C	Zweck
pursue 1 E	verfolgen, recherchieren
put across 5 E	verständlich machen, vermitteln
put off 11 G	aufschieben
put sth on the spike 1 E	etw. nicht weiter verfolgen

q

quota 12 G	Quote
quote 4 B	Kostenvoranschlag

r

raft 12 B	Floß
railcard 7 D	Bahnkarte
range of 2 F	*hier*: Vielzahl an; Auswahl an

rate 7 D	*hier*: Tarif
reasonable 6 I	vernünftig, angemessen
receiver 1 I	Empfänger
recipient 10 I	Empfänger(in)
recite 10 K	vortragen, rezitieren
recommendation 2 C	Empfehlung
reconcile with 3 H	in Einklang bringen mit, miteinander vereinbaren
records 9 D	Unterlagen, Aufzeichnungen
recruit 6 B	einstellen, anstellen
recruitment policy 6 K	Einstellungspolitik
rectify 5 E	verbessern, korrigieren
red tide 12 C	giftige Algenpest
redevelopment 6 M	Sanierung
refer to 1 C	*hier*: bezeichnen
refer to 11 I	sich beziehen auf, verweisen auf
referendum 8 A	Volksentscheid
reflect 1 D	(wider)spiegeln
refugee disaster 1 B	Flüchtlingselend
registered company 5 J	eingetragene Firma
rehearsal 11 A	(Theater-)Probe
reject 10 E	ablehnen, zurückweisen
rejection slip 11 B	Absage
relay 7 G	weiterleiten
release 1 G	Freilassung
release 9 G	freisetzen
reliable 7 F	zuverlässig
relic 11 C	Überbleibsel, Relikt
reminder 8 K	Erinnerung, Mahnung
remit 11 B	Aufgabe, Auftrag
remote 3 B	entfernt, abgelegen
remote control 8 C	Fernbedienung
repack 12 C	umsetzen
report for duty 7 C	sich zum Dienst melden
reports 10 F	Berichte
request 5 E	erbitten, ersuchen um
requirement 8 E	Bedürfnis, Anspruch
requirement 11 B	Voraussetzung, Erfordernis
residence 5 J	Aufenthalt, Wohnsitz
resident 5 J	Einwohner(in)
resign 10 J	zurücktreten von, aufgeben, verzichten auf
resort 4 I	Urlaubsort
restored 7 A	restauriert
restrict 12 G	begrenzen, beschränken
retain 3 D	*hier*: beibehalten, bewahren
retired 5 C	im Ruhestand, pensioniert
re-train 10 I	umschulen
return ticket 7 D	Rückfahrkarte
revenue 5 J	Einnahmen, Einkünfte
review 1 B	Kritik, Besprechung
revise 10 E	überarbeiten, revidieren
revision 8 E	Überholen, Revision
revive 11 I	wiederbeleben
rewarding 2 H	lohnend, dankbar (*Aufgabe*)
ribbon 10 D	Band

rigorous 9 G streng
rivalry 11 F Rivalität
robotics 4 D Robotertechnik
rocky 4 I felsig
roll 3 B Brötchen
rolling stock 7 F rollendes Material, Fahrzeuge
rope 12 B Schnur, Seil, Leine
rose window 7 J Fensterrose
rotating engine 6 M Rotationsmaschine
rouse 1 G aufrütteln, wachrufen
rubbish 9 I Abfall, Müll
rugged 4 I zerklüftet
run 7 E betreiben, unterhalten
run-down 11 J heruntergekommen
running shoes 13 I Joggingschuhe
rural 3 H ländlich
rush hour 7 D Stoßzeit(en), Hauptverkehrszeit(en)

S

salmon 3 C Lachs
sample 3 E probieren, kosten
satisfaction 6 L Befriedigung
satisfactory 9 E befriedigend, zufriedenstellend
scallop 12 F Jakobsmuschel
scattered around 2 J verstreut liegen in
schedule 1 E *hier*: Terminplan
schedule 7 C Fahrplan
scheme 6 B *hier*: Programm
scholar 2 J Gelehrte(r)
sciences 2 C Naturwissenschaften
screen 8 C Bildschirm
screw 2 J Schraube
script 11 I Schrift
scrutinise 10 F untersuchen, genau prüfen
sculptor 4 I Bildhauer
seal 4 B versiegeln
seat reservation 7 B Platzreservierung
seed 12 C Samen
self-contained 6 H separat, unabhängig
self-contained 10 J distanziert
self-government 5 I Selbstverwaltung
senior 4 E höher, leitend
senior citizens 7 D Senioren, ältere Bürger
sense of belonging 2 I Zugehörigkeitsgefühl
sensitive 2 H empfindlich, reizbar
sermon 1 B Predigt
service 4 B (*Geräte*) warten, Inspektion machen; Kundendienst, Inspektion, Wartung
session 10 G Sitzung(speriode)
set apart from 6 F sich abheben, unterscheiden von
set eyes on 1 B zu Gesicht bekommen
set off 9 G (*zu etw.*) führen, bringen
set the presses rolling 1 E die Druckerpresse ins Rollen bringen
set up 9 G gründen, errichten

setting 10 L	Umgebung
setting 11 C	Rahmen, Schauplatz
settle 12 I	sich niederlassen
set-up 2 C	Organisation, Drum und Dran
sewage 9 E	Abwasser
share 7 E	Aktie
sharpen 13 E	schärfen
shell 12 C	Schale
shellfish 12 A	Schalen-, Krustentier(e)
shift 7 A	Schicht
shipwreck 12 I	Schiffbruch
shore 9 K	Ufer
shore 12 C	Strand
short term 4 E	kurzfristig
signalling 7 F	Signalübermittlung
significant 1 G	bedeutend, wichtig
signpost 3 C	Wegweiser
single ticket 7 D	Fahrkarte für einfache Fahrt
site 2 E	Platz, Stelle
sizeable 12 B	beträchtlich, ansehnlich
skill 6 G	Fähigkeit, Fertigkeit
slogan 13 G	Werbespruch
smoked 3 C	geräuchert
smooth 3 F	*hier*: weich
sniff 13 H	schnüffeln
snooker 4 F	Snooker (*dem Billiard verwandtes Spiel*)
soak 9 F	einweichen
sober 11 G	nüchtern
socialise 2 E	sich unterhalten, gesellschaftlich verkehren
solicitor 6 B	Rechtsanwalt, -anwältin, *der/die nicht vor Gericht plädiert*
sommelier 5 E	Weinverkoster
sort out 3 E	besprechen, klären
source of income 12 A	Einnahmequelle
space 13 G	Platz, Raum, Fläche
spacecraft 9 D	Raumfahrt
span 6 M	sich spannen, führen über
spark a debate 1 G	eine Diskussion auslösen
sparkling 9 F	sprudelnd, perlend
spawn 9 G	laichen
special requests 7 B	Sonderwünsche
spelling 11 I	Schreibweise
spiritual 'high' 1 B	Hochstimmung
sponsor 8 I	unterstützen, fördern
spreadsheet 8 J	Tabellenkalkulation(sprogramm)
squint 8 B	Schielen
stable 2 H	gefestigt, beständig
stage 8 E	Phase
stagecoach 3 D	Postkutsche
staging post (stage post) 3 D	Postkutschenstation
stained glass 7 J	Buntglas
stairhead 11 C	oberster Treppenabsatz
stately 11 C	stattlich

stately 12 I	herrschaftlich
steak and kidney pie 3 C	Fleischpastete mit Nieren
steam 7 A	Dampf
steam engine 7 I	Dampflok
still 9 F	Destillierapparat
stock exchange 7 E	Börse
stocking 5 H	Strumpf
stockings 12 C	Strümpfe; *hier*: längliche Netze
store 5 D	Lager, Vorrat
store 8 C	speichern
story 1 B	*hier*: Artikel
straight A grade 2 C	*entspricht etwa einer glatten Eins*
straightforward 8 G	einfach, unkompliziert
stretch 12 C	(sich) spannen
stringer 1 F	(freie/r) Lokalreporter(in), Berichterstatter(in) vor Ort
strip down 4 B	auseinandernehmen, zerlegen
strip off 12 C	entfernen
stronghold 9 K	Festung
strut at sb 10 F	sich aufblasen vor jmdm.
stuff 6 F	Zeug
stunning 13 F	überwältigend, großartig
subconscious 13 H	unterbewußt
sub-editor 1 E	Redakteur(in)
subject 1 G	*hier*: Untertan
subject 11 A	Thema
subscribe to 1 I	abonnieren
subsidise 7 E	subventionieren, unterstützen
substantial 7 F	wesentlich
substitute 6 K	Ersatz
suit 1 C	*hier*: befriedigen
suitability 6 G	Eignung
suitable 11 C	passend
sun-worship(ping) 5 C	Sonnenanbetung
supervise 8 A	beaufsichtigen, überwachen
supervisor 11 G	Aufsicht; Leiter(in)
supervisory 7 G	beaufsichtigend, überwachend
supplement 1 C	Beilage, Magazin
supplement 5 G	*hier*: Zuschlag
supplement 12 B	ergänzen
supplier 3 E	Lieferant(in)
support 7 G	*hier*: stützen
Supreme Governor of the Church of England 1 B	Oberhaupt der Anglikanischen Kirche
surface 8 C	Oberfläche
Surface Mount Technology 8 E	*etwa*: Oberflächenmontagetechnologie
surrounded by 9 J	umgeben von
surveying 2 C	Inspektion
survive 12 B	überleben
sustain 11 C	*hier*: tragen
sustain 12 G	erhalten
sweep the board 13 F	alle Preise gewinnen, abräumen
sweeping 6 L	drastisch, überragend

t

tabloid 1 B	Boulevardzeitung; Sensationspresse
take on 7 F	übernehmen
take on board 5 F	aufnehmen
take over 8 I	übernehmen, ablösen
take up 4 A	(*Karriere*) einschlagen
tangible 10 D	greifbar, handfest, real
tank 12 C	Kessel, Behälter
target at 13 H	(ab)zielen auf, als Zielgruppe haben
tartan 8 K	Schottenkaro
tasting 3 E	Kostprobe, Probieren
taxpayer 7 E	Steuerzahler(in)
technician 4 F	Techniker(in)
teetotal 3 G	abstinent
temporary 6 I	befristet, vorübergehend
tempt 4 F	verführen, verleiten
tend to 3 E	neigen, tendieren zu
test-tube baby 1 G	Retortenbaby
thin out 12 C	ausdünnen
three-fold 11 B	dreifach
tide 5 G	Flut, Gezeiten
tie 3 D	Bindung
tighten up on 9 E	strenger werden, härter durchgreifen bei
till 3 E	(Laden-)Kasse
timber 3 H	Holz
time-consuming 10 B	zeitaufwendig, -raubend
tin 4 I	Zinn
tin 9 I	Dose
tip 4 I	Spitze
tip-off 1 E	Tip, Wink
toll 3 C	Maut, Straßenzoll
tower 8 C	Turm, Tower (*stehendes Computergehäuse*)
toxic 12 D	giftig, Gift-
toxicity 12 D	Giftgehalt
toxin 12 D	Giftstoff
trace 6 L	ausfindig machen, auffinden
tracks 7 F	Schienen, Gleise
trainee 2 C	Auszubildende(r), Volontär(in), Praktikant(in)
transform 2 J	umwandeln
treasure 7 J	Kostbarkeit, Schatz
treasured 11 J	geschätzt, in Ehren gehalten
treatment of 9 C	Behandlung, Umgang mit
trial packet 13 I	Probepackung
tricky 13 H	schwierig, knifflig
try for 9 E	sich bemühen um
tuition 4 D	Unterricht
turn up 3 E	auftauchen, erscheinen
typify 11 J	verkörpern

u

unbiased 1 D	unvoreingenommen, neutral
undergraduate 2 J	Student(in)
undertaking 13 B	Projekt, Unternehmen
ungirdled 11 C	lose, offen, nicht zugebunden

unique 3 G	einzigartig
unmanageable 11 E	*hier*: schwer verständlich
unspoilt 3 H	unberührt; unverdorben
up-and-coming 1 B	vielversprechend, gefragt
up-market 13 D	anspruchsvoll, exklusiv
user friendly 8 G	benutzerfreundlich
utilities 7 E	Versorgungseinrichtungen

v

valuable 11 J	wertvoll
van 13 H	Lieferwagen, Transporter
vast bulk 7 F	Großteil
vector 4 C	Vektor
the very 5 E	genau der/die/das
vibrant 10 K	dynamisch, pulsierend
virtually 2 C	praktisch, fast, nahezu
vision 13 G	*hier*: Bild
visual 13 D	grafischer Entwurf
visual 13 G	Seh-, optisch
vocation 1 B	Berufung; Begabung
vocational 2 F	berufsbildend
voluntary 10 B	freiwillig
vote 10 E	(Wahl-)Stimme; wählen, abstimmen
voter 10 E	Wähler(in)
vowel 3 A	Vokal
vox pops 10 K	Meinungsumfrage

w

wages *pl* 3 E	Lohn, Löhne
warehouse 1 F	Lager(haus)
waste disposal 9 A	Müllbeseitigung, Abfallentsorgung
watch-tower 11 C	Wachturm
wealthy 2 G	wohlhabend
weigh 12 C	wiegen
weld 4 B	(zusammen)schweißen
wharf (*pl* -ves) 13 K	Kai
wheel-chair 7 B	Rollstuhl
whitefish 12 G	Weißfisch
white-washed 4 I	weiß getüncht
wink 11 G	zwinkern, blinzeln
wobbly 13 F	wacklig
wobbly dessert 13 F	Wackelpudding, Götterspeise
word processing 8 B	Textverarbeitung
work experience 6 G	Berufserfahrung
work-experience placement 6 H	Praktikum, Weiterbildung
workforce 5 E	Arbeitskräfte
workplace 4 C	Arbeitsplatz
worthwhile 3 G	lohnend, *hier*: lebenswert

x

X-ray 1 G	Röntgenstrahl

y

year out 6 F	einjähriger Auslandsaufenthalt
yeast 3 F	Hefe

Crossword puzzle

(*Solution page 241*)

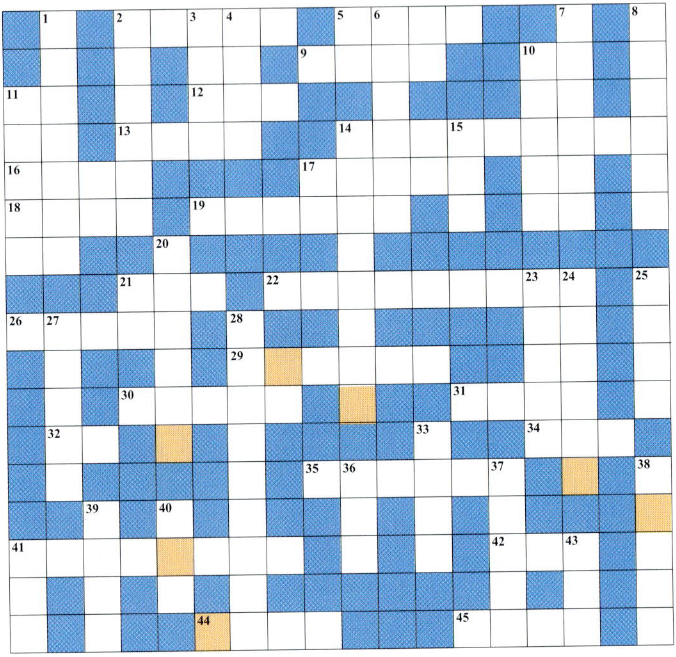

Across:

2 part of the UK
5 school examination at 16
9 synonym for target or objective
12 opposite of wet
13 'Over the sea to ...' is a famous song about one of the Hebrides Islands.
14 university town
16 city in the North of England
17 The members of the House of ... are not elected.
18 synonym for large town
19 small fishing town in the South-West of Ireland
21 river in Scotland near Balmoral
22 William the Conqueror's hunting ground
26 Wilde's first name
29 the capital of Ireland
30 The highest mountain in Britain is Ben ... .
31 nickname for Birmingham
32 You have to write your ... if you're looking for a job.
34 favourite British drink
35 political party
41 fishing village in Cornwall
42 short for Gross Domestic Product
44 Irish writer
45 Newcastle's river

Down:

1 The Sun is the archetypical ... newspaper.
2 Scotland is famous for its many ... distilleries.
3 'My Fair ...' is a musical based on a play by 44 Across.
4 an Irish name for Ireland
5 synonym for proceed
6 London's tallest landmark is ... Wharf Tower.
7 England's capital
8 synonym for TV or computer monitor
10 author of 'Gulliver's Travels'
11 author of 'Dubliners'
14 the westernmost county in England
15 mad cow disease
20 one of the Channel Islands
23 very dark Irish drink
24 London's river
25 British measure for liquids
27 You can buy shares on the ... exchange.
28 the capital of Scotland
33 Scottish word for lake
36 short for advertisements
37 British sport
38 synonym for problem or concern
39 traditional Scottish family group
40 Glenys Kinnock is an ... .
41 where you would go to have a drink with friends
43 Steak and kidney ... is a typical English meal.

The letters in the orange squares make the title of a famous novel